Student Problem

MW01252621

for use with

Corporate Finance

Fifth Edition

Stephen A. Ross
Massachusetts Institute of Technology

Randolph W. Westerfield
University of Southern California

Jeffrey Jaffe
University of Pennsylvania

Prepared by
Robert C. Hanson
Eastern Michigan University

Boston   Burr Ridge, IL   Dubuque, IA   Madison, WI   New York   San Francisco   St. Louis
Bangkok   Bogotá   Caracas   Lisbon   London   Madrid
Mexico City   Milan   New Delhi   Seoul   Singapore   Sydney   Taipei   Toronto

Irwin/McGraw-Hill

A Division of The McGraw·Hill Companies

Student Problem Manual for use with
CORPORATE FINANCE

2 3 4 5 6 7 8 9 0 MAZ/MAZ 9 3 2 1 0 9

ISBN 0-256-26195-4

http://www.mhhe.com

PREFACE

This revised Student Problem Manual to accompany the fifth edition of *Corporate Finance* by Professors Stephen A. Ross, Randolph W. Westerfield, and Jeffrey F. Jaffe is intended to be an integral part of your effort to master the principles of modern corporate finance. This Manual will be useful to you in several ways as you study and learn corporate finance. It will help you study by concisely summarizing the learning objectives of each chapter and providing an outline of the chapter's important points. This guide provides over 500 worked-out problems to help you understand the application of financial principles, and to assist you in solving end-of-chapter problems. The worked-out problems and concept test questions will help you prepare for exams by providing additional practice solving problems and by refreshing your knowledge of key concepts. The fifth edition includes over 200 new and revised problems with solutions. Many of these additional problems reflect new or revised material in the fifth edition of *Corporate Finance*, while other problems are specifically designed to complement the end-of-chapter problems in the text.

Organization of the Student Problem Manual

The organization of this guide closely parallels that of the text. Problem Manual chapters are organized as follows:

Chapter Mission Statement. A concise summary of the learning objectives of each chapter is provided followed by an outline of the key concepts discussed in the chapter. This will provide you an overview of what financial concepts will be discussed in the chapter and help you organize your studying.

Concept Test. A series of 15 to 20 fill-in-the-blank questions are provided for you to test your understanding of the essential concepts presented in the chapter. The test allows you to evaluate your grasp of key concepts by comparing your answers to those provided.

Problems. An average of 18 detailed problems are provided in each chapter. Many problems are designed to guide you through a difficult application of a financial concept.

Solutions. A detailed worked-out solution is provided for each problem. In many cases, a detailed discussion is provided to help you understand the underlying concept addressed by the problem.

Many of the problems build on each other in order to provide you with a step-by-step learning guide. To aid in this process, detailed solutions are provided at the end of each chapter. This organization encourages you to try solving the problems on your own before looking at our solution. You'll get a lot more out of the problems and a better understanding of the underlying financial concepts if you struggle on your own to find the answer before looking at our solution. Most problems were solved on a hand-held financial calculator with answers rounded off to three or four decimal places. Your answers may slightly differ from ours if you use financial tables or use a different rounding procedure.

Preface

Acknowledgments

I would like to acknowledge the contribution of R. Bruce Swensen and Bradford D. Jordan who ably prepared the second edition of the Student Problem Manual. Their work established the foundation for subsequent editions. A great deal of credit must go to both of them for initially developing a truly valuable learning tool to complement *Corporate Finance*. The author also thanks Brian Kluger and Charles Wildman for their careful review of the third edition. Finally, thanks go to Michele Janicek at Irwin/McGraw-Hill for her support and assistance in preparing the fifth edition.

Robert C. Hanson
Ann Arbor, Michigan
May 1998

iv

TABLE OF CONTENTS

CHAPTER 1

INTRODUCTION TO CORPORATE FINANCE

CHAPTER MISSION STATEMENT

Chapter 1 provides the student an overview of modern corporate finance and the issues facing the financial manager. The chapter addresses these issues from the set-of-contracts perspective. The modern corporate form of organization is described and compared to proprietorships and partnerships. Investment and financing decisions facing the firm are reviewed from the context of value creation. Securities issued by the firm are characterized as contingent claims on the value of the firm. Finally, the chapter explores the structure of financial markets.

The key concepts discussed in Chapter 1 are outlined below.

- ♦What is corporate finance
    - ●balance-sheet model
    - ●capital structure
    - ●financial manager
- ♦Value creation
- ♦Corporate securities as contingent claims
- ♦The firm
    - ●sole proprietorship
    - ●partnership
    - ●corporation
- ♦Goals of the corporation
    - ●set-of-contracts perspective
    - ●principal-agent relationship
    - ●managerial goals
    - ●shareholder goals
    - ●separation of ownership and control
- ♦Financial markets
    - ●capital markets
    - ●money markets
    - ●primary market
    - ●secondary market
    - ●auction markets
    - ●dealer markets

CONCEPT TEST

1. Corporate finance addresses three basic issues: _____, _____, and _____.

2. An important job of the financial manager is to _____.

3. Debt and equity securities are _____ on the value of the firm.

4. Short-term assets are called _____ assets. Long-term assets are called _____ assets.

5.   A _____ is a claim on the assets of a firm, either in the form of a debt or an equity share.

6.   The mixture of debt and equity that a firm uses to finance its purchases of assets is called the firm's _____.

7.   The decision regarding which fixed assets to buy is called the _____ decision.

8.   A debt or obligation that must be repaid within a year is called a _____.

9.   The difference between a firm's current assets and current liabilities is called the firm's _____.

10. Since the payments to the creditors and the owners of a firm depend on the value of the firm, bonds and stocks are said to be _____ on the value of the firm.

11. A business owned by a single person is a _____.

12. In a partnership, all the partners have unlimited liability for partnership debts.

13. In a partnership, there are two kinds of partners. The _____ partners have unlimited liability, whereas the _____ partners have limited liability.

14. The rules and procedures by which a corporation governs itself are contained in the corporate _____.

15. All corporations must prepare a document called the _____ describing the number of shares which may be issued, the business purpose, the intended life, and other details.

16. Corporations have advantages over proprietorships and partnerships because of the _____.

17. The primary disadvantage of the corporate form of organization is _____ of corporate income.

18. The primary goal of the corporation is maximization of _____.

19. Because management goals may conflict with shareholder goals, an _____ problem is said to exist.

20. A frequently cited management goal is maximization of _____.

21. The costs associated with aligning shareholder goals and management goals are called _____ costs.

22. When financial markets are classified according to the maturity of the financial instruments, the two types of markets are _____ markets and _____ markets.

23. The _____ market is the market for short-term debt instruments.

24. A market in which firms continuously stand ready to buy and sell is a _____ market.

25. The New York Stock Exchange is an example of a secondary market which functions as an _____ market.

26. A stock that trades on the NYSE is said to be _____ on the exchange.

27. All trading in a particular stock on the NYSE is handled by an individual known as a _____.

28. The dealer market for equities is called the _____ market.

29. When a security is first offered to the public, it is said to be trading in the _____ market. Later, it trades in the _____ market.

30. Trading at a given location and the immediate availability of prices distinguishes an _____ market from a _____ market.

ANSWERS TO CONCEPT TEST

1. capital budgeting; capital structure; net working capital
2. create value
3. contingent claims
4. current; fixed
5. security
6. capital structure
7. capital budgeting
8. current liability
9. net working capital
10. contingent claims
11. sole proprietorship
12. general
13. general; limited
14. bylaws
15. articles of incorporation
16. separation of ownership from management
17. double taxation
18. shareholder wealth
19. agency
20. corporate wealth
21. agency
22. money; capital
23. money
24. dealer
25. auction
26. listed
27. specialist
28. over-the-counter
29. primary; secondary
30. auction; dealer

CHAPTER 2

ACCOUNTING STATEMENTS AND CASH FLOW

CHAPTER MISSION STATEMENT

Chapter 2 reviews the basic financial statements of a firm and shows how information from these statements can be used to determine cash flow. The balance sheet provides a snapshot of the firm's assets, liabilities, and shareholders' equity on the last day of the fiscal year. The income statement and statement of financial cash flow provide a view of the firm's activities over the preceding fiscal year. Financial statements report values based on historical cost and income based on accrued revenues and expenses. The chapter emphasizes, however, that financial managers are concerned about the market values of the firm's assets and liabilities and the firm's cash flow, which ultimately determines these values. The chapter demonstrates how financial managers and others can use information in financial statements to derive cash flows going to the firm, to creditors, and to stockholders. Appendix A reviews financial ratios used to assess the health and vitality of the firm, Appendix B explains the statement of cash flows, and Appendix C concludes with a discussion of current tax rates.

The major concepts discussed in Chapter 2 are outlined below.

- ♦ Balance Sheet
  - accounting liquidity
  - dcbt versus equity
  - value versus cost
- ♦ Income Statement
  - GAAP
  - noncash items
  - time and costs
  - fixed versus variable costs
  - product versus period costs
- ♦ Net Working Capital
  - changes in net working capital
- ♦ Financial Cash Flow
  - to the firm
  - to creditors
  - to shareholders
  - total cash flow
  - operating cash flow

CONCEPT TEST

1. Stockholders' equity is defined as the difference between the firm's _____ and _____.

2. The _____ reports accounting values of the firm's assets, liabilities, and stockholders' equity on a particular date.

3. The _____ in the balance sheet are listed in order by the time it takes to convert them into cash.

4. The _____ in the balance sheet are listed in the order in which they must be paid.

5. An asset that can be converted to cash quickly and easily is considered a _____ asset.

6. The fixed asset values shown on a firm's balance sheet are not current market values; Instead, these assets are shown at _____.

7. For accounting purposes, revenue is shown on the income statement when it _____, not necessarily when payment is received.

8. One reason that net income is not the same as cash from operations is that some expenses are _____ deductions.

9. The two most common noncash expenses are _____ and _____.

10. Accounting costs are usually classified as either _____ costs or _____ costs.

11. Costs of goods sold are _____ costs, while selling, general and administrative expenses are _____ costs.

12. Operating cash flow is calculated as _____ + _____ − _____.

13. Total cash flow to the firm is operating cash flow − capital spending − _____.

14. Cash flow to creditors is calculated as _____ + _____ − _____.

15. Cash flow to stockholders is calculated as _____ + _____ − _____.

For questions 16-25, indicate whether the action represents an increase (addition) to net working capital, which uses up cash flow, or a decrease (reduction) in net working capital, which generates cash flow.

16. Inventory decreases by $345.

17. Accounts receivable increases by $38.

18. Cash balance increases by $303

19. Accounts payable increase by $30.

20. Notes payable decrease by $83.

21. Inventory is purchased with cash.

22.   A corporate jet is purchased with cash.

23.   Proceeds from the sale of long term debt are used to pay off a short-term bank loan.

24.   A cash dividend is paid.

25.   A credit customer pays a bill.

For questions 26-28, indicate whether the action represents an increase or decrease in the cash flow of the firm.

26.   Acquisition of fixed assets.

27.   An addition to net working capital.

28.   Increase in depreciation.

For questions 29-31, indicate whether the action represents an increase or decrease in cash flow to investors in the firm.

29.   Firm issues long term debt.

30.   Cash dividends are increased.

31.   Firm repurchases common stock.

ANSWERS TO CONCEPT TEST

1.	assets; liabilities		16.	reduction
2.	balance sheet		17.	addition
3.	assets		18.	addition
4.	liabilities		19.	reduction
5.	liquid		20.	no change
6.	historical cost		21.	no change
7.	accrues		22.	reduction
8.	noncash		23.	addition
9.	depreciation; deferred taxes		24.	reduction
10.	product; period		25.	no change
11.	product; period		26.	decrease
12.	EBIT; depreciation; current taxes		27.	decrease
13.	additions to net working capital		28.	increase
14.	interest; repayments of long-term debt; proceeds from new long-term debt		29.	decrease
			30.	increase
15.	dividends; stock repurchased; stock issued		31.	increase

PROBLEMS

Use the financial statements shown below for Arcadia Enterprises to answer problems 1-5. Except for per share values and unless otherwise indicated dollar amounts are in thousands.

Arcadia Enterprises
Balance Sheet
December 31
($ thousands)

Assets			Liabilities and Owners' Equity		
	1996	1997		1996	1997
Current assets			Current liabilities		
Cash	$29,553	$31,749	Accts payable	$8,772	$7,713
Accts receivable	52,532	52,211	Notes payable	22,757	25,670
Inventory	109,662	113,273	Other	35,062	35,678
Total current assets	191,747	197,233	Total current liabilities	66,591	69,061
			Long-term debt	62,441	66,081
			Deferred taxes	2,519	1,380
Fixed assets			Stockholders' equity		
Net plant and			Common stock	21,330	21,909
equipment	140,106		Capital surplus	45,658	53,650
			Accumulated retained earnings	133,314	
Total fixed assets	140,106	_____	Total owners' equity	200,302	_____
Total assets	$331,853	$_____	Total liabilities and owners' equity	$331,853	$_____

Arcadia Enterprises
Income Statement
1997
($ thousands)

Net sales	$376,280
Cost of goods sold	
Operating expenses	57,845
Depreciation	20,734
Earnings before interest and taxes	_____
Interest paid	1,128
Taxable income	_____
Taxes	
Currently payable	$
Deferred	$ (1,139)
Net Income	$_____
Retained earnings	$
Dividends	$6,489

**Arcadia Enterprises
Financial Cash Flow
1997
($ thousands)**

Cash flow of the firm

Operating cash flow $42,288
  (EBIT plus depreciation minus taxes)

Capital spending   (42,727)
  (Acquisition of fixed assets minus
   sale of fixed assets)

Additions to net working capital   (3,016)

Total $ (3,455)

Cash flow to investors in the firm

Debt $(2,512)
  (Interest plus retirement of debt
   minus long-term debt financing)

Equity   (2,082)
  (Dividends plus repurchase of equity
   minus new equity)

Total $(4,594)

Problem 1

Arcadia acquires a new office building for $75 million while at the same time selling an old warehouse for its book value of $32.273 million. What is the value of net plant and equipment for 1997?

Problem 2

Cost of goods sold is 70% of net sales and taxes currently payable equal $13,890. What is the firm's net income for 1997? How much net income goes toward retained earnings?

Problem 3

If the par value of Arcadia's common stock is $2.50 per share, what was the net increase in the number of shares outstanding from 1996 to 1997?

Problem 4

Assume that during 1997 Arcadia both issued and repurchased shares of common stock at the same market price (Note: number of shares issued - number of shares repurchased = 231,600 shares). What was this price?

Problem 5

Using values from the balance sheet show that, as the statement of financial cash flow indicates, additions to net working capital are $3,016 thousand.

Problem 6

The Apricot Company in 1996 had notes payable of $1,200, accounts payable of $2,400, and long-term debt of $3,000. The corresponding entries for 1997 are $1,600, $2,000, and $2,800. For assets, Apricot had in 1996 $800 in cash, $400 in marketable securities, and $1,800 of inventory. The corresponding entries for 1997 are $500, $300, and $2,000. Accounts receivable at the end of 1996 were $900 and $800 at the end of 1997. Apricot's net plant and equipment was $6,000 in 1996 and $8,000 in 1997. Construct Apricot Company's balance sheet for 1996 and 1997.

Problem 7

Apricot Company had sales of $1,000 during 1997 cost of goods sold was $400, depreciation was $100, and paid $160 of interest. The tax rate is 35% and all taxes are paid currently. What is Apricot's net income for the year?

Problem 8

Calculate Apricot's operating cash flow for 1997 using the information in problem 7.

Problem 9

During 1997 Apricot sold $2,400 worth of stock and used the entire proceeds to buy fixed assets. There was no new long-term borrowing, and dividends of $120 were paid. Based on this information and the financial statements in previous problems construct the firm's statement of financial cash flow.

Problem 10

Compare Apricot's operating cash flow with its total cash flow. Do you expect total cash flow to be positive or negative?

Problem 11

Use the following information about the Aspen Corporation to calculate cash flow of the firm in 1997. The tax rate is 35%.

	1996	1997
Sales	$5,575	$7,225
Costs	2,625	3,592
Depreciation	1,045	1,045
Interest	250	316
Dividends	875	900
Current assets	2,850	3,340
Fixed assets	14,175	14,692
Current liabilities	2,210	2,515
Long-term debt	5,875	6,665

Problem 12

Calculate the cash flow to Aspen's long-term creditors and to its stockholders in 1997.

SOLUTIONS

Solution 1

From Arcadia's income statement depreciation is $20,734, thus the historical cost of existing assets (including warehouse) in 1997 is $140,106 − 20,734 = $119,372. From this value subtract the book value of the warehouse and add the cost of the new office building. The value of net plant and equipment on December 31, 1997 is then $119,372 − 32,273 + 75,000 = $162,099.

Solution 2

Cost of goods sold is .70 × $376,280 = $263,396; earnings before interest and taxes is $34,305; taxable income is $33,177; taxes equal $12,751 = $13,890 − $1,139; net income is $20,426; and retained earnings increase by $13,937. For 1997, Accumulated Retained Earnings becomes $133,314 + $13,937 = $147,251.

Solution 3

The balance sheet indicates that common stock increased by $21,909 − 21,330 = $579 thousand. Thus, the net number of new shares issued was $579 thousand/$2.50 per share = 231,600 shares.

Solution 4

The income statement indicates that dividends for 1997 were $6,489, while the statement of financial cash flow indicates that cash flow to equity holders was $(2,082). Thus, net new equity financing was $6,489 − (2,082) = $8,571. Given that 231,600 shares were issued, then the market price was $8,571 thousand/231,600 shares = $37.00 per share. Alternately, the price can be found by considering the per share change from 1996 to 1997 in (common stock + capital surplus).

Solution 5

Total current assets are $191,747 and $197,233 for 1996 and 1997, respectively. Total current liabilities are $66,591 and $69,061 for 1996 and 1997, respectively. The change in net working capital from 1996 to 1997 was:

	1996	1997	Change
Current assets	191,747	197,233	5,486
Current liabilities	66,591	69,061	2,470
Net working capital	125,156	128,172	3,016

Thus, net working capital increased by $3,016 representing a use of cash flow by the firm.

Solution 6

Apricot Company
Balance Sheet
December 31
($ thousands)

Assets			Liabilities and Owners' Equity		
	1996	1997		1996	1997
Current assets			Current liabilities		
Cash	$ 800	$ 500	Accts payable	$ 2,400	$2,000
Marketable securities	400	300	Notes payable	1,200	1,600
Accts receivable	900	800			
Inventory	1,800	2,000			
Total current assets	3,900	3,600	Total current liabilities	3,600	3,600
			Long-term debt	3,000	2,800
Fixed assets			Stockholders' equity		
Net plant and equipment	6,000	8,000	Common stock	3,300	5,200
Total fixed assets	6,000	8,000	Total owners' equity	3,300	5,200
Total assets	$9,900	$11,600	Total liabilities and owners' equity	$9,900	$11,600

Note: Stockholders' equity is a residual item, equal to total assets less current liabilities less long term debt.

Solution 7

Apricot Company
Income Statement
1997
($ thousands)

Net sales	$1,000
Cost of goods sold	400
Depreciation	100
Earnings before interest and taxes	500
Interest paid	160
Taxable income	340
Taxes	119
Net Income	$ 221

Solution 8

Cash flow from operations is:

	Earnings before interest and taxes	$ 500
+	Depreciation	100
−	Taxes	119
=	Cash flow from operations	$ 481

Note: Depreciation must be added to EBIT since this noncash expense was previously subtracted from revenues to find taxable income.

Solution 9

Apricot Company
Financial Cash Flow
1997
($ thousands)

<u>Cash flow of the firm</u>

Operating cash flow	$ 481
(EBIT plus depreciation minus taxes)	
Capital spending	(2,100)
(Acquisition of fixed assets minus	
sale of fixed assets)	
Additions to net working capital	300
Total	$ <u>(1,319)</u>

<u>Cash flow to investors in the firm</u>

Debt	$ 360
(Interest plus retirement of debt	
minus long-term debt financing)	
Equity	(1,679)
(Dividends plus repurchase of equity	
minus new equity)	
Total	$ <u>(1,319)</u>

Solution notes: From the balance sheet we see that net fixed assets increased by $2,000, from the income statement depreciation of existing assets was $100, while $2,400 of new assets were purchased. Thus, assets sold must be $2,400 − 2,000 − 100 = $300. Net equity increased by $1,900, retained earnings were $221 − 120 = $101, and new equity was sold for $2,400. Thus, repurchased equity was $2,400 + 101 − 1,900 = $601.

Solution 10

From problem 8 cash flow from operations is:

	Earnings before interest and taxes	$ 500
+	Depreciation	100
−	Taxes	119
=	Cash flow from operations	$ 481

Total cash flow to the firm is:

Operating cash flow	$ 481
Net capital spending	(2,100)
Addition to net working capital	300
Total cash flow	$ (1,319)

Note that total cash flow is negative and includes adjustments for capital spending and changes to net working capital. Net working capital decreased by $300 between 1996 and 1997 and represents a cash inflow to the firm. Growing firms typically have negative total cash flow (in the short run).

Solution 11

Cash flow to the firm is Aspen's 1997 cash flow that results from operations, capital spending, and changes in net working capital. Operating cash flow equals EBIT ($2,588 = $7,225 − 3,592 − 1,045) plus depreciation ($1,045) less taxes ($795) or $2,838. Net capital spending equals the increase in fixed assets plus depreciation ($14,692 − $14,175 + $1,045 = $1,562). Additions to net working capital equal the change in current assets less the change in current liabilities ($490 − $305 = $185). Cash flow to the firm equals $2,838 − $1,562 − $185 = $1,091.

Solution 12

Cash flow to long-term creditors equals interest payments net of increases in long-term debt ($316 − ($6,665 − $5,875) = −$474. In 1997, funds from issuing long-term debt exceeded interest paid by $474 Cash flow to stockholders equals dividends plus the repurchase of stock. From the information provided, the balance sheet value of shareholders' equity (Total Assets − Total Liabilities) declined from $8,940 in 1996 to $8,852 in 1997. Net income in 1997 was $1,477, Aspen paid dividends of $900, and additions to retained earning were $577. This suggests that Aspen repurchased $665 of common stock. Cash flow to shareholders equals $1,565 = $665 + $900. To summarize:

Cash flow of the firm	$1,091
= Cash flow to long-term creditors	($474)
+ Cash flow to stockholders	$1,565

APPENDIX 2A

FINANCIAL STATEMENT ANALYSIS

Financial managers, financial analysts, and security analysts, among others, organize information from financial statements into financial ratios in order to evaluate a firm's financial health and profitability. Typically, managers will look for trends in the ratios and compare with other firms in the industry. From the financial managers point of view, however, inferences must be made with caution since most ratios are based on accounting values rather than market values. Ratios are usually classified into five areas: (1) short-term solvency, (2) activity, (3) financial leverage, (4) profitability, and (5) value.

CONCEPT TEST

A1.   The current ratio is defined as _____ divided by _____.

A2.   The quick ratio is similar to the current ratio except that _____ is deducted from current assets.

A3.   Total asset turnover is defined as _____ divided by _____.

A4.   The ACP is _____ divided by _____.

A5.   The days in inventory is calculated as _____ divided by _____.

A6.   Earnings before interest and taxes divided by interest expense is called the _____ ratio.

A7.   Three common measures of financial leverage are the _____ ratio, the _____ ratio, and the _____.

A8.   Net profit margin is _____ divided by _____.

A9.   Net return on assets is defined as _____ divided by _____.

A10.   Return on equity is defined as _____ divided by _____.

A11.   Return on equity can be written as the product of _____, _____, and the _____.

A12.   The _____ is calculated by dividing annualized dividends per share by current market price per share.

A13.   The _____ ratio is the market price per share divided by the book value per share.

A14.   The _____ is a measure of the return to the firm's stockholders.

A15.   The _____ measures the firm's ability to meet its interest obligations.

ANSWERS TO CONCEPT TEST

A1.   current assets; current liabilities
A2.   inventory
A3.   operating revenues; average total assets
A4.   days in period; receivables turnover
A5.   days in period; inventory turnover
A6.   coverage
A7.   debt; debt-to-equity; equity multiplier
A8.   net income; sales

A9.   net income; average total assets
A10. net income; average shareholders' equity
A11. profit margin; asset turnover; equity multiplier
A12. dividend yield
A13. market-to-book value
A14. return on equity
A15. interest coverage ratio

PROBLEMS

Problems A1 to A6 refer to the Arcadia Enterprises example presented above.

Problem A1

Use the 1997 financial statement information for Arcadia Enterprises, presented above, to fill in the following table:

Financial Ratios for Arcadia Enterprises

Short-term solvency ratios

Current ratio	_____
Quick ratio	_____

Activity ratios

Total asset turnover	_____
Inventory turnover	_____
Receivables turnover	_____

Financial leverage ratios

Debt ratio   _____
Debt-to-equity ratio   _____
Equity multiplier   _____
Interest coverage   _____

Profitability ratios

Net profit margin   _____
Return on assets   _____
Return on equity   _____

Problem A2

Use the du Pont method to compute ROA and ROE for Arcadia Enterprises.

Problem A3

Acadia's current stock price is $37.00 per share. The firm has 8,763,600 share outstanding. What is Arcadia's dividend yield if dividends per share remain constant?

Problem A4

What is Arcadia's market-to-book ratio if the stock price is $37.00 per share?

Problem A5

What is Arcadia's price-to-earnings (P/E) ratio?

Problem A6

Assume that the replacement value of Arcadia's <u>fixed</u> assets is 25% higher than book value. Further assume that all debt sells at par value and that working capital is carried at replacement value. What is Arcadia's Tobin's Q ratio for 1997?

Problem A7

If the debt-to-equity ratio is 1/2, what is the total debt ratio? What is the equity multiplier?

Problem A8

If ROE is 16% and the debt ratio is 1/2, what is ROA?

Problem A9

Suppose that beginning inventory is $1,000 and ending inventory is $1,200. Sales for the year are $14,000. Cost of goods sold is 70% of sales. Compute days in inventory.

SOLUTIONS

Solution A1

Financial Ratios for Arcadia Enterprises

Short-term solvency ratios

Current ratio	2.86
Quick ratio	1.22

Activity ratios

Total asset turnover	1.09
Inventory turnover	2.36
Receivables turnover	7.18

Financial leverage ratios

Debt ratio	0.38
Debt-to-equity ratio	0.61
Equity multiplier	1.61
Interest coverage	30.41

Profitability ratios

Net profit margin	5.43%
Return on assets	5.92%
Return on equity	9.66%

Solution A2

Based on the du Pont method, ROA for Arcadia is:

$$ROA = 5.43\%(1.09) = 5.92\%$$

ROE is:

$$ROE = 5.43\%(1.09)(1.61) = 5.92\%(1.61) = 9.53\%$$

This is not exactly the same as the 9.66% above because the equity multiplier is not based on average values for the year. If you calculate the equity multiplier using average values, you should get 1.63, and the du Pont method will indicate $5.43\%(1.09)(1.63) = 9.65\%$.

Solution A3

Arcadia paid total dividends of $6,489,000 in 1997, or $6,489,000/8,763,600 shares = $0.74 per share. The dividend yield is $0.74/$37.00 = .0200 or 2.00%.

Solution A4

Book value per share is the balance sheet value for shareholder's equity divided by the number of shares outstanding. Book value per share is $222,810 thousand/8,763.6 thousand shares = $25.42 per share. Therefore, the market-to-book ratio is $37.00/$25.42 = 1.46.

Solution A5

Arcadia's net income per share equals $20,426,000/8,763,600 = $2.33 per share, and the P/E ratio is $37.00/$2.33 = 15.87.

Solution A6

Tobin's Q is the ratio of the market value of the firm's debt plus equity to the replacement value of the firm's assets. The market value of debt (as assumed) is just its book value of $136,522 thousand, while the market value of equity is the stock price times the number of shares outstanding $37.00 (8,763,600 shares) = $324,253,200. The replacement value of the fixed assets is $202,623,750 while the replacement value of the firms current assets is (as assumed) $197,233 thousand. Thus, Arcadia's Q-ratio is ($136,522 + $324,253.2)/($202,623.75 + $197,233) = $460,775.2/$399,856.75 = 1.15.

Solution A7

If the debt-to-equity ratio is 1/2, the firm has $.50 in debt for every $1 in equity. This means the firm has $.50 in debt for every $1.50 in value, so the total debt ratio is .3333. The firm also has $1 in equity for every $1.50 in value, so the equity multiplier is 1.5.

Solution A8

The firm has $.50 in equity for every $1 in value, so the equity multiplier is 2. From the du Pont method, ROA $\times$ (2) = ROE = .16, so ROA is 8%.

Solution A9

Average inventory is $1,100, so the inventory turnover is $[.70(\$14,000/\$1,100)] = 8.91$. The days in inventory is (365/8.91) = 40.97 days.

APPENDIX 2B

STATEMENT OF CASH FLOWS

Appendix 2B reviews the Statement of Cash Flows that firms must provide in their Annual Report along with the Balance Sheet, Income Statement, and Statement of Retained Earnings. This statement provides the details behind changes in accounting cash. The Statement of Cash Flows is comprised of three components: cash flow from operating activities, cash flow from investing activities, and cash flow from financing activities. The bottom line is the change in cash on the balance sheet.

CONCEPT TEST

B1. Cash flow from operating activities equals net income plus _____ expenses minus changes in _____ assets (except cash) and _____ liabilities.

B2. Increases in current assets from one year to the next _____ cash flow from operations.

B3. Increases in current liabilities from one year to the next _____ cash flow from operations.

B4. Cash flow from investing activities equals net _____.

B5. Cash flow from financing activities equals cash flow to and from _____ and _____.

B6. The sum of all three categories of cash flow equals _____ on the balance sheet.

ANSWERS TO CONCEPT TEST

B1. noncash, current, current
B2. reduces
B3. increases

B4. capital expenditures
B5. creditors, owners
B6. change in cash

PROBLEMS

Use the financial statements for Arcadia Enterprises presented earlier for the following problems. In addition to the information presented earlier in problems 1-5, assume that Arcadia issues $15,227,000 worth of common stock and issues $8,305,000 worth of long-term debt.

Problem B1

Fill in the following table of cash flows from operating activities.

Arcadia Enterprises
1997
($ thousands)

Cash flow from operating activities

Net income	$
Depreciation	
Deferred taxes	(1,139)
Change in assets and liabilities	
Accounts receivable	
Inventories	
Accounts payable	
Other	616
Cash flow from operating activities	$

Problem B2

Fill in the following table of cash flow from investing activity.

Arcadia Enterprises
1997
($ thousands)

Cash flow from investing activities

Acquisition of fixed assets	$
Sales of fixed assets	
Cash flow from investing activities	$

Problem B3

Fill in the following table of cash flow from financing activity.

Arcadia Enterprises
1997
($ thousands)

Cash flow from financing activities

Change in notes payable	$
Retirement of long-term debt	
Proceeds from long-term debt sales	8,305
Dividends	
Repurchase of stock	
Proceeds from new stock issue	15,227
Cash flow from financing activity	$

Problem B4

Show that the change in balance sheet cash from 1996 to 1997 equals the cash flow from operating, investing, and financing activities.

SOLUTIONS

Solution B1

Arcadia Enterprises
1997
($ thousands)

Cash flow from operating activities

Net income	$20,426
Depreciation	20,734
Deferred taxes	(1,139)
Change in assets and liabilities	
Accounts receivable	321
Inventories	(3,611)
Accounts payable	(1,059)
Other	616
Cash flow from operating activities	$36,288

Solution B2

Arcadia Enterprises
1997
($ thousands)

Cash flow from investing activities

Acquisition of fixed assets	$(75,000)
Sales of fixed assets	32,273
Cash flow from investing activities	$(42,727)

Solution B3

Arcadia Enterprises
1997
($ thousands)

Cash flow from financing activities

Change in notes payable	$2,913
Retirement of long-term debt	(4,665)
Proceeds from long-term debt sales	8,305
Dividends	(6,489)
Repurchase of stock	(6,656)
Proceeds from new stock issue	15,227
Cash flow from financing activity	$8,635

Solution B4

From 1996 to 1997 Arcadia's cash balance increases by $2,196 = $31,749 - $29,553. The operating, investing, and financing cash flows equal $36,426 - $42,727 + $8,635 = $2,196.

APPENDIX 2C

TAX RATES

Appendix 2C presents the U.S. federal tax rates for individuals and corporations.

CONCEPT TEST

C1.   Under current tax law, the maximum marginal tax rate for individuals is _____.

C2.   Under current tax law, the maximum marginal tax rate for corporations is _____.

C3.   The maximum marginal tax rate for corporations applies to income between _____ and _____.

C4.   Most large profitable corporations face a marginal tax rate of _____.

C5.   When a corporation owns between 20% and 80% of another corporation, _____ percent of the dividends received from the other corporation is exempt from federal taxes.

C6.   Tax law permits corporations to carry tax losses forward up to _____ years and back for as many as _____ years.

ANSWERS TO CONCEPT TEST

C1.   39.6%   C4.   35%
C2.   39%   C5.   80%
C3. $100,001; $335,000   C6.   20; 2

CHAPTER 3

FINANCIAL MARKETS AND NET PRESENT VALUE:
FIRST PRINCIPLES OF FINANCE (ADVANCED)

CHAPTER MISSION STATEMENT

The purpose of this chapter is to provide the student an understanding of why financial markets exist and how they facilitate consumption and investment decisions by individuals and investment decisions by firms. A perfectly competitive financial market is defined. The existence of a competitive financial market leads to the principle that the investment decision is separate from the consumption decision. The concept of net present value (NPV) is introduced; NPV is probably the single most important concept in corporate finance. Corporations seek out investments in real assets that have positive net present values since these investments are worth more than they cost.

The major concepts presented in the chapter are outlined below.

- ◆Financial market economy
  - ●financial instruments
  - ●anonymous market
  - ●financial intermediaries
  - ●market clearing
  - ●equilibrium rate of interest
- ◆Making consumption choices
- ◆Competitive market
  - ●perfect markets
  - ●price takers
  - ●arbitrage
- ◆Basic principle of investment decision making
  - ●separation theorem
- ◆Net present value rule
  - ●maximize company value

CONCEPT TEST

1. A financial instrument that is a promise to pay the owner as it comes due is called a _____ instrument.

2. When total funds demanded by borrowers equals the amount that lenders wish to loan, then the market is said to _____.

3. If the amount borrowers wish to borrow is greater than the amount lenders wish to loan out, then the interest rate will _____.

4. An institution that matches buyers and sellers of money (borrowers and lenders) is called a _____.

5.   A financial market in which borrowers and lenders do not actually meet is called an _____ market.

6.   The interest rate that clears the market is called the _____ rate of interest.

7.   If no individual in a market can have an impact on the market price, then market participants are called _____.

8.   A financial market in which trading is costless, information is freely available, and no trader has a significant impact on price is called a _____.

9.   Simultaneous buying and selling activities that earn guaranteed profits and require no net investment are called _____ opportunities.

10.   The idea that investment decisions can be made without reference to an individual's consumption preferences or income pattern is called the _____.

11.   A _____ is the amount to which an initial dollar amount will grow when interest is compounded at a specified interest rate for a specified number of years.

12.   The difference between the current worth of an investment and its cost is called the _____ of the investment.

13.   The value that the financial market would place on a future cash flow is called the _____ of that cash flow.

14.   The interest rate prevailing in the financial markets provides a _____ against which proposed investments can be compared.

15.   "An investment is acceptable only if it is superior to alternatives in the financial market" is a statement of the _____.

16.   The financial manager acts in the best interests of the shareholders by choosing investments to _____.

17.   The NPV rule depends on the presence of _____.

ANSWERS TO CONCEPT TEST

1. bearer
2. clear
3. rise
4. financial intermediary
5. anonymous
6. equilibrium rate of interest
7. price takers
8. perfectly competitive financial market
9. arbitrage

10. separation theorem
11. future value
12. net present value (NPV)
13. present value (PV)
14. benchmark
15. first principle of investment decision making
16. maximize NPV
17. competitive financial markets

PROBLEMS

Problem 1

An investor's income is $100,000 this year and $120,000 next year. She plans to consume $80,000 this year and $143,200 next year. If this difference between her income and consumption patterns results from a financial market transaction, what is the market interest rate?

Problem 2

An individual has an income of $5000 this year and $8000 next year. If the market rate of interest is 15%, what is the most he can consume this year? Next year?

Problem 3

Given the information in problem 2, complete the following table:

This year's consumption	Next year's consumption
$ 0	
5,000	
8,000	
10,000	
12,000	

Problem 4

An investment in real assets requires an initial outlay of $2 million. It promises to pay $2.18 million in one year. The market interest rate is 10%. Is this a good investment? What is the rate of return on this investment?

Problem 5

In problem 4, what is the present value of the future cash flow? What is the net present value (NPV) of the investment?

Problem 6

Calculate the present value for each of the following cash flows to be received or paid one year hence:

Future cash flow	Interest rate	Present value
$ 10,000	10%	
153,200	5%	
153,200	10%	
(183,840)	20%	
(120,600)	9%	

Problem 7

As a newly-coined MBA embarking on a career in consulting, you naturally must own a Lexus GS300 that costs $47,200. You also have to spend $3,600 on a blue pin-stripe suit, braces, ties, and $5,400 to furnish your apartment. These expenses must be paid immediately. Your salary this year will be $72,000 plus a bonus of unknown amount. Routine living expenses will be $36,000 paid at year end. You plan to borrow against income to pay for current consumption. If income arrives at year end, how much bonus will need in order to have enough funds to pay off the loan? The market interest rate is 14%.

Problem 8

Becky wants to consume equal dollar amounts this year and next year. Becky's current income is $48,000, paid on December 31st; next December 31st she will be paid $60,000. The interest rate is 12%. How much will Becky consume each year?

Problem 9

Brian does not believe in saving and is interested only in maximizing current consumption. His income is $49,000 this year and $50,000 next year. He has three investment opportunities, each of which costs $5,000. One will pay $6000, one will pay $7000, and one will pay $8000 the following year. The market interest rate is 25%. What is the net present value of each of the investments? How much can Brian spend today?

Problem 10

If you deposit $10,000 today in a bank account paying 10.38%, how much will you have in one year; that is, what is the future value of your investment? If you need $12,000 in one year, how much do you have to deposit today?

Problem 11

Barbara has current income of $60 and her income next year is zero. Given this income pattern, she prefers to consume $20 this year. Barbara has an investment opportunity. If she accepts this investment opportunity, she could consume, at most, $80 this year with no consumption next year. Alternately, she could consume, at most, $100 next year with no consumption this year. However, if she accepts the investment, her preference is to consume $60 next period.

What is the net present value of the investment? What is the market interest rate? Ignoring the investment, what would Barbara choose to consume next period? What is the most she could consume next period if she ignores the investment opportunity? If Barbara accepts the investment opportunity, what will she consume this period?

Problem 12

An individual has the opportunity to invest $1000 today to acquire an asset which will generate $300 in income one year from today and which can be sold for $900 at that time. Use the first principle of investment decision-making to determine the minimum level of the market interest rate for which the investment would be attractive.

Problem 13

Beverly has $40,000 on hand and expects her income next year to be $48,000. She would like to consume $50,000 today by borrowing the additional $10,000 from a bank at the market rate of 20%. A friend, however, suggests that she should instead borrow $15,000 from the bank and invest the additional $5,000 in an investment project that will return $12,000 in one year. The friend believes that this will make Beverly better off. What should she do?

Problem 14

In the above example, what is the net present value of the $5,000 investment?

Problem 15

Continuing with problems 13 and 14, what is the most Beverly can consume today without borrowing against next years income of $48,000? Stated differently, what is the most she can spend today and still spend $48,000 next year?

Problem 16

An investment project requires an initial outlay of $1,250. The cash inflow from this investment will be $1,475 one year from today. The market rate of interest is 20%. Find the net present value of the investment.

Problem 17

The Balsam Company's only asset is $100,000 cash in the bank collecting 20% interest. Balsam has an investment opportunity that will cost $30,000 and will produce a net present value (NPV) of $7,500. If Balsam makes the investment, what will be the new value of the firm?

Problem 18

What is the value of Balsam next year, now that the firm has made its positive net present value investment?

Problem 19

Balsam's $30,000 investment in real assets has a net present value (NPV) of $7,500. What rate of return did Balsam receive on its investment.

Problem 20

Brenda is the sole owner of the Baize Company, a maker of men's hats. The firm presently has $120,000 cash in the bank, $40,000 of which will soon be used to invest in real assets. Brenda believes that the investment will produce $50,625 next year. The interest rate is 12.5%. What is the largest salary that Brenda could pay herself today? 80,000

Problem 21

An entrepreneur has purchased an asset for $2 million which will produce a cash inflow of $3 million one year from today. He plans to issue 1,000 shares of common stock to himself and sell 9,000 shares of stock to the general public. His business, which consists entirely of this one asset, will cease to exist after one year. The market rate of interest is 20%, and the future cash inflow to the firm is guaranteed. At what price per share should the entrepreneur sell the common stock? What gain will the entrepreneur realize?

Problem 22

A firm has an investment opportunity but no cash on hand. The opportunity requires a $200,000 investment and will produce a cash flow of $250,000 next year. The firm will issue 1,000 shares and use the proceeds to pay for the project. What price should the firm set for each share if the market rate of interest is 15%?

SOLUTIONS

Solution 1

The $20,000 she doesn't consume this year is invested at rate r and the resulting future amount plus next year's $120,000 must equal next year's consumption of $143,200. To find the market rate of interest solve for the value of r in the following equation:

$$\$20,000(1+r) + \$120,000 = \$143,200$$

$$(1+r) = (\$143,200 - \$120,000)/\$20,000$$

$$(1+r) = 1.160$$

$$r = .160 \ \text{ or } 16.0\%$$

Solution 2

The maximum he can consume this year is [$5000 + ($8000/1.15)] = $11,956.52. The maximum possible consumption next year is [$5000(1.15) + 8000] = $13,750. Notice that each dollar received one year from now is worth ($1/1.15) = $.87 today, so [$13,750 × (1/1.15)] = $11,956.52. This is a good way to check your answer.

Solution 3

This year's consumption	Next year's consumption
$ 0	$ 13,750
5,000	8,000
8,000	4,550
10,000	2,250
12,000	not possible

The information provided indicates that the maximum that can be consumed today is $11,956.52 (see problem 2). If, however, it were possible to borrow against income in later years, this individual could consume $12,000 this year by borrowing ($8,000/1.15) = $6956.52 and paying back $8,000 next year and borrowing an additional ($12,000 − $11,956.52) = $43.48 this year and repaying the loan plus interest in two years. The payment at that time would be $57.50. (Compounding over a period of more than one year is covered in Chapter 4)

Solution 4

If you invest $2 million at the 10% market rate of interest, you will have ($2 million) × (1.10) = $2.2 million in one year. By the first principle of investment decision making, the investment in real assets, which provides only $2.18 million, is not a good investment.

The rate of return for the investment is [($2.18 million − $2 million)/$2 million] = 9%, which is less than the market interest rate.

Solution 5

Each future dollar is worth ($1/1.10) = $.909 today, so the present value is [$2.18 million × (1/1.10)] = $1.982 million. The net present value is:

($1.982 million − $2 million) = −$.0182 million = −$18,181.82

Thus, by investing $2 million in this project your wealth decreases by $18,181.82.

Solution 6

Future cash flow	Interest rate	Present value
$ 10,000	10%	$ 9,090.91
153,200	5%	145,904.76
153,200	10%	139,272.73
(183,840)	20%	(153,200.00)
(120,600)	9%	(110,642.20)

In the second and third cases, notice that the future cash flow is the same, but the present value is greater when the market interest rate is 5% than for a market interest rate of 10%. This result illustrates the fact that present value and interest rates are inversely related.

Solution 7

Right now (t=0) you need to borrow a total of ($47,200 + $3600 + $5,400) = $56,200. At the end of the year (t=1) you will pay back $64,068 (= $56,200 × 1.14) and will pay $36,000 in living expenses. Since your income is $72,000, you will need a bonus of $28,068 (= $64,068 + $36,000 − $72,000) in order to pay all your bills.

Solution 8

First consider how much Becky could consume next year if she consumes nothing today. At most, next year she could consume $60,000 + $48,000(1.12) = $113,760. Now, let x be how much Becky consumes each year. Then,

$$x + x(1.12) = \$113,760$$

$$x = \$113,760/2.12 = \$53,660.38$$

Note that to consume $53,660.38 this year Becky must borrow $5,660.38 against next year's income. Next year Becky will pay back $5,660.38(1.12) = $6,339.63, and consume $60,000 − $6,339.63 = $53,660.37.

Solution 9

The net present values of the three investments are -$200, $600, and $1,400, respectively. Brian will not accept the first one since it has a negative net present value, but he will accept the other two.

Brian can spend his current income of $49,000 less the $10,000 investment, plus the present value of next year's income, which is ($65,000/1.25) = $52,000. Thus Brian can spend $91,000 today. To check this, notice that Brian can borrow $52,000 against the future income of $65,000 (i.e., $50,000 plus $15,000 investment income). He will thus have to repay [$52,000(1.25)] = $65,000, which will leave him with exactly zero for next year's consumption, as planned. Note also that this investment strategy provides Brian more consumption than spending all of this years income ($49,000) plus what Brian could borrow against next year's income ($40,000=$50,000/1.25).

Solution 10

If you deposit $10,000, you will have ($10,000)(1.1038) = $11,038 at the end of the year. If you need $12,000, you will have to deposit ($12,000/1.1038) = $10,871.53 today.

Solution 11

The net present value of the investment is ($80 – $60) = $20. The interest rate is found by solving for r in the following equation:

$$\$100/(1 + r) = \$80$$

The interest rate is therefore 25%. If Barbara ignores the investment opportunity, she would consume ($60 – $20)(1.25) = $50 next year. Without the investment, the most she could consume next period is ($60)(1.25) = $75. With the investment, Barbara will consume [($100 – $60)/1.25] = $32 this period.

Solution 12

Substitute the relevant values (PV = $1000; FV = $1200) into either the future value formula or the present value formula, and then solve for the interest rate r. Using the future value formula:

$$FV = PV \times (1 + r)$$

$$\$1200 = \$1000 \times (1 + r)$$

$$1 + r = 1.20$$

$$r = .20 \text{ or } r = 20\%$$

For values of greater than 20%, the investment in the asset described above is inferior to the market opportunity; for values of r less than 20%, the investment in the asset is superior to the market opportunity.

Solution 13

If Beverly borrows $10,000 at 20 % to satisfy her consumption plan, then next year she will pay back $12,000 (=$10,000 × 1.20) and have $36,000 (=$48,000 – $12,000) to consume. On the other hand, if she follows her friend's advise and borrows $15,000 and invests $5,000 in the project, then next year she will pay back $18,000 (=$15,000×1.20) and will be able to consume $42,000 (=$48,000 + $12,000 – $18,000). Thus, by investing in the project she can consume the same today and an additional $6,000 next year.

Solution 14

The $5,000 investment returns $12,000 in one year. The present value of this payoff at the market rate of 20% is $10,000. Thus, the net present value of the investment is

$$NPV = -\$5,000 + \$12,000/1.20 = \$5,000.$$

Solution 15

Clearly, Beverly could spend the $40,000 she has on hand and next year spend the $48,000 income. But a better solution is to invest $5,000 in the project and borrow $10,000 at 20% against the project's payoff of $12,000. With this strategy, she could spend $45,000 (=$40,000 – $5,000 + $10,000) today and use the project's $12,000 payoff to pay down the loan.

Solution 16

The net present value of the $1,250 investment is

$$NPV = -\$1,250 + \$1,475/1.20 = -\$20.83.$$

If the $1,250 was invested at the market rate of 20%, then next year it would be worth $1,500, or $25 more than with the investment project. The present value of this difference is $25/1.20 = $20.83.

Solution 17

Balsam's value before the investment decision is $100,000. After the decision, the value of the firm increases by the net present value of the investment. Thus, the new value is

$$\$100,000 + \$7,500 = \$107,500.$$

This value is also equal to the sum of remaining cash in the bank, the cost of the new asset, and the asset's NPV: $70,000 + $30,000 + $7,500.

Solution 18

Next year, the firm will be worth $107,500(1.20) = $129,000. Another way to look at next years value is as follows. The $70,000 cash balance will be worth $70,000(1.20) = $84,000 next year; the present value of the investment is $30,000 + $7,500 = $37,500, the future value is $37,500(1.20) = $45,000. The future value of the firm is $84,000 + $45,000 = $129,000.

Solution 19

From problem 18, the future value of the investment is ($30,000 + $7,500)(1.20) = $45,000. Therefore, Balsam's rate of return was

$$($45,000/$30,000) - 1 = .50 \text{ or } 50\%$$

Note that a $30,000 investment in the financial markets would have a future value of $30,000(1.20) = $36,000. The present value of the real asset's extra return is the project's NPV

$$($45,000 - $36,000)/1.20 = $9,000/1.20 = $7,500$$

Solution 20

Brenda could invest $40,000 in the project and then borrow $50,625/1.125 = $45,000 against future income. This amount combined with the $80,000 cash balance will provide Brenda a maximum salary of $45,000 + $80,000 = $125,000. Alternatively, Brenda could make the investment and then sell the company. In this case she would receive $80,000 + $40,000 + NPV = $120,000 + $5,000 = $125,000.

Solution 21

The present value of the future cash inflow is $2.5 million. Each of the 10,000 shares, therefore, is worth $250. In other words, an investor who purchases a share for $250 today will receive $300 one year from today. This investment provides a rate of return equal to the 20% market rate of interest. If the entrepreneur chose to issue all 10,000 shares to the general public, he would realize a gain of $500 thousand, which is equal to the net present value of the investment in the asset. By selling 9,000 shares, he has realized a gain of $450 thousand; that is, he sold nine-tenths of his $2 million investment ($1.8 million) for $2.25 million. The remaining $50 thousand is an unrealized gain, unless he also chooses to sell the additional 1,000 shares. This illustrates a general principle, new shareholders get a fair return on their investment (in this case 20%) while the existing shareholder (the entrepreneur) gets the NPV provided by the project.

Solution 22

The firm will use the $250,000 payoff next year to provide new shareholders a fair 15% return. Today's value of the 1,000 shares should be equal to the present value of $250,000.

$$\text{Value of shares} = $250,000/1.15 = $217,391.30.$$

Thus, the share price should be $217.39. The firm actually raises $217,391.30, uses $200,000 for the project, and keeps the remaining $17,391.30 for the present owners, which is the net present value of the project.

CHAPTER 4

NET PRESENT VALUE

CHAPTER MISSION STATEMENT

The purpose of Chapter 4 is to acquaint students with the time-value-of-money concept and the mathematics of calculating present and future values of multiple cash flows. The importance of compound interest is stressed. Simplifying formulas are developed and worked-out problems are presented to demonstrate their application.

The key concepts are outlined below.

> ◆Time-value-of-money
> ◆Present and future values
> > ●Single period
> > ●Multi-periods
> > ●Compound interest
> > ●Compounding periods
> ◆Simplifying formulas
> > ●Perpetuity
> > ●Growing perpetuity
> > ●Annuity
> > ●Growing annuity

CONCEPT TEST

1. When money is invested in the financial markets for multiple time periods and the interest is reinvested, the money is said to earn interest on _____ or _____ interest.

2. An interest rate is quoted as "10% compounded daily;" the 10% interest rate is an example of a _____ interest rate.

3. If 10% compounded daily is equivalent to 10.5156% compounded annually, then 10.5156% is the _____ interest rate. Are these rates equivalent?

4. The expression $(1 + r)^T$ is called a _____.

5. The expression $[1/(1 + r)^T$ is called a _____.

6. For a given stated rate, the effective rate is _____ (higher/lower) the more often the rate is compounded during the year.

7. If an interest rate is compounded an infinite number of times during the year, this is called _____ compounding.

8.   A _____ is a constant series of cash flows, occurring at regular intervals, which continues forever.

9.   An _____ is a constant series of cash flows, occurring at regular intervals, which continues for a fixed number of periods.

10.   The expression PV = [C/(r − g)] is used to find the present value of a _____.

ANSWERS TO CONCEPT TEST

1.	interest; compound	6.	higher
2.	stated annual	7.	continuous
3.	effective annual; yes	8.	perpetuity
4.	future value factor	9.	annuity
5.	present value factor	10.	growing perpetuity

PROBLEMS

Problem 1

What is the present value of $1,000 to be received in 5 years if the market interest rate is 13%?

Problem 2

What is the future value of $1,000 dollars invested at 13% for 5 years?

Problem 3

For each of the following future values, compute the present value.

Future value	Years	Interest rate	Present value
$ 498	7	13%	
1,033	3	6	
14,784	23	4	
898,156	4	31	

Problem 4

For each of the following present values, compute the future value.

Present value	Years	Interest rate	Future value
$ 123	13	13%	
4,555	8	8	
74,484	5	10	
167,332	9	1	

Problem 5

An investment offers cash flows of –$1243, $400, $889, $432 each year starting at time zero. The market interest rate is 12%. Is this a good investment?

Problem 6

An investment offers cash flows of $300, –$200, –$100 each year starting at time zero. Is this a good investment if the market rate of interest is 15%?

Problem 7

A local bank is offering 9% interest, compounded monthly, on savings accounts. If you deposit $1,500 today, how much will you have in 3 years? How much will you have in 3.5 years?

Problem 8

For each of the following, calculate the effective annual rate:

Stated rate	Number of times compounded	Effective Rate
5%	semiannually	
11%	quarterly	
16%	daily	
20%	infinite	

Problem 9

You have just joined the reputable investment banking firm of R. B. Carter & Associates, Ltd. They have offered you two different salary arrangements. You can have $50,000 per year for the next 3 years or $25,000 per year for the next 3 years, along with a $50,000 signing bonus today. If the market interest rate is 16%, compounded quarterly, which salary arrangement should you prefer?

Problem 10

Suppose the effective annual rate for a loan is 8% and the loan requires monthly payments. What is the stated rate?

Problem 11

You're tapped out, but your cousin, who has a reputation for avarice, offers you "four for five on payday;" this means you borrow $4 today and you must repay $5, 6 days from now, when you get your next paycheck. What effective annual interest rate is your cousin charging you for this loan?

Problem 12

A local bank is offering an account that has an effective annual interest rate of 12.75%. If the bank is using continuous compounding, what is the stated rate?

Problem 13

Solve for the unknown time period in each of the following:

Present value	Years	Interest rate	Future value
$ 100		12%	$ 350
123		10	351
4,100		5	8,523
10,543		6	26,783

Problem 14

Solve for the unknown interest rate in each of the following:

Present value	Years	Interest rate	Future value
$ 123	6		$ 218
1,000	5		3052
4,100	7		8,523
10,543	12		21,215

Problem 15

Suppose you are offered an investment that pays 11.55% continuously compounded. How long will it take for your money to double?

Problem 16

You expect to receive an annuity of $1,000 per year for the next five years (that is, date 1 to date 5). The market rate of interest is 12%. Assuming that you do not spend any of the income at any other time, what is the maximum you can spend from these payments at date 5? At date 0? At date 3?

Problem 17

An investment will increase in value by 270% over the next 17 years. What is the annual interest rate which, when compounded quarterly, provides this return?

Problem 18

Consider a perpetuity which pays $100 per year; the market rate of interest is 10%. What is the present value of the perpetuity? What is the present value of the perpetuity at date 3? What is the present value at date n? Under what circumstances does the value of a perpetuity change?

Problem 19

A firm invests $3 million in a project which will yield a perpetuity of $1 million per year. What is the discount rate r for which this project's net present value is $1.5 million?

Problem 20

Your life-long dream is to climb 29,028 foot Mount Everest. The expedition will cost $72,000, which you plan to save over the next 6 years. How much must you save each month to accumulate sufficient funds if your deposits earn a stated interest rate of 6% per annum compounded monthly?

Problem 21

Ten years from now, you plan on taking a year's unpaid vacation and sailing across the Pacific from Hawaii to Australia. You estimate that expenses, e.g., boat, crew, provisions, etc., will be $5000 per month over the 12-month journey. How much money will you need in the bank at the start of the trip in order to withdraw $5000 per month for expenses? The interest rate is 8.4%, compounded monthly. Assume that all payments are made at the end of the month.

Problem 22

What lump sum should you deposit in the bank today so that you will have enough money ten years from now for your trip? Recall that the interest rate is 8.4%, compounded monthly.

Problem 23

The lump sum deposit in problem 21 is out of the question given your current financial state. Instead, you believe that a systematic monthly savings plan is better. How much should you deposit monthly to insure sufficient funds in ten years for your trip?

Problem 24

You have reconsidered the monthly savings plan in problem 22, and have now decided to save a fixed percentage of your salary each month. The difference is that you expect your salary to increase at an annual rate of 2.4% compounded monthly; thus your monthly savings will also increase at the same rate. Your present salary is $4,000 per month. The interest rate remains at 8.4% compounded monthly. What percent of your monthly salary should you save?

Problem 25

An Alaskan company has received a franchise, in perpetuity, to build a pipeline from Alaska to Southern California. The pipeline will transport fresh melted glacier water to thirsty residents of the Golden State. The project will take nine years to complete at a cost of $24 million per year. Water will start flowing nine years from now, and the first water bill will be due 12 months later. The company assumes that it can raise water rates by 4% per year. The interest rate is 8%. What is the minimum first year's payment that will allow the company to just break-even? How much would the company have to charge to break-even if rates must remain constant?

Problem 26

You would like to start saving for you daughter's college education. Eighteen years from now your daughter will embark on a four-year undergraduate program at a private university. At the beginning of each of the four years you expect to pay $25,000 up front in college related expenses. How much should you save each month for the next 18 years in order to have enough funds in the bank to pay all four years' expenses when they arise? Assume that the stated interest rate is 9% per year.

Problem 27

How much would you have to save each month if you continued to save, while your daughter was in school, until you pay the last $25,000?

Problem 28

How much would you have to save each month if you increased your saving each month to match your expected 6% per year (0.5% per month) increase in salary? Assume that you save until the last $25,000 payment.

SOLUTIONS

Solution 1

The present value is $[\$1,000/(1.13)^5] = \$542.76$.

Solution 2

The future value is $[\$1,000(1.13)^5] = \$1,842.44$.

Solution 3

Future value	Years	Interest rate	Present value
$ 498	7	13%	$ 211.68
1,033	3	6	484.31
14,784	23	4	5,998.26
898,156	4	31	304,976.65

Solution 4

Present value	Years	Interest rate	Future value
$ 123	13	13%	$ 602.46
4,555	8	8	8,430.99
74,484	5	10	119,957.23
167,332	9	1	183,008.54

Solution 5

Compute the net present value for the investment as follows:

$$NPV = -\$1243 + (\$400/1.12) + (\$889/1.12^2) + (\$432/1.12^3) = \$130.337$$

Since the net present value is positive, the investment is acceptable.

Solution 6

The net present value is:

$$\$300 - (\$200/1.15) - (\$100/1.15^2) = \$50.473$$

Since the NPV is positive, this is an acceptable investment.

Solution note: In this case, the first cash flow is positive, while the subsequent cash flows are negative. This fact does not affect the calculation of the net present value, although it would affect the application of the internal rate of return criterion (discussed in chapter 6). These cash flows should be thought of as a loan. This is an acceptable 'investment' because the $300 we receive today is greater than the present value of the future cash outflows.

Solution 7

The interest rate is actually (.09/12) = .0075 or .75% per month. The future value factors for 36 months (3 years) and 42 months (3.5 years) are:

$$(1.0075)^{36} = 1.30865$$

$$(1.0075)^{42} = 1.36865$$

Multiply the future value factor times the $1,500 deposit; you will have $1,962.97 in 3 years and $2,052.97 in 3.5 years. Mathematically, you can get the same answer by compounding the effective annual rate over the number of years, 2 or 2.5 years. For example, the effective annual rate is:

$$[1 + (.09/12)]^{12} - 1 = .093807 \text{ or } 9.3807\% \text{ per year.}$$

After 3.5 years, you will have:

$$\$1,500(1.093807)^{3.5} = \$2,052.97.$$

Solution 8

Stated rate	Number of times compounded	Effective Rate
5%	semiannually	5.063%
11%	quarterly	11.462
16%	daily	17.347
20%	infinite	22.140

Note: With an infinite number of compounding periods the relationship between the stated rate and the effective rate is $\ln(1 + r_{eff}) = r_{stated}$.

Solution 9

The effective annual rate is 16.986%. The present value of $50,000 for 3 years is $110,504.31. The present value of $25,000 for 3 years is half as much, or $55,252.16. The total value of this option is $105,252.16. You should select the $50,000 per year option since it has a higher present value.

Solution 10

We need to solve the following equation for r:

$$[1 + (r/12)]^{12} - 1 = .08.$$

$$[1 + (r/12)]^{12} = 1.08.$$

Find the twelfth root of 1.08:

$$(1.08)^{1/12} = 1.006434.$$

Thus, $r/12 = 1.006434 - 1 = .006434$ and $r = 7.7208\%$.

Note: The twelfth root may be found using a calculator with a y^x function where in this case x=1/12. Alternatively, using natural logarithms,

let $z = (1.08)^{1/12}$, then taking the log of both sides

$$\ln z = (1/12)\ln(1.08) = .006413$$

Solving for z, $z = e^{\ln z} = e^{.006413} = 1.006434$,

where e is the base of the natural logarithm system and is approximately equal to 2.7183.

Solution 11

The interest rate is $[(5/4) - 1] = 25\%$ for 6 days. There are about $(365/6) = 60.8333$ such periods in a year. The effective rate is thus 1.25 raised to the power 60.8333, minus 1. This works out to be a nice round 78.59 million percent. This seems somewhat high; so maybe doing business with relatives is not such a good idea.

Solution 12

We need to solve for r in the following equation:

$$e^r - 1 = .1275$$

$$e^r = 1.1275$$

Take the log of both sides,

$$\ln (e^r) = \ln (1.1275)$$

$$r \ln(e) = r = .1200$$

Note: By definition, $\ln (e) = 1$.

Solution 13

Present value	Years	Interest rate	Future value
$ 100	11.05	12%	$ 350
123	11.00	10	351
4,100	15.00	5	8,523
10,543	16.00	6	26,783

Note: Your financial calculator may only return an integer number of periods, thus you may need to solve for n in the following formula

$$FV = PV (1 + r)^n.$$

Solution 14

Present value	Years	Interest rate	Future value
$ 123	6	10%	$ 218
1,000	5	25	3052
4,100	7	11	8,523
10,543	12	6	21,215

Solution 15

There are two ways to solve this problem. First, calculate the effective annual rate and then find out how long it would take to double your money at that rate. The effective annual rate is $r_{eff} = 12.24\%$,

$$1 + r_{eff} = e^{.1155}$$

The time it takes to double solves the following

$$(1.1224)^t = 2.0,$$

so it will take 6 years to double your money. Alternatively, solve the following equation for t:

$$\$1(e^{.1155t}) = \$2.$$

Solve for by taking the natural log of 2 and dividing by .1155; the solution is 6.00 years.

Solution 16

The first question requires that you find the future value of the annuity. This can be done as follows:

$$FV = \$1,000 \times [1.12^4 + 1.12^3 + 1.12^2 + 1.12^1 + 1]$$

$$= \$1,000 \times [6.35285] = \$6,352.85$$

Note that the term in square brackets is a future value annuity factor, which can be found in any set of present/future value tables. This calculation indicates that you could invest your first $1,000 payment, to be received at date 1, for a period of four years, at a 12% rate; the second payment could be invested for three years, and so on; the proceeds of these investments could then be spent at date 5.

The second question requires that you find the present value of the annuity. This can be done as follows:

$$PV = \$1,000 \ [1/(1.12)^1 + 1/(1.12)^2 + 1/(1.12)^3$$

$$+ \ 1/(1.12)^4 + 1/(1.12)^5]$$

$$= \$1,000 \ [3.60478] = \$3,604.78.$$

The term in square brackets is a present value annuity factor, which can be found in any set of present value tables. This calculation indicates that you could borrow $3,604.78 today, at a 12% interest rate, and repay the loan in five annual installments of $1,000 each.

The third question requires that you invest the first two payments and borrow against the last two payments in order to spend the maximum possible at date 3. The maximum possible consumption at date 3 is $5,064.45 = $1,000 $[1.12^2 + 1.12^1 + 1 + 1/(1.12)^1 + 1/(1.12)^2]$.

Solution 17

Solve the following equation for r (where PV is the beginning amount):

$$PV \ (1 + r/4)^{68} = FV = PV(1 + 2.70) = 3.70PV$$

$$(1 + r/4)^{68} = \ 3.70$$

$$r/4 = (3.70)^{1/68} - 1 = .019426$$

Therefore, r = .07770 or 7.770%. Note: (FV − PV)/PV = 2.70 or 270%; $(3.70)^{1/68}$ is the 68th root of 3.70 or 1.019426.

Solution 18

The present value of the perpetuity is given by the following formula:

$$PV = C/r = \$100/.10 = \$1,000$$

Three years from now (or n years from now) the value of the perpetuity is still $1,000. An investor who purchases the perpetuity at any subsequent date is purchasing a perpetual series of payments, regardless of the date. The value of the perpetuity changes only if the market rate of interest changes.

Solution 19

Solve the following equation for r:

$$-\$3,000,000 + (\$1,000,000)/r = \$1,500,000$$

The solution is r = .2222 or 22.22%. For values of r less than 22.22%, the NPV of the project is greater than $1.500,000.

Solution 20

The $72,000 goal is the future value of an annuity. With a periodic rate of 0.5% per month for 72 months, the monthly payment solves the following future value of an annuity equation.

$$(1/.005)[(1.005)^{72} - 1] \times PMT = 72,000$$

$$PMT = \$833.25$$

Notice that the future value of a t-period annuity is just the present value of a t-period annuity times the future value factor $(1 + r)^t$.

Alternatively, you can find the present value of $72,000 $(=72,000/(1.005)^{72} = 50,277.77)$ and set this equal to the present value of an 72-month annuity.

$$\$50,277.77 = (1/.005)[1 - 1/(1.005)^{72}] \times PMT$$

$$PMT = \$50,277.77/60.3395 = \$833.25$$

Solution 21

Calculate the present value at date 10 of a 12-month annuity of $5000 per month. The monthly interest rate is 8.4%/12 = .7%. The present value of an annuity factor is

$$(1/.007)[1 - 1/(1.007)^{12}] = 11.4714$$

Thus, the amount required is $5,000(11.4714) = 57,357.

Solution 22

Find the present value (PV) such that the future value (FV) is $57,357.

$$PV = FV/(1.007)^{120} = \$57,357/2.3096 = \$24,834$$

Solution 23

Find the annuity payment such that its future value is $57,357, or equivalently, find an annuity payment such that its present value is $24,834.

$$FV = \$57,357 = (PMT/.007)[(1.007)^{120} - 1] = PMT(187.0855)$$

$$PMT = \$57,357/187.0855 = \$306.58$$

or, using present values

$$PV = \$24,834 = (PMT/.007)[1 - 1/(1.007)^{120}] = PMT(81.0035)$$

$$PMT = \$24,834/81.0035 = \$306.58$$

Solution 24

This is an example of a growing annuity. The present value of an annuity whose first payment is C, which grows at rate g for T periods, when the interest rate per period is r, is:

$$PV = C[1 - ((1 + g)/(1 + r))^{T}]/(r - g)$$

In this problem we want to solve for C, given that PV = $24,834, g = 2.4%/12 = .2%, r = 8.4%/12 = .7%, and T = 120. Thus,

$$\$24,834 = C[1 - ((1.002)/(1.007))^{120}]/(.007 - .002)$$

$$\$24,834 = C(89.9424)$$

$$C = \$24,834/89.9424 = \$276.11$$

Remember that C represents the payment at date 1 when your salary will be $4,000(1.002) = $4,008. The percentage of your salary that you must save is $276.11/$4008 = .0689 or 6.89%.

Solution 25

This problem involves a nine-year annuity, a growing perpetuity, and a perpetuity. To break-even, the present value of the revenues must equal the present value of the costs. The present value of the project's cost is

$$PV(Cost) = \$24 \text{ million } (1/.08)[1 - 1/(1.08)^{9}] = \$150 \text{ million}$$

If revenues start at date 10 and grow at 4% per year, the present value today (date 0) is

$$PV(Revenues) = [C/(.08 - .04)] [1/(1.08)^{9}]$$

Note that the first term in square brackets finds the present value at date 9 of a growing perpetuity starting at date 10, while the second term in square brackets discounts this value back nine years to the present. Setting this equal to $150 million and solving for C find

$$\$150 \text{ million} = [C/.04] \, [.500]$$

$$C = \$12 \text{ million}$$

Thus, the firm should charge $12 million the first year and 4% higher each subsequent year. If, on the other hand, the payment must remain constant, then the break-even rate becomes

$$PV = \$150 \text{ million} = [C/.08] \, [1/(1.08)^9]$$

$$C = \$150 \text{ million} \, (.08/.5) = \$24 \text{ million}$$

Interestingly, if the company pays out $24 million per year for nine years, and then a year later starts receiving $24 million per year forever, the company just breaks-even. By break-even we mean, of course, the company receives a fair rate of return on its investment.

Solution 26

The first step in finding your monthly saving requirement is to calculate how much you would need in the bank after 18 years so that you could withdraw $25,000 at year 18 and $25,000 each year for the next three years. This amount is the present value of a three year annuity plus $25,000:

$$PV(\text{year } 18) = \$25,000 \, (1/.09381)[1 - 1/(1.09381)^3] + \$25,000 = \$87,855.12$$

Note that we use the effective rate of 9.381%, rather than the stated rate of 9%, for consistency with monthly compounding that we will use later to find the monthly payment.

To find the monthly payment, set $87,855.12 as the future value of a 216 (=12×18) period annuity:

$$\$87,855.12 = PMT \times (1/.0075)[(1.0075)^{216} - 1]$$

$$PMT = \$163.80$$

Thus, you would save $163.80 each month for 216 months, at which time you would withdraw $25,000 for the first year's expenses. Without making additional deposits, you would withdraw $25,000 at the end of months 228, 240, and 252.

Solution 27

In this problem, monthly deposits continue through month 252. The future value at month 252 of the four $25,000 payments is

$$\$114,972.17 = \$25,000 \ (1/.09381)[(1.09381)^4 - 1]$$

Again, we use the effective rate of 9.381% for annual compounding. Set this value equal to the future value of a 252-period annuity with unknown payment, and a compounding rate of 0.75% per period.

$$\$114.972.17 = PMT \times (1/.0075)[(1.0075)^{252} - 1]$$

$$PMT = \$154.73$$

Now, you make deposits each month for 252 months. You withdraw $25,000 at months 216, 228, 240, and 252, at which time the account will be exhausted.

Solution 28

The solution proceeds as in the previous problem by finding the future value (=$114,972.17) at month 252 of the four $25,000 payments. The next step is to find the present value of this amount.

$$PV = \$114,972.17/(1.0075)^{252} = \$17,491.98$$

Set this present value equal to the present value of a growing annuity (equation 4.15 in the text). You expect your monthly payments to grow along with your salary at 0.5% per month. You can find the initial monthly payment by setting the $17,491.98 equal to the present value of a growing annuity:

$$\$17,491.98 = PMT \times [\ \frac{1}{r-g} - \frac{1}{r-g} \times (\frac{1+g}{1+r})^T\ ]$$

Set r = 0.0075, g = 0.0050, and T = 252, and solve for PMT = $93.98. Thus, your first payment is $93.98 and payments will grow by 0.5% each month:

$$\$93.98, \$94.45, \$94.92 \dots \$328.63 \text{ at month } 252.$$

Note that the last payment equals $93.98(1.005)^{251}$.

CHAPTER 5

HOW TO VALUE BONDS AND STOCKS

CHAPTER MISSION STATEMENT

Chapter 5 demonstrates how the mathematics of compounding and discounting is used to value bonds and stocks. The values of pure discount bonds, level coupon bonds, and perpetual bonds are determined. The valuation of common and preferred stock is shown. The discussion places special emphasis on dividend patterns that follow growing perpetuities and growing annuities. The concept of the net present value of a growth opportunity (NPVGO) is introduced and illustrated through examples. The relationship between the firm's growth rate and reinvested earnings is shown, along with the influence of growth on a firm's price to earnings ratio, and the firm's value. The Appendix discusses the term structure of interest rates.

The key topics are outlined below.

- ♦Bond values
  - ●pure discount bonds
  - ●level-coupon bonds
  - ●perpetual bonds (consols)
  - ●yield to maturity
- ♦Stock values
  - ●dividends and capital gains
  - ●zero growth dividends
  - ●constant growth dividends
  - ●differential growth dividends
- ♦Growth rates
  - ●retention ratio
  - ●return on equity
- ♦Growth opportunities
- ♦NPVGO model (Advanced)
- ♦Price-earnings ratio and growth opportunities

CONCEPT TEST

1. A bond that promises a single payment at a future date is called a _____ bond or _____ bond.

2. A _____ promises regular coupon interest payments, as well as a specified principal payment at the maturity date.

3. Bonds that are outstanding forever are called _____ or _____.

4. The regular cash payments for a level-coupon bond are called _____.

5. A financial instrument that promises a fixed payment every period for a set number of periods is called an _____.

6. The amount that a bond pays when it matures is called the bond's _____ and is typically $_____.

7. Bond prices and bond yields are _____ related. This means that bond prices _____ when interest rates rise.

8. A bond pays a coupon of $120. If the market interest rate is 10%, then the bond will sell at a _____. If the market interest rate is 15%. then the bond will sell at a _____.

9. The value of a share of common stock is equal to the _____ of all future dividends.

10. Growth in earnings will occur when total investment exceeds _____.

11. The earnings growth rate equals _____ times return on _____.

12. The present value per share of a future investment's net present value is referred to as _____.

13. The firm's price-to-earnings ratio is _____ related to the firm's discount rate.

14. Firms that have good growth opportunities will likely have a _____ P/E ratio.

ANSWERS TO CONCEPT TEST

1. pure discount; zero-coupon
2. level-coupon bond
3. perpetuities; consols
4. coupon payments or 'coupons'
5. annuity
6. face value; 1000
7. inversely; fall

8. premium; discount
9. present value
10. depreciation
11. retention ratio; retained earnings
12. NPVGO
13. negatively
14. high

PROBLEMS

Problem 1

The Cottonwood Corporation has issued a 5-year pure discount bond with a face value of $1,000; the market rate of interest is 8%. Calculate the bond's current value.

Problem 2

What is the value of a consol that pays $250 every 6 months when the annual market interest rate is 14%?

Problem 3

The Chestnut Company has a level-coupon bond outstanding (face value = $1,000) that pays $120 per year and has 10 years to maturity. If the yield for similar bonds is currently 14%. what is the bond's value?

Problem 4

Suppose the Chestnut Company's bond required semiannual coupon interest payments. What would be its value?

Problem 5

You are thinking about investing in a $1,000 face value bond which will mature in two years. The bond has an 8% coupon and pays interest semiannually. The current yield to maturity on similar bonds is 6%, and rates are not expected to change. What is the bond's price today and after each interest payment?

Problem 6

A $1,000 face value bond that matures in 20 years has a coupon rate of 12% and pays interest semiannually. What is the value of this bond today if similar bonds have a 10% yield to maturity? What would be the bond's value if yields suddenly increase to 14%?

Problem 7

Convex, Inc., has just paid a $2 annual dividend on its common stock. The dividend is expected to increase at a constant 8% per year indefinitely. If the required rate of return on Convex's stock is 16%, what is its current value?

Problem 8

Cyprus Corporation's next annual dividend is expected to be $4. The growth rate in dividends over the following three years is forecasted at 15%. After that, Cyprus's growth rate is anticipated to equal the industry average of 5%. If the required rate of return is 18%, what is the current value of the stock?

Problem 9

The Cougar Co. has a level-coupon bond outstanding with a $90 coupon interest payment, payable annually. The bond has 20 years to maturity, and similar bonds currently yield 7%. By prior agreement the company will skip the coupon payments in years 8, 9, and 10. These coupons will be repaid without interest at maturity. What is the bond's value?

Problem 10

The dividend paid this year (date 0) on a share of common stock is $10. Assuming dividends grow at a 5% rate for the foreseeable future, and that the required rate of return is 10%, what is the value of the stock today? Last year (date −1)? Next year (date +1)?

Problem 11

A firm just paid a dividend of $2.20 per share of common stock and the current stock price is $57.75. Dividends are expected to grow at a 5% rate for the foreseeable future. What is the current rate of return for this stock? If in the past dividends grew at 10% per year, for example, the current dividend is 10% higher than its predecessor, what were the stock prices over the past two years?

Problem 12

A company pays a current dividend of $1.20 per share on its common stock. The annual dividend will increase by 3%, 4% and 5%, respectively, over the next three years, and then by 6% per year thereafter. The appropriate discount rate is 12%. What is the current price of the stock? What is the capital gain (or loss) on the stock over the past year?

Problem 13

The current price of a stock (P_0) is $20 and last year's price (P_{-1}) was $18.87. The current year's dividend (Div_0) is $2. Assume a constant growth rate (g) in dividends and stock price. What is the stock's rate of return for the coming year?

Problem 14

Canyon Recreational Products has earnings of $1.60 per share and plans to pay a $0.64 dividend. In the past Canyon Rec. Prod. has earned a return of 25% on its investments, and the firm believes this will continue in the future. At what rate do you expect Canyon's earnings to grow?

Problem 15

Continuing with the previous problem, what will be Canyon Recreational Product's earnings and dividends next year if the firm maintains its dividend payout policy?

Problem 16

A corporation issues a bond today with a $1,000 face value, an 8% coupon interest rate, and maturity in 25 years. An investor purchases the bond for $1,000. What is the yield to maturity?

Problem 17

Suppose that the investor bought the bond described in the previous problem for $900. What is the yield maturity?

Problem 18

Suppose that the bond described in the previous two problems has a price of $1,100 five years after it is issued. What is the yield to maturity at that time?

Problem 19

A pure discount bond is selling for $400; it has a face value of $1,000 and the maturity date is 14 years from today. What is the rate of return, or yield to maturity, for the bond?

Problem 20

A share of preferred stock with a $12 annual dividend is selling for $75. What is the rate of return for the preferred stock?

Problem 21

The Coachella Gold Mining Company just paid a $4.50 per share dividend, the company's 100th consecutive annual dividend. The future does not look bright, however. The mine is virtually depleted, and earnings are expected to decline 10% per year for the foreseeable future. Carlos Del Oro, the company's president, plans to continue the firm's policy of paying out 45% of earnings as dividends for the next five years. After five years the firm will liquidate all assets, and then use the proceeds to buy back all outstanding shares six years from now at $9.566 per share. The required rate of return on the firm's stock is 20%. What is today's stock price?

Problem 22

Cummaquid Seafoods expects to earn $1.25 million per year for the foreseeable future selling fresh seafood to restaurants on Cape Cod. The company sees a profit opportunity in setting up its own restaurant that will specialize in clams, scallops, and lobster. This new operation will require a one-time investment next year of $500,000 and is expected to generate additional earnings of $130,000 per year forever starting the following year. Cummaquid's discount rate is 12%. What is the value of Cummaquid before the new investment is announced? What is the firm's value after the announcement? What is the net present value of the growth opportunity (NPVGO)?

Problem 23

The Cape Cod Cranberry Company has been harvesting cranberries and producing cranberry sauce since 1749. The demand for cranberry sauce has been remarkably stable over this period; in fact, earnings have been $1,479 thousand per year for the last 100 years, and no change is expected in the future. However, for the last 20 years the firm has been contemplating the introduction of a new product to celebrate the firm's 250th birthday. The new product will require a $750 thousand investment two years from now and will produce a 30% return starting in year three. Since the new product is related to the firm's 250th birthday, income from the project will last only five years. Cape Cod's cost of capital is 6%. What is the value of the firm if the new project is not undertaken? What is the value of the firm if the new project proceeds as planned?

Problem 24

What is Cape Cod Cranberry Company's price-to-earnings ratio?

SOLUTIONS

Solution 1

Because the bond pays out a single lump sum of $1,000 in 5 years, and the interest rate is 8%, the value is $[\$1,000/(1.08)^5] = \$680.58$.

Solution 2

The interest rate is 7% every 6 months, so the value of this perpetuity is $3,571.43 (=$250/.07) .

Solution 3

The bond's value is the present value of the coupon payments plus the present value of the $1,000 face amount:

$$PV = \$120/(1.14) + \$120/(1.14)^2 + ...$$

$$+ \$120/(1.14)^{10} + \$1,000/(1.14)^{10}$$

$$= \$120 \, (5.2161) + \$1,000 \, (.2697) = \$895.68$$

Solution 4

The coupon payments are now $60 per period for 20 time periods; the relevant discount rate is 7%. The present value is:

$$PV = \$60/(1.07) + \$60/(1.07)^2 + ...$$

$$+ \$60/(1.07)^{20} + \$1,000/(1.07)^{20}$$

$$= \$60 \, (10.5940) + \$1,000 \, (.2584) = \$894.06$$

Solution 5

The bond's price is the present value of all future interest and principal payments discounted at the yield to maturity. Since interest payments occur semiannually, each interest payment is $1,000(.08)/2 = $40.00, and the discount rate is 6%/2 = 3% per six-month period. The bond values are

$$PV_0 = \$40/(1.03) + \$40/(1.03)^2 + ... + \$1,040/(1.03)^4 = \$1,037.17$$

$$PV_1 = \$40/(1.03) + \$40/(1.03)^2 + \$1,040/(1.03)^3 = \$1,028.29$$

$$PV_2 = \$40/(1.03) + \$1,040/(1.03)^2 = \$1,019.14$$

$$PV_3 = \$1,040/(1.03) = \$1,009.71$$

Note that your return should be the prevailing yield to maturity 6% per year or 3% per six-months. Over the first six-month period your return consists of a $40/$1,037.17 = .0386 or 3.86% interest yield and a capital loss of ($1,028.29 − $1,037.17)/$1,037.17 = −.0086 or −.86%. Total return equals 3.86% − .86% = 3.00%.

Solution 6

With a yield to maturity of 10% per annum, the value of this 20-year bond paying interest of $60 semiannually is

$$PV = \$60/(1.05) + \$60/(1.05)^2 + ...$$

$$+ \$60/(1.05)^{40} + \$1,000/(1.05)^{40}$$

$$= \$60 (17.1591) + \$1,000 (.1420) = \$1,171.55$$

The bond sells at a premium because the current yield is less than the coupon rate. Now, if the yield suddenly jumps to 14%, above the coupon rate, the bond will sell at a discount

$$PV = \$60/(1.07) + \$60/(1.07)^2 + ...$$

$$+ \$60/(1.07)^{40} + \$1,000/(1.07)^{40}$$

$$= \$60 (13.3317) + \$1,000 (.0668) = \$866.68.$$

Solution 7

Since the growth rate in dividends is constant, the value of the stock is $[Div_1/(r - g)]$. The next dividend is expected to be $[\$2(1 + .08)] = \$2.16$, so the value is $[\$2.16/(.16 - .08)] = \$27.00$.

Solution 8

The current value of the stock is equal to the present value of the dividends from the high growth phase plus the present value of the stock price when the high growth phase ends. Notice that the next dividend Div_1 is forecasted at $4. To calculate the stock price at date 4, we must first determine the date 5 dividend (Div_5):

$$Div_5 = Div_1 \times (1.15)^3 \times (1.05) = \$6.39$$

The price at date 4 is thus $[\$6.39/(.18 - .05)] = \$49.15$. The present value of this amount is $[\$49.15/(1.18)^4] = \$25.35$. We can calculate the PV of the first four dividend payments as follows:

Year (t)	Growth rate (g)	Expected Dividend	Present Value
1	15%	$4.00	$3.39
2	15%	$4.60	$3.30
3	15%	$5.29	$3.22
4	15%	$6.08	$3.14

The total present value for the first four dividend payments is $13.05. The share value is thus ($25.35 + $13.05) = $38.40.

Solution 9

This problem can be solved by calculating the present value of each coupon payment, plus the present value of the face value. An easier approach is to calculate the present value under the assumption that all the coupons are paid; then deduct the present value of the coupons that are skipped and add the present value of the coupons paid at maturity. The value of the bond (ignoring the skipped and repaid coupons) is $1,211.88 (check this for practice). The present value of the skipped coupons is:

$$PV = \$90/(1.07)^8 + \$90/(1.07)^9 + \$90/(1.07)^{10} = \$147.09$$

At maturity, an extra (3)($90) = $270 will be paid. The present value of this $270 is $69.77. Thus the value of the bond is ($1,211.88 - $147.09 + $69.77) = $1,134.56.

Solution 10

The value today is:

$$P_0 = Div_1/(r - g) = \$10(1.05)/(.10 - .05) = \$210.00$$

The value last year was:

$$P_{-1} = Div_0/(r - g) = \$10/(.10 - .05) = \$200.00$$

The value next year will be:

$$P_{+1} = Div_2/(r - g) = \$10(1.05)^2/(.10 - .05) = \$220.50$$

Note that the stock price grows at 5% per year.

Solution 11

Substitute $P_0 = \$57.75$, $Div_0=2.20$, $g=.05$ into the following equation and solve for r:

$$P_0 = \$57.75 = Div_1/(r - g) = \$2.20(1.05)/(r - .05)$$

Solving for r, the rate of return is = .09 or 9%. In order to determine the capital gain (or loss) find the value of the stock last year (P_{-1}). Because at time $t = -1$ and $t = -2$ dividends were not expected to grow at a constant rate forever, we can not use the constant growth formula to find earlier prices. Instead, we can just discount the current dividend and stock price at the rate of return found above.

$$P_{-1} = (Div_0 + P_0)/(1 + r) = (\$2.20 + \$57.75)/(1.09) = \$55.00$$

$$P_{-2} = (Div_{-1} + P_{-1})/(1 + r) = (\$2.00 + \$55.00)/(1.09) = \$52.29.$$

Solution 12

Dividends for the next three years are determined as follows:

$$Div_1 = \$1.20 \times (1.03) = \$1.24$$

$$Div_2 = \$1.20 \times (1.03) \times (1.04) = \$1.29$$

$$Div_3 = \$1.20 (1.03) \times (1.04) \times (1.05) = \$1.35$$

The year 3 price is:

$$P_3 = Div_4/(r - g) = \$1.35(1.06)/(.12 - .06) = \$23.83$$

The current price (P_0) is the present value of the next three year's dividends plus the present value of P_3, discounted at 12%; P_0 is $20.06. In order to find the capital gain, we must determine last year's price (P_{-1}) by finding the present value of the dividends Div_0 to Div_3, discounted to last year, plus the present value of P_3, also discounted to last year; P_{-1} is equal to $18.98, so that the capital gain is ($20.06 - $ 18.98) = $1.08.

Bonds and Stocks

Solution 13

This problem can be solved by rewriting the following equation and solving for r:

$$P_0 = Div_1/(r - g)$$

$$r = (Div_1/P_0) + g$$

We know that $P_0 = \$20$. We can determine the values of both g and Div_1 from the information given. The growth rate for dividends is the same as the growth rate for stock price; since the price increased from $18.87 to $20, g is 6%. Applying the growth rate to dividends, we see that $Div_1 = [\$2(1.06)] = \$2.12$. Substituting these values, we find that r = .166 or 16.6%.

Solution 14

A firm's growth rate is determined by the fraction of earnings that it reinvests back into the firm and the return it gets on these investments. For Canyon Recreational Products, its growth rate is

$$g = \text{Retention ratio} \times \text{Return on retained earnings}$$

$$g = (1 - 0.64/1.60) \times .25$$

$$g = .60 \times .25 = .15$$

Solution 15

Next year's earnings and dividends should be 15% higher than present levels. That is, earnings will be

$$\text{Next year's earnings} = \$1.60(1.15) = \$1.84$$

$$\text{Next year's dividend} = \$0.64(1.15) = \$0.736$$

To see this, Canyon retains $0.96 (=$1.60 - $0.64) which earns a 25% return. Thus, next year this $0.96 investment will contribute $0.24 (=$0.94 × 0.25) to earnings. New earnings will be $1.60 + $0.24 = $1.84. If Canyon pays out 40% of earnings as dividends, then next years dividend will be $1.84 × 0.40 = $0.736.

Solution 16

The yield to maturity is the value of r in the following equation, where A^T_r is the present value of an annuity factor for T periods at rate r:

$$PV = (C \times A^T_r) + \$1,000/(1 + r)^T$$

$$PV = \$1,000 = (\$80 \times A^{25}_r) + \$1,000/(1 + r)^{25}$$

Trial-and-error indicates that the solution is r = .08 or 8%; that is, when r = .08, the present value of the future payments is exactly $1,000. However, this problem should be solved by inspection by realizing that the $80 coupon payment is 8% of the face value of the bond. Consider an investor who deposits $1,000 in an account which pays $80 interest each year; the investor withdraws each interest payment but leaves the principal on deposit for 25 years, at which time she withdraws the $1,000. Clearly, the investor has earned 8% interest on her principal and, since she has not left any interest on deposit to accumulate compound interest, 8% is the rate of return for the deposit. Similarly, the yield to maturity for the bond is 8%, the same as the coupon interest rate. The result is true regardless of the time period; that is, an investor who buys a bond for its $1,000 face value receives a yield to maturity equal to the coupon interest rate.

Solution 17

The yield to maturity is the value of r in the following equation:

$$PV = (C \times A^T_r) + \$1,000/(1 + r)^T$$

$$PV = \$900 = (\$80 \times A^{25}_r) + \$1,000/(1 + r)^{25}$$

We determined in the previous problem that the yield to maturity is 8% when the price of the bond is $1,000. Now, the purchase price is less than $1,000, so that the yield to maturity must be greater than 8%. Therefore, using trial-and-error, we first guess that the yield to maturity is 10%, and calculate the present value:

$$PV = (\$80 \times A^{25}_{10\%}) + \$1,000/(1.10)^{25}$$

$$PV = (\$80 \times 9.077) + \$1,000/(1.10)^{25} = \$818.46$$

Since a price of $818.46 implies a yield to maturity of 10%, the yield to maturity for the $900 price is less than 10%. If we now guess that the yield is 9%, we find that the present value is $901.77. Therefore, the yield to maturity is slightly greater than 9%. The precise value of the yield to maturity is 9.0197%, as determined using a financial calculator.

Solution 18

The yield to maturity is the value of r in the following equation:

$$PV = (C \times A^T_r) + \$1,000/(1 + r)^T$$

$$PV = \$1,100 = (\$80 \times A^{20}_r) + \$1,000/(1 + r)^{20}$$

We know that the yield to maturity is less than the coupon rate because the bond is selling at a premium. Therefore, we will initially guess that r = 6%, and calculate PV = $1,229.40. Our second guess is that r = 7%, and PV = $1,105.94. Therefore, the yield to maturity is slightly greater than 7%; the exact value is 7.0522%.

Solution 19

Substitute PV = $400, FV = $1,000 and T = 14 into the following equation and solve for r:

$$FV = PV \, (1 + r)^T$$

$$\$1,000 = \$400 \, (1 + r)^{14}$$

$$2.50 = (1 + r)^{14}$$

$$r = (2.50)^{1/14} - 1 = .0676 \text{ or } 6.76\%$$

Solution 20

Ordinary preferred stock pay a constant dividend in perpetuity. Thus, substitute C=$12 and PV=$75 into the following equation and solve for r:

$$PV = C/r$$

$$\$75 = \$12/r$$

Therefore, r = .16 or 16%.

Solution 21

Today's stock price is the present value of the next five dividends plus the present value of the price shareholders will receive in year six. Next year's dividend will be 45% of next year's earnings, which will be 10% less than this year's earnings. Since the payout ratio is .45 and this year's dividend is $4.50, then this year's earnings must be $10.00 per share. Next year's earnings will be $10.00(.9) = $9.00 and the dividend will be $9.00(.45) = $4.05. Thereafter, dividends will decline by 10% per year along with earnings. Thus, today's stock price is

$$P_0 = \$4.05/(1.20) + \$3.645/(1.20)^2 + ...$$

$$+ 2.657/(1.20)^5 + \$9.566/(1.20)^6 = \$13.50$$

Note that since dividends are expected to decline at a constant 10% per year forever, the constant dividend growth model can be used to determine today's price. That is,

$$P_0 = Div_1/(r - g) = \$4.05/[.20 - (-.10)] =$$

$$\$4.05/.30 = \$13.50$$

Solution 22

If Cummaquid maintains existing operations, its value is

$$\text{Value} = \$1.25 \text{ million}/.12 = \$10.417 \text{ million}.$$

The value of the investment opportunity is

$$\text{Value of opportunity} = \$130,000/.12 = \$1,083,333.$$

The net present value of the opportunity is

$$\text{NPV of opportunity} = \$1,083,333. - \$500,000$$

$$\text{NPV} = \$583,333.$$

This is the NPV next year. This year the NPV is

$$\text{PV (NPV)} = \$583,333./(1.12) = \$520,833.$$

This is the investment's NPVGO. Thus, after the announcement of the investment opportunity, Cummaquid's value will increase to

$$\text{Value} = \$10,416,667. + \$520,833. = \$10,937,500.$$

Solution 23

Clearly, Cape Cod Cranberry is an example of a cash cow. Thus, the value of the firm if no new investments are made and earnings remain constant for the foreseeable future is

$$\text{PV} = E/r = \$1,479/.06 = \$24,650 \text{ thousand}$$

The value of the firm today if it undertakes the new investment two years from now depends on the investment's net present value. The net present value is

$$\text{NPV(year 2)} = -\$750 + [\$750(.30)]\ A^5_{6\%}$$

$$= -\$750 + [\$225]\ 4.2124 = \$197.79 \text{ thousand}$$

The value of the firm is its value as a cash cow plus the present value (at time zero) of all future investment NPVs. The latter value is the net present value of growth opportunities (NPVGO). Thus, the value of Cape Cod Cranberry is

$$\text{PV} = \text{cash cow} + \text{NPVGO}$$

$$= \$24,650 + \$197.79/(1.06)^2$$

$$= \$24,650 + \$176 = \$24,826 \text{ thousand}$$

Solution 24

Since the number of shares outstanding is not known, the P/E ratio will be calculated using total firm value divided by total earnings. From the previous problem, PV = cash cow + NPVGO, thus

$$P/E = PV/earnings = \$24,826/\$1,479 = 16.8$$

The P/E ratio may also be expressed as

$$P/E = 1/r + NPVGO/earnings$$

$$= 1/.06 + \$176/\$1,479 = 16.8$$

Notice that the P/E ratio is the inverse of the cost of capital only when NPVGO equals zero.

APPENDIX 5A

TERM STRUCTURE OF INTEREST RATES

The appendix briefly describes the term structure of interest rates. For convenience, we generally assume that interest rates do not depend on a bond's term to maturity and that interest rates are constant over time. In practice, this is clearly not the case. Longer maturity bonds usually command a higher return, and interest rates vary over time as (among other factors) inflation concerns change. Spot rates, future rates, and the term structure are defined. Two theories of term structure are discussed: expectations hypothesis and the liquidity preference hypothesis.

CONCEPT TEST

A1. Interest rates observed in the market place at time zero are called _____.

A2. Interest rates that are hypothesized to exist in future periods are called _____.

A3. The relationship between spot rates on pure discount bonds and the maturity of the bonds is known as _____.

A4. The expectations theory suggests that the forward rate _____ the future spot rate.

A5. The liquidity preference theory suggests that when investors' time horizon is shorter than the maturity of bonds, then the forward rate should _____ the future spot rate.

A6. The interest rate appropriate for discounting a cash flow to be received in year 5 is called the 5-year _____ rate.

ANSWERS TO CONCEPT TEST

A1. spot rates
A2. forward rates
A3. term structure of interest rates

A4. equals
A5. exceed
A6. spot

PROBLEMS

Problem A1

Consider two $1,000 par value zero-coupon bonds. Bond A matures next year and is currently priced at $952.38. Bond B matures two years from now and its price is $873.44. Calculate the one- and two-year spot rates and the forward rate.

Problem A2

Extending the previous problem, assume that the three year spot rate is 11%. What is today's price of bond C, a three-year, $1,000 face value, zero-coupon bond? What is the forward rate for year 3?

Problem A3

The one-, two-, and three-year spot rates are $r_1 = 12\%$, $r_2 = 13\%$, and $r_3 = 14\%$. Determine the price and yield-to-maturity of a three-year, $1,000 face value, 10% coupon bond.

SOLUTIONS

Solution A1

The one-year spot rate, r_1 is obtained from bond A:

$$\$952.38 = \$1,000/(1 + r_1)$$

$$r_1 = .050 \text{ or } 5.0\%$$

The two-year spot rate, r_2, is obtained from bond B:

$$\$873.44 = \$1,000/(1 + r_2)^2$$

$$r_2 = .070 \text{ or } 7.0\%$$

The forward rate is found using both spot rates. In equilibrium, investing in bond A today, receiving the $1,000 face value next year, and reinvesting the $1,000 in a new one-year zero-coupon bond should produce the same return as investing in bond B today. The future hypothetical one-year rate is the forward rate, f_2. Thus, the forward rate is

$$(1 + r_1)(1 + f_2) = (1 + r_2)^2$$

$$(1 + .05)(1 + f_2) = (1.07)^2$$

$$f_2 = (1.07)^2/(1.05) - 1 = .0904 \text{ or } 9.04\%$$

Solution A2

The price of the new three-year bond is

$$PV = \$1,000/(1.11)^3 = \$731.19$$

Investing in bond C for three years must provide the same return as investing in bond B for two years and a one-year bond over year three. At time zero, the expected rate on the one-year bond is the forward rate for year three, f_3. The forward rate is found from

$$(1 + r_2)^2 (1 + f_3) = (1 + r_3)^3$$

$$(1 + .07)^2 (1 + f_3) = (1.11)^3$$

$$f_2 = (1.11)^3/(1.07)^2 - 1 = .1945 \text{ or } 19.45\%$$

Note that if you invest $731.19 in bond C you will get back $1,000 at the end of year three. If you invest $731.19 in bond B for two years you will receive $837.14; reinvest this over year three at f_3 and you end up with $837.14(1.1945) = \$999.96$ (or $1,000 with rounding error). On the other hand, you could invest $731.19 in three consecutive one year bonds: Bond A for one year, a bond with forward rate f_2 for the second year, and a bond with forward rate f_3 for the third year. After three years you would have $731.19(1.05)(1.0904)(1.1945) = \$999.98$.

Solution A3

The bond pays $100 interest in years one and two, then in year three the bond matures and the holder receives the $100 interest plus the $1,000 principal payment. First, use the spot rates to determine the bond's price:

$$P = \frac{\$100}{(1.12)} + \frac{\$100}{(1.13)^2} + \frac{\$1,100}{(1.14)^3} = \$910.07$$

Now, use the bond price of $910.07 to find the yield to maturity. For the yield to maturity, in the following equation solve for y:

$$\$910.07 = \frac{\$100}{(1+y)} + \frac{\$100}{(1+y)^2} + \frac{\$1,100}{(1+y)^3}$$

Using a financial calculator, or by trial and error, to find y, the yield to maturity equals 13.865%. In other words, the present value of the interest and principal payments discounting at 13.865% equals the bond price of $910.07. Note that spot rates determine the bond's price, and that yield to maturity is then derived from this price.

CHAPTER 6

SOME ALTERNATIVE INVESTMENT RULES

CHAPTER MISSION STATEMENT

The purpose of this chapter is to review commonly used investment rules in addition to the net present value rule. Rules such as payback period, discounted payback period, accounting rate of return are inferior to methods using discounted cash flows, such as the internal rate of return or net present value. The internal rate of return criterion provides the correct accept-reject decision in most cases, but it suffers from such problems as multiple rates of return and may be difficult to use with mutually exclusive projects, projects with different scale, or differences in the timing of cash flows. The profitability index is another common decision rule which is particularly useful when capital rationing is present.

Key concepts presented in Chapter 6 are outlined below.

- ◆Why net present value
    - ●proper use of cash flows
    - ●shareholders benefit
- ◆Alternate investment rules
    - ●payback period
    - ●discounted payback period
    - ●average accounting return
- ◆Internal rate of return
    - ●multiple rates of return
    - ●mutually exclusive projects
    - ●projects of different scale
    - ●timing of cash flows
- ◆Profitability index
    - ●independent projects
    - ●mutually exclusive projects
    - ●capital rationing

CONCEPT TEST

1. The length of time until the sum of a project's cash flows equals the initial investment is called the _____.

2. The length of time until the sum of a project's discounted cash flows equals the initial investment is called the _____.

3. Since the payback period criterion requires simply adding a project's cash flows, it ignores the _____.

4. A deficiency common to both the payback period and discounted payback period rules is that the _____ must be arbitrarily selected.

5. The major advantage of the payback period rule is its _____.

6.   The average accounting return (AAR) is defined as _____ divided by _____.

7.   The AAR requires that the _____ be arbitrarily specified.

8.   A deficiency common to both the AAR criterion and the payback period criterion is that both ignore the _____.

9.   The internal rate of return (IRR) is the discount rate at which the NPV is _____.

10. The profitability index is the ratio of the _____ to the _____.

11. When a firm is considering two or more potential investments, of which only one can be accepted, then the investments are said to be _____.

12. An _____ is an investment whose acceptance or rejection does not affect, and is not affected by, the acceptance or rejection of any other projects.

13. If the cash flows for a project change signs more than once, then the IRR criterion may fail to identify an acceptable project because of the _____ problem.

14. If a project is acceptable according to the discounted payback period criterion, is it necessarily acceptable by the net present value criterion?

15. The internal rate of return is the rate of return (or discount rate) which equates the present value of the _____ with the _____ of the investment.

16. If a project is acceptable according to the payback period criterion, then it is necessarily acceptable by the NPV criterion only if the required rate of return is _____.

17. If a project is acceptable according to the profitability index rule, is it necessarily acceptable according to the net present value criterion?

18. Suppose a project's cash flows are a level perpetuity. In this case, the payback period is the same as one divided by _____.

19. Solving for the internal rate of return is equivalent to solving for the yield to maturity of a _____.

20. If the first cash flow for an investment is positive and all the remaining cash flows are negative, then the internal rate of return criterion becomes: "Accept the investment if the IRR is _____ the required return."

21. If, due to limited funds availability, a firm has more profitable investments than it can accept, then _____ is said to exist.

22. If funds are limited in the current period, then the _____ criterion may be useful for choosing among positive NPV investments.

23. If we are comparing two investments, does the one with the higher internal rate of return necessarily have the higher net present value?

24. In practice, the most commonly used capital budgeting techniques are _____ techniques.

25. The profitability index criterion states that a project is acceptable if the index value is greater than _____.

ANSWERS TO CONCEPT TEST

1.	payback period	13.	multiple rates of return
2.	discounted payback period	14.	yes
3.	time value of money	15.	cash inflows; cash outlay
4.	cutoff period	16.	zero
5.	simplicity	17.	yes
6.	average net income; average book value	18.	the IRR
7.	target AAR	19.	level coupon bond
8.	time value of money	20.	less than
9.	zero	21.	capital rationing
10.	PV of future cash flows; initial investment	22.	profitability index
		23.	no
11.	mutually exclusive	24.	discounted cash flow
12.	independent investment project	25.	one

PROBLEMS

For Problems 1-5, use the following cash flows for projects A and B:

A: (-$2,300, $600, $750, $800, $1,000)
B: (-$2,300, $1,100, $950, $500, $450)

Problem 1

Calculate the payback period for projects A and B.

Problem 2

If the discount rate is 14%, what is the discounted payback period for project A? For project B?

Problem 3

Calculate (by trial-and-error) the internal rate of return for projects A and B.

Problem 4

If A and B are mutually exclusive and the required rate of return is 5%, which project should be accepted?

Problem 5

If the discount rate is 14%, and A and B are mutually exclusive, which project should be accepted? At what discount rate will we be indifferent between A and B?

Problem 6

Compute the internal rate of return for the following investments:

$$(-\$60, \$155, -\$100) \text{ and } (\$60, -\$155, \$100)$$

How do you interpret the results in terms of the IRR rule?

Problem 7

You have been asked to analyze the investment ($-\$51$, $\$100$, $-\$50$). Compute the internal rate of return for this investment. Is the investment acceptable? The required return is unknown.

Problem 8

Calculate the internal rate of return for an investment with the following cash flows: ($\$792$, $-\$1,780$, $\$1,000$).

Problem 9

For the investment identified in Problem 8, determine the acceptability of the investment when the required rate of return is 10%; when the required rate of return is 12%; when the required rate of return is 14%.

Problem 10

Consider the following abbreviated financial statements for a proposed investment:

Year	0	1	2	3	4
Gross book value	$160	$160	$160	$160	$160
– accumulated depreciation		40	80	120	160
Net book value	160	120	80	40	0
Sales		$ 95	$ 90	$ 97	$ 80
Costs		33	30	25	10
Depreciation		40	40	40	40
Taxes (@50%)		11	10	16	15
Net Income		$ 11	$ 10	$ 16	$ 15

What is the average accounting return? What is the internal rate of return?

Problem 11

You have the opportunity to borrow $8,000, to be repaid in yearly installments of $2,200 at the end of each of the next five years. Use the IRR criterion to determine whether this loan is preferable to borrowing at the market rate of 11.5%.

Problem 12

An investment costs $125 and produces cash inflows of $15 per year in perpetuity.
What is the IRR of this investment?

Problem 13

An investment of $210 produces a perpetual stream of cash inflows. Next year, the cash inflow will be $10.50, and the cash inflow will grow at 5% per year. What is the internal rate of return on this investment?

Problem 14

The Dioxal Oil Company is in the process of cleaning up a minor oil spill. The firm could do the work with one cleanup team or two teams. One team would cost of $25 per month for five months. The two-team alternative would cost $40 per month for three months. If two teams are used, the firm can restart refining sooner and collect $10 in earnings in months 4 and 5. Should Dioxal use one or two teams to clean up the oil spill? Base your decision on IRR.

Problem 15

A firm is considering the following mutually exclusive investment projects:

Project A requires an initial outlay of $500 and will return $120 per year for the next seven years. Project B requires an initial outlay of $5,000 and will return $1,350 per year for the next five years.

The required rate of return is 10%. Use the net present value criterion to determine which investment is preferable.

Problem 16

Calculate the internal rate of return for each of the investment projects described in Problem 15.

Problem 17

Calculate the profitability index for each of the investment projects described in Problem 15.

Problem 18

Again, refer to the two investments identified in Problem 15; calculate the internal rate of return, the profitability index, and the net present value for the incremental investment (B-A).

Problem 19

The Daisy Manufacturing Company has the opportunity to invest in four independent projects whose cash flows are shown below. Calculate the IRR and NPV of each project. The appropriate discount rate is 15%.

Project	CF_0	CF_1	CF_2
A	-$10	$10	$10
B	-$15	$8	$12
C	-$10	$5	$15
D	-$25	$16	$24

Problem 20

The investment opportunity confronting Daisy is short-lived, however, and Daisy must commit to the projects immediately. Daisy has only $25 in cash available and has no hope of raising additional capital before the investment opportunity disappears. In which project, or projects, should Daisy invest?

Problem 21

Dreadnought Mills must pick between two operating plans that use different technologies in its new weaving mill. Cash flows for these plans are shown below. Calculate the internal rate of return for each plan. Dreadnought's chief operating officer believes that Plan A looks best because of a one-year payback period. Do you agree?

Year:	0	1	2	3
Plan A	-$8,000	$8,000	$800	$800
Plan B	-$8,000	$900	$900	$10,000

Problem 22

Before deciding on a plan, Dreadnought's President wants to see the net present values of each plan. The appropriate discount rate is uncertain, so calculate the NPV of each plan using rates of 10%, 15%, and 20%. Do these calculations support Plan A or Plan B?

Problem 23

Since the appropriate discount rate is uncertain, find the rate at which Dreadnought Mills would be indifferent between Plan A and Plan B.

SOLUTIONS

Solution 1

The sum of the first three cash flows for project A is $2,150, and the sum of the first four cash flows is $3,150, so the payback period for A is between three and four years. After three years, A is within $150 of paying back the initial cost. The cash flow in the fourth year is $1,000. The fractional year is thus ($150/$1,000) = .15, so we could say the payback period is 3.15 years.

The payback period for project B is 2.5 years.

Chapter 6

Solution 2

The sum of the four discounted cash flows for project A is $2,235.47, so A does not pay back its initial cost. For B, the sum of the four discounted cash flows is $2,299.83, so the discounted payback period is almost exactly four years.

Solution 3

The solution to Problem 2 provides some useful information for solving this problem. For project B, the discounted payback period is almost exactly equal to the life of the project, so the internal rate of return must be slightly less than 14%. The exact value of the IRR is 13.996%. For project A, the NPV is -$64.53 at a 14% discount rate, so the IRR is somewhat less than 14%. At discount rates of 12% and 13% the NPVs of A are $38.55 and -$13.91. Therefore, the IRR must be between 12% and 14%. The exact value is 12.73%.

Solution 4

Using a discount rate of 5% the NPV for A is $465.47 and the NPV for B is $411.43. Therefore, A is preferred even though it has the lower IRR, 12.73% versus 14.00%.

Solution 5

From Problem 3, A has a negative NPV at a 14% discount rate (-$64.53) and should be rejected. B has a NPV of essentially zero (-$0.17), thus B is borderline acceptable and definitely preferred to A.

To solve for the rate at which we are indifferent between A and B, we need to compute the discount rate such that A and B have the same net present value:

$$NPV\ A = NPV\ B$$

This is equivalent to finding the discount rate such that:

$$NPV\ A - NPV\ B = 0$$

This is solved by finding the internal rate of return for the incremental cash flows for an investment (A - B): ($0, -$500, -$200, $300, $550). This rate is found by trial and error or with the use of a financial calculator; the latter approach indicates that the rate is 8.57%. At this discount rate, both A and B have a NPV of $233.50.

Solution 6

Since the cash flows for each of these investments change sign more than once, each investment may have more than one internal rate of return. These can be determined by trial and error, but since these cash flows extend over only three time periods, it is possible to solve algebraically for the two IRR values. Consider, for example, the first of the two investments. The IRR is the rate r which is a solution to the following equation:

$$\$60 \ = \ \frac{\$155}{(1+r)} \ - \ \frac{\$100}{(1+r)^2}$$

Algebraically, this is a quadratic equation; let $x = 1/(1+r)$, then the equation can be written as:

$$\$155x \ - \ \$100x^2 \ - \ \$60 \ = \ 0$$

In general, a quadratic equation has two solutions ($x=.80$ and $x=.75$), which can be determined directly by using the quadratic formula. The two solutions here are $r_1 = .25$ or 25% and $r_2 = .3333$ or 33.33%. These same values are the two solutions for the second investment above.

To interpret these results, we can compute the net present value at a rate between the two IRRs. At a discount rate of 30%, for example, the NPV is +$.06 for the first investment and -$.06 for the second. We should accept the first investment only if our required rate of return is between 25% and 33.33%, and we should accept the second one only if our required return is outside the range 25% to 33.33%. This conclusion derives from the fact that a quadratic equation, when graphed, has the shape of a parabola, so that the net present value must be either exclusively negative or exclusively positive between the two solutions identified here, and has the opposite sign outside the range of the two solutions.

Solution 7

This is a problem designed to keep graduate students out of trouble by keeping them busy. There is no IRR! All this means is that there is no real number for which the NPV is zero. At any discount rate, the NPV is negative, so the required return is irrelevant. This result can also be demonstrated algebraically because the IRR is the solution to a quadratic equation, as discussed in the solution to Problem 6. For this problem, however, the quadratic equation does not have a solution.

Solution 8

Because the sign of the cash flows changes twice, there are two IRRs for this problem. These can be determined using trial and error, and they can also be determined algebraically since the problem can be formulated as a quadratic equation. (Note that the way financial calculators handle the multiple solution problem varies from model to model. Most require that you input a guess. But some calculators will not provide both solutions. Furthermore, a computer spreadsheet program will generally provide one solution at a time; in order to determine the second solution, you must be aware of the fact that a second solution exists in order to derive the second solution) The two values of the internal rate of return are 11.1111% and 13.6364%.

Solution 9

This problem can be solved using the net present value criterion by simply calculating the NPV for the investment at each value of the required rate of return. The net present values are $.26, -$.09, and $.06. respectively for the three required rates. These results indicate that the investment is acceptable if the required rate of return is either 10% or 14%, but it is unacceptable if the required rate of return is 12%. These results can be understood algebraically by noting that the quadratic equation in this problem has negative net present value for values of r between the two solutions derived in Problem 8 and positive net present value for values of r outside the range of the two solutions. Therefore, the investment is unacceptable if the required rate of return is any value between 11.1111% and 13.6364%, and is acceptable otherwise.

Solution 10

The average net income is [($11 + $10 + $16 + $15)/4] = $13. The average book value is $80, so the AAR is 16.25%.

To compute the internal rate of return, the cash flows must first be tabulated. As indicated in Chapter 2, operating cash flow can be derived by adding depreciation to net income, so that cash flows are $51, $50, $56, and $55, respectively over the four year period. (Note: the calculation of cash flows is discussed in greater detail in Chapter 7) The initial investment is $160. Using trial and error, it can be shown that the IRR is approximately 12%; the exact value is 12.0608%.

Solution 11

We can use the trial and error process or a financial calculator to find the interest rate for this loan. Since the loan payments are in the form of an annuity, however, it is more efficient to take advantage of this fact and solve for the interest rate directly, either using a present value annuity factor table or the annuity functions of a financial calculator. The interest rate is the value of r that is the solution to the following equation:

$$PV = PMT \times \text{Annuity Factor}$$

$$\$8,000 = \$2,200 \times A^5_r$$

The value of the annuity factor in the above equation is 3.6364. Referring to an annuity table, we find that the present value annuity factor is 3.6048 for r = 12% and T=5; Therefore, the interest rate on the loan is somewhat less than 12%. The exact value of r, determined using the annuity functions of a financial calculator, is 11.6488%. It is clear that borrowing at the market rate of 11.5% is preferable to borrowing at the higher rate indicated in this example. This is consistent with the IRR criterion for financial opportunities which begin with an inflow; that is, such opportunities are acceptable only if the internal rate of return (i.e., the interest rate for the loan) is less than the market rate of interest.

Solution 12

The internal rate of return is just the discount rate that makes the net present value equal zero. Thus, IRR is the rate r which solves the following equation.

$$NPV = 0 = -\$125 + \$15/r$$

$$r = \$15/\$125 = .12 \text{ or } 12\%$$

Solution 13

The IRR is found by finding the discount rate, r, which makes the investment's NPV=0. The cash flows from the investment are an example of a growing perpetuity. Thus, the NPV is

$$NPV = -\$210 + \$10.50/(r - .05)$$

Setting NPV=0 and solving for r, we find that IRR = .10 or 10%.

Solution 14

Dioxal has two mutually exclusive projects: one team or two teams. Evaluating mutually exclusive projects using IRR requires that you examine the incremental cash flows. That is, you look at the rate of return you receive on your incremental investment. In Dioxal's case, the objective is to determine the lowest cost means of cleaning up the oil spill. The incremental cash flows associated with the second team are shown in the following table.

Teams	1	2	3	4	5
2	-40	-40	-40	+10	+10
1	-25	-25	-25	-25	-25
2 - 1	-15	-15	-15	+35	+35

The internal rate of return for the incremental cash flow, 2 - 1, is 19.03%. This indicates that Dioxal is getting a 19.03% return on the extra costs required for the second team. If Dioxal's cost of capital is less than 19.03% then two teams make sense; otherwise Dioxal should use only one team. To see the economic logic of this, calculate the present value of the costs at two rates, say 15% and 25%, surrounding the IRR. At 15%, the cost of one team is -$83.8, while two teams cost -$80.6. At 25%, one team costs -$67.2, two teams cost -$70.7. Therefore, if the cost of capital is less than 19%, two teams cost less.

Solution 15

Because the returns for each investment are in the form of an annuity, we can use the present value annuity factors to determine the net present values. For project A:

$$NPV = -\$500 + \$120 \times A^7_{.10} = -\$500 + \$120 \times 4.8684 = \$84.21.$$

Therefore, the net present value for project A is $84.21. Similarly, the net present value for project B is $117.56. The net present value criterion indicates that B is the preferred alternative. (Note that there may be an additional problem here arising from the difference in the life of the two assets; if the assets perform a comparable task, the shorter life of project A may imply that a new investment in a replacement is required sooner for A than for B. This possibility is addressed in Chapter 7.)

Solution 16

Because the returns for each project are in the form of an annuity, we can estimate the IRRs using trial and error or we can determine the exact values using the annuity functions of a financial calculator. The latter approach indicates that the internal rates of return are 14.9500% and 10.9162% for projects A and B, respectively. In spite of the fact that project A has the higher IRR, the solution to Problem 15 indicates that project B is preferable. This is an example of the scale problem discussed in the chapter.

Solution 17

The profitability index is defined as the ratio of the present value of the future cash flows divided by the initial investment. For project A, the profitability index is ($584.21/$500) = 1.168. For project B, the profitability index is ($5,117.56/$5,000) = 1.024. If these two projects were independent of each other, both would be acceptable according to the profitability index criterion because each of the above values is greater than 1.0. This conclusion is consistent with that implied by the net present value and internal rate of return criteria for independent projects. However, since the projects are in fact mutually exclusive, the profitability index criterion can not be used to select the preferred alternative.

Solution 18

The cash flows for the incremental investment (B - A) are:

(-$4,500, $1,230, $1,230, $1,230, $1,230, $1,230, -$120, -$120)

The internal rate of return for (B - A) is 10.3009%, the present value is $4,533.35, the profitability index is 1.007, and the net present value is $33.35. All three criteria indicate that the incremental investment (B - A) is acceptable; it is always true that the three criteria applied to the incremental investment result in the same decision. Consequently, since project A is acceptable and the incremental investment (B - A) is acceptable, then project B is preferred. We have demonstrated that the internal rate of return and profitability index criteria, when applied to the incremental investment, result in the same decision derived by applying the NPV criterion in Problem 15.

Solution 19

Project	CF_0	CF_1	CF_2	IRR(%)	NPV
A	-$10	$10	$10	61.8	$6.26
B	-$15	$ 8	$12	20.0	$1.03
C	-$10	$ 5	$15	50.0	$5.69
D	-$25	$16	$24	35.1	$7.06

All four projects are good investments since in each case the IRR exceeds the discount rate and the NPV is positive.

Solution 20

This is a problem in capital rationing. Daisy has only $25 in cash available, but collectively the projects require an investment of $60. Thus, although all projects have a positive NPV as indicated in Problem 19, the firm cannot invest in all four projects. To select which project or projects to invest in, the profitability index of each project must be determined. Looking solely at NPV is not sufficient if capital rationing is present. The profitability index is the present value of all cash flows subsequent to the initial investment divided by the initial cash outflow.

Project	CF_0	CF_1	CF_2	IRR(%)	NPV	PI
A	-$10	$10	$10	61.8	$6.26	1.63
B	-$15	$ 8	$12	20.0	$1.03	1.07
C	-$10	$ 5	$15	50.0	$5.69	1.57
D	-$25	$16	$24	35.1	$7.06	1.28

When ranked by profitability, project A is the most attractive, followed by C, D, and B. This ranking indicates that Daisy should invest in projects A and C, using up $20 of the $25 cash available. Essentially, the remaining $5 is invested in the financial market where NPV−0. Note that the NPV of A and C equals $11.95, higher than any other possible combination.

Solution 21

The internal rates of return (IRR) for Dreadnought's plans are shown in the following table.

Year:	0	1	2	3	IRR
Plan A	-$8,000	$8,000	$800	$800	16.04%
Plan B	-$8,000	$900	$900	$10,000	15.20%

Judging by the internal rates of returns, Plan A seems the better choice because its internal rate of return exceeds Plan B's internal rate of return. But a correct decision can not be made without considering the appropriate discount rate for the project.

Solution 22

Net present values for these plans are shown below.

Rate:	10%	15%	20%	IRR
Plan A	$535	$87	-$315	16.04%
Plan B	$1,075	$38	-$838	15.20%

These net present values show that Plan B is preferred at low discount rates, 10%, while Plan A is preferred at higher rates, 15%, and neither plan would be acceptable with a discount rate of 20%.

Solution 23

Dreadnought would be indifferent between plans at a rate that is between 10% and 15%. This rate would be the internal rate of return of the incremental project Plan A - Plan B. When the discount rate is 14.54%, both plans have an NPV of $126.

Year:	0	1	2	3	IRR
Plan A	-$8,000	$8,000	$800	$800	16.04%
Plan B	-$8,000	$900	$900	$10,000	15.20%
A - B	$0	$7,100	-$100	-$9,200	14.54%

CHAPTER 7

NET PRESENT VALUE AND CAPITAL BUDGETING

CHAPTER MISSION STATEMENT

The purpose of Chapter 7 is to illustrate, through worked out examples, how the concepts of discounted cash flow and net present value are used in practice to evaluate capital budgeting decisions. The practical problems of identifying the relevant incremental cash flows are discussed. The affects of inflation on interest rates and cash flows are described. The proper method of evaluating mutually exclusive projects with different lives is analyzed. An appendix discusses depreciation.

The key concepts discussed in Chapter 7 are outlined below.

- ♦Incremental cash flows
  - ●sunk costs
  - ●opportunity costs
  - ●side effects
  - ●investment and salvage
  - ●net working capital
  - ●taxes
- ♦Inflation and capital budgeting
  - ●interest rates and inflation
  - ●cash flow and inflation
  - ●discounting real and nominal cash flows
- ♦Investments of unequal lives
  - ●replacement chains
  - ●equivalent annual cost
  - ●replacement decisions

CONCEPT TEST

1. The difference in the firm's cash flows with and without a project is called the _____ for that project.

2. Relevant project cash flows consist of two parts: _____ and _____.

3. A cost that the firm incurred regardless of whether it accepts or rejects a particular project is called a _____.

4. A cost that is associated with using an asset which could be used in a different way is called an _____.

5. Suppose one project has the effect of increasing the cash flow to another project. This increase is an incremental cash flow and is an example of a _____.

6. When Hershey Foods introduced Hershey's Kisses with Almonds, if sales of the regular Hershey's Kisses declined, this decline would be an example of _____.

7. Cash revenues in a particular year are equal to booked sales less the change in _____.

8. Cash costs in a particular year are equal to booked operating costs and taxes less the change in _____.

9. Suppose we are considering two machines which are mutually exclusive and which have different useful lives; if the machine chosen will be replaced at the end of its life, then we use the _____ method to evaluate the decision.

10. Costs that change as the quantity of output changes are called _____.

11. Costs that do not change when output changes are called _____.

12. Interest rates that have not been adjusted for the effect of inflation are called _____ interest rates.

13. Interest rates that have been adjusted for the effect of inflation are called _____ interest rates.

14. The discount rate used in capital budgeting is normally stated in _____ terms.

15. The depreciation tax shield _____ after-tax cash flow by _____ taxes.

16. The depreciation tax shield is often discounted at the _____ since it is viewed as essentially _____.

17. A firm's "tax books" are likely to show _____ earnings than its "stockholders' books".

For Questions 18-22, answer 'yes' if the cash flow is incremental and 'no' if it is not.

18. The cost of an environmental impact study before the study is commissioned.

19. The cost of an environmental impact study after the study has been completed.

20. A change in credit terms that results in more credit sales.

21. A new project's share of total corporate fixed overhead that existed before accepting the project.

22. The change in total fixed corporate overhead that results from a new project.

ANSWERS TO CONCEPT TEST

1.	incremental cash flow	12.	nominal
2.	operating cash flow; capital requirements	13.	real
		14.	nominal
3.	sunk cost	15.	increases; decreasing
4.	opportunity cost	16.	riskless rate; riskless
5.	side effect	17.	lower
6.	erosion	18.	yes
7.	accounts receivable	19.	no
8.	accounts payable	20.	yes
9.	equivalent annual cost (EAC)	21.	no
10.	variable costs	22.	yes
11.	fixed costs		

PROBLEMS

Use the following information to solve Problems 1-5:

The Datum Co. has recently completed a $200,000, two-year marketing study. Based on the results of the study, Datum has estimated that 6,000 of its new electro-optical data scanning hardware, known as "DataScan," could be sold annually over the next 8 years, at a price of $8,000 each. Variable costs per unit are $4,400, and fixed costs total $5.4 million per year.

Start-up costs include $17.6 million to build production facilities, $1.5 million for land, and $4 million in net working capital. The $17.6 million facility will be depreciated on a straight-line basis to a value of zero over the eight-year life of the project. At the end of the project's life, the facilities (including the land) will be sold for an estimated $4.7 million. The value of the land is not expected to change during the eight year period.

Finally, start-up would also entail tax-deductible expenses of $0.4 million at year zero. Datum is an ongoing, profitable business and pays taxes at a 35% rate on all income and capital gains. Datum has a 20% opportunity cost for projects such as this one.

Problem 1

What operating cash flow does the "DataScan" project generate for years 1 through 7?

Problem 2

Express the operating cash flows from Problem 1 in terms of after-tax revenues, after-tax expenses, and the depreciation tax shield. What is the marginal contribution to cash flow of each of the three components?

Problem 3

What is the initial cash flow at year 0?

Problem 4

What is the terminal year cash flow?

Problem 5

What are the internal rate of return and net present value of the "DataScan" project?

Problem 6

Deciduous Inc. is a leading manufacturer of shake roof shingles. The company is considering two alternative production methods. The costs and lives associated with each are:

Year	Method 1 Cost	Method 2 Cost
0	$900	$800
1	20	80
2	20	80
3	20	80
4		80

The relevant opportunity cost of capital is 10%. Assuming that Deciduous will not replace the equipment when it wears out, which production method should the firm buy?

Problem 7

Consider the data from Problem 6 and assume that Deciduous is going to replace the equipment when it wears out. Which method should the firm purchase?

Problem 8

You have been asked to value orange groves belonging to the Roll Corporation. The groves produce 1.6 billion oranges per year. Oranges currently sell for $.10 per 100. With normal maintenance, this level of production can be sustained indefinitely (assuming no unexpected hard freezes occur). Variable costs (primarily upkeep and harvesting) are $1.2 million per year. Fixed costs are negligible. The nominal discount rate is 18%, and the inflation rate is 10%. Assuming that orange prices and the variable costs change with inflation, what is the value of the groves? (Ignore taxes and depreciation.)

Problem 9

Suppose that, for the data in Problem 8, prices increase at the inflation rate, but costs only increase at half the inflation rate. What is the value of the orange groves?

Problem 10

Doukhobor, Ltd., is considering replacing its four old wheat milling machines with a single new model. The old machines are worth $100 apiece today, each costs $30 per year to operate, and each will be worth $5 when it wears out in four years. All machines are replaced when they wear out. A new machine costs $1000 to buy and install, costs $20 per year to operate, lasts eight years, and can be sold for $100 when it wears out. The relevant opportunity cost is 12%. Should Doukhobor replace now or later?

Problem 11

Dendrite Landscaping must decide whether to replace an aging backhoe with a new model. The old backhoe needs continuous maintenance to work reliably, and maintenance is becoming increasingly costly. Next year these costs are expected to be $1,500, and costs will double each year. Dendrite could sell the old backhoe today for $4,000. Resale values will decline 50% per year. A new backhoe would cost $12,000, incur maintenance costs of $900 per year, and last for 5 years. After 5-years, the new backhoe could be sold for $1,500. There are no taxes and the appropriate discount rate is 12%. Maintenance costs are paid at year end. Should Dendrite replace the backhoe now or later?

Problem 12

Deciduous Inc. is deciding whether or not to enter the aluminum siding business. Projected sales, total net working capital (NWC) requirements, and capital investments are:

Year	Sales	NWC	Investment
0	$ 0	$400	$20,000
1	5,000	500	
2	6,000	500	
3	9,000	700	
4-6	10,000	700	

Variable costs are 60% of sales, and fixed costs are negligible. The $20,000 in production equipment will be depreciated on a straight-line basis, to a value of zero, over a five-year period. The equipment will actually be worth $10,000 if salvaged in six years. The required rate of return is 10% and the firm's tax rate is 34%. Should Deciduous embark on this new line of business?

Problem 13

For Problem 12, assume that the inflation rate is 8% and that all the data in the problem (including the discount rate) are in real terms. Is the aluminum siding business attractive now? Why do we get a different answer?

Problem 14

The Cape Cod Cranberry Company must choose between two bog skimmers. Skimmer 1 is made in Maine, costs $7,500, will last 5 years, and requires $150 per year maintenance. Skimmer 2 is made in Michigan, costs $9,900, lasts 7 years, and requires only $127 per year maintenance. The discount rate is 8%. Which skimmer should Cape Cod Cranberry purchase? Assume that whichever skimmer is purchased, Cape Code will continue using that type of skimmer forever. Also, assume that all cash flows are after tax.

Problem 15

The Datum Corporation invested $10,000 in a new minicomputer which is expected to last six years and have no salvable value. Datum has the choice of depreciating the computer using the five-year class schedule or straight line over five years. Assume that the incremental income from the computer is $5,000 per year and the tax rate is 34%. What are the total taxes remitted to the government under each choice of depreciation? What is the present value of the total tax bill? Which method should Datum choose? Assume a 12% discount rate.

Problem 16

Datum decides to sell the minicomputer after three years. What will be the tax consequences if the selling price is $5,000? What if the price is $2,000? Assume that Datum used the five-year class depreciation schedule, and ignore the half year convention for the salvage year.

Problem 17

The Dakota Biscuit Company has embarked on a new cookie project which will last five years. Dakota expects first year's sales of their new cookie to be $12,000. Over the following three years, unit sales will remain constant but prices will rise at the inflation rate of 10% Dakota expects to maintain inventory equal to 9% of next year's sales, and accounts receivable less accounts payable should equal 5% of current year sales. All credit accounts are settled at the end of the next year, i.e., essentially, there is a one year lag in payment of 5% of sales. There are no incremental cash balances. What are Dakota's net working capital requirements for this project?

Problem 18

From Problem 17, what cash flows are associated with Dakota's net working capital requirements?

Problem 19

Datum expects to sell 5,000 hard drives next year. Sales will increase to 7,500 the following year, and to 6,000 the third year at which time the line will be discontinued. The current (time zero) price is $400 per unit, while costs are $150 per unit. Generally, Datum can increase prices to offset inflation, but competitive pressures will cause a 2% decline in real prices. Unit costs rise with inflation which is expected to be 5%. Incremental depreciation is $50,000 per year. Datum's tax rate is 34%. What are the project's operating cash flows?

Problem 20

If Datum's real discount rate is 6%, what is the present value of the cash flows in Problem 19?

Problem 21

Now suppose Datum decides that since the depreciation tax shield is relatively certain, it should be discounted at the nominal riskless rate of 6%. Now what is the present value of the cash flows?

SOLUTIONS

Solution 1

Revenues, expenses and depreciation are expected to be constant for years 1 through 7. In addition, there are no capital requirements in any of these years. so the cash flows will be identical for these years. Annual revenue will be [($8,900)(6,000)] = $48 million. Annual depreciation is ($17.6 million/8 years) = $2.2 million. Annual variable costs will be [($4,400)(6,000)] = $26.4 million and total operating costs equal ($26.4 million + $5.4 million) = $31.8 million. Taxable income is ($48 million − $31.8 million − $2.2 million) = $14 million and taxes are [(.35)($14 million)] = $4.9 million, so that net income is $9.1 million. Operating cash flow equals $11.3 million, which equals revenues minus operating costs minus taxes, or equivalently net income plus depreciation, $11.3 million.

Solution 2

Operating cash flow can be written as:

$$\text{Revenues } (1 - T_c) - \text{Expenses } (1 - T_c) + (T_c) \text{ Depreciation} =$$

$$(\$48 \text{ million})(.65) - (\$31.8 \text{ million})(.65) + (.35)(\$2.2 \text{ million}) =$$

$$\$31.20 \text{ million} - \$20.67 \text{ million} + \$0.77 \text{ million} = \$11.3 \text{ million}$$

The three terms above are, respectively, the after-tax revenues. after-tax expenses and the depreciation tax-shield. The marginal contributions of each term to operating cash flows are, respectively, $.65 per dollar of increase in revenues, $.65 per dollar of decrease in expenses, and $.35 per dollar of increase in depreciation.

Solution 3

The year 0 cash outflows are: $17.6 million to build production facilities, $1.5 million for land, $4 million in working capital, and the after-tax cost of the tax-deductible $0.4 million in expenses, or [($0.4 million)(.65)] = $0.26 million. The total of these outflows is $23.36 million. Note that the test market expense is a sunk cost, so it is excluded from this calculation.

Solution 4

The year 8 operating cash flow will be $11.3 million, as determined in Problem 1. Additional calculations are necessary in order to determine the capital requirements. First, the company will sell the land for $1.5 million. Second, the plant and equipment will be sold for ($4.7 million − $1.5 million) = $3.2 million. The plant and equipment will be depreciated to a book value of zero. The difference between the book value and the sale proceeds is taxable as a recapture of excess depreciation, so the firm will net [($3.2 million)(.65)] = $2.08 million from the sale. The land cannot be depreciated, so its book value is $1.5 million.

Finally, the $4 million in working capital will be recovered. This happens as, among other things, accounts are paid, inventory is sold off, and working cash balances are freed up. The total year 8 cash inflow is $18.88 (=$11.3 + $7.58) million.

Solution note: in reality, some portion of working capital would be recovered in later years, or not be recovered at all because of bad debts, inventory losses ('shrinkage'), and so forth.

Solution 5

The cash flows for this project consist of −$23.36 million in year 0, $11.3 million in years 1 through 7, and $18.88 million in year 8. The present value of the cash inflows for years 1 through 8, discounted at 20%, equals $45.123 million, so that the net present value is $21.763 million. The internal rate of return is 46.84%. Thus, Datum should proceed with the project.

Solution 6

The present value of the operating costs for Methods 1 and 2 are $949.74 and $1053.59, respectively. If the equipment is not to be replaced, then Method 1 should be selected because it has the lower present value of costs.

Solution 7

If the equipment will be replaced, then we need to calculate the equivalent annual cost (EAC) for each method. For Method 1, an annuity of $381.90 per year has a present value of $949.74, so that the costs associated with this method are equivalent to paying $381.90 each year for three years. For Method 2, the EAC is $332.38. The firm should select Method 2 because it has the lower EAC.

Solution 8

Revenues from sales of 1.6 billion oranges, at $.001 apiece, are equal to $1.6 million. Since we are ignoring both taxes and depreciation, operating cash flow is equal to revenues minus expenses or ($1.6 million − $1.2 million) = $.4 million per year. At this point, it's tempting to treat the $.4 million as a perpetuity, and divide by .18 to calculate the present value. This would not be correct. The $.4 million annual cash flow is in current dollars and therefore does not reflect future inflation. The 18% discount rate does reflect future inflation, so we are being inconsistent by dividing a real cash flow by a nominal discount rate.

To be consistent, we must modify the above calculation by using either the nominal cash flows or the real discount rate. We will demonstrate that the approaches are equivalent by using both procedures. The real discount rate is $[(1.18/1.10) - 1] = 7.2727\%$. The present value of the perpetuity is ($400,000/.072727) = $5.5 million. Alternatively, we could use the formula for a growing perpetuity to determine the present value. The nominal cash flow grows by 10% per year. The year 1 cash flow is thus ($400,000)(1.1) = $440,000. To find the present value of a growing perpetuity, divide the year-1 cash flow by the discount rate less the growth rate; therefore, the present value is $[(\$440,000)/(.18 - .10)] = \$5.5$ million.

Solution 9

If the costs increase by only 5% per year, then in real terms, the costs are decreasing. As a result, it is easier to solve this problem using nominal cash flows.

Next year's revenues are expected to be $[(\$1.6\text{ million})(1.10)] = \$1.76$ million. The present value of the future revenues is $[(\$1.76\text{ million})/(.18 - .10)] = \$22$ million. Next year's costs are expected to be $[(\$1.2\text{ million})(1.05)] = \$1.26$ million. It follows then that the present value of future costs is $[(\$1.26\text{ million})/(.18 - .05)] = \$9.692$ million. The value of the groves is ($22 - $9.692) million = $12.308 million.

Solution 10

If we decide to keep the four old machines, then we forgo the $100 each that we could receive by selling; this is an opportunity cost. The present value of the costs of keeping the old equipment is $[4(\$100 + \$30(3.03735) - \$5(.6355))] = [4(\$187.94)] = \$751.77$. The present value of the costs for the new equipment is $1058.96. However, the old equipment has a shorter life than the new equipment. The decision here can be regarded as a choice between two mutually exclusive alternatives with unequal lives. The alternatives are to 'purchase' the old machines (that is, not sell the old machines) or to purchase the new one. In other words, we compute the EAC for each alternative. The EAC of keeping the old equipment is $[\$61.88(4)] = \$247.51$. The EAC for the new equipment is $213.17. Therefore, Doukhobor Ltd. should replace the existing equipment now.

Solution 11

Dendrite will decide whether to replace the backhoe by comparing the cost of keeping the old backhoe for one more year with the equivalent annual cost of a new backhoe. The equivalent annual cost of the new backhoe is

$$\text{EAC(new)} = \text{PV Costs/Annuity factor}$$

$$\text{PV Costs} = \$12,000 + \$900 \times \text{Annuity Factor} - \$1,500/(1.12)^5$$

$$\text{PV Costs} = \$12,000 + \$900 \times 3.6048 - \$851.14 = \$14,393.16$$

$$\text{EAC(new)} = \$14,393.16/3.6048 = \$3,992.78.$$

Where Annuity Factor = 3.6048, and the $1,500 disposal value is negative because it offsets costs that are shown as positive values.

The maintenance costs and resale values of the old backhoe are shown below.

Year	Maintenance	Resale
0		$4,000
1	$1,500	2,000
2	3,000	1,000
3	6,000	500

The cost of keeping the old backhoe for one year is

$$PV_0 = \$4,000 + \$1,500/1.12 - \$2,000/1.12 = \$3,553.57$$

At time 1, the future value of this is $3,980.00 = $3,553.57(1.12)

If the old backhoe is kept for one year and then replaced in two years, the cost is

$$PV_1 = \$2,000 + \$3,000/1.12 - \$1,000/1.12 = \$3,785.71$$

At time 2 the future value of this is $4,240.00 = $3,785.71(1.12)

The following table summarizes the costs associated with each decision:

Decision	1	2	3	4
Replace at t=0	$3,992.78	$3,992.78	$3,992.78	$3,992.78
Replace at t=1	$3,980.00	$3,992.78	$3,992.78	$3,992.78
Replace at t=2		$4,240.00	$3,992.78	$3,992.78

The lowest cost decision is to replace the backhoe at year two.

Solution 12

We can calculate the cash flows as follows:

Year	0	1	2	3	4-5	6
Revenues		$5,000	$6,000	$9,000	$1,000	$10,000
Operating costs		3,000	3,600	5,400	0	6,000
Depreciation		4,000	4,000	4,000	6,000	0
					4,000	
Operating cash flow		$2,680	$2,944	$3,736	0	$ 2,640
Working capital	400	100	0	200	0	(700)
Investment	20,000					
Salvage value						6,600
Capital requirements	20,400	100	0	200	0	(7,300)
Cash flow	$(20,400)	$2,580	$2,944	$3,536	$4,000	$9,940

The present value of the future cash flows, discounted at the 10% required rate of return, is $18,261.77, and the net present value is ($18,261.77 − $20,400) = −$2,138.23. Deciduous should stick with shake shingles and not enter the aluminum siding business.

Solution 13

The nominal cash flows for years 1 through 6 are indicated below; the year 0 cash flows are identical to those in Problem 12. Notice that depreciation is not adjusted for inflation because the depreciation charge is based on cost and is therefore unaffected by inflation.

Year	1	2	3	4	5	6
Revenues	$5,400	$6,998	$11,337	$13,605	$14,693	$15,869
Operating costs	3,240	4,199	6,802	8,163	8,816	9,521
Depreciation	4,000	4,000	4,000	4,000	4000	0
Operating cash flow	$2,786	$3,207	$4,353	$4,952	$5,239	$ 4,190
Working capital	108	0	252	0	0	(1,111)
Investment						
Salvage value						10,473
Capital requirements	108	0	252	0	0	(11,584)
Cash flow	$2,678	$3,207	$4,101	$4,952	$5,239	$15,774

The nominal discount rate is $[(1.10)(1.08) - 1] = .1880$ or 18.8%. Using this discount rate, the present value of the cash flows is $17,283.48 and the net present value of the investment is $-$3,116.52.

This result differs from that in Problem 12 because the depreciation deduction is not adjusted for inflation. As a result, the real depreciation tax shield declines in value and real taxes increase. The net present value decreases by the present value of the increase in taxes.

Solution 14

This is an investment decision involving mutually exclusive projects with unequal lives. Comparing present value of costs is inappropriate in this case. Cape Cod Cranberry instead should select the skimmer with the lowest equivalent annual cost. Skimmer 1: PV(costs) = $7,500 + $150(3.9927) = $8,099 where 3.9927 is the present value annuity factor; EAC = $8,099/3.9927 = $2,028. Skimmer 2: PV(costs) = $9,900 + $127(5.2064) = $10,561 where 5.2064 is the present value annuity factor; EAC = $10,561/5.2064 = $2,028. Since both skimmers have the same EAC, Cape Cod Cranberry should be indifferent between the two.

Solution 15

Year	1	2	3	4	5	6
Revenues	$5,000	$5,000	$5,000	$5,000	$5,000	$5,000
Depreciation	2,000	3,200	1,920	1,152	1,152	576
Taxable income	3,000	1,800	3,080	3,848	3,848	4,424
Taxes (5-year class)	1,020	612	1,047	1,308	1,308	1,504
Revenues	$5,000	$5,000	$5,000	$5,000	$5,000	$5,000
Depreciation	2,000	2,000	2,000	2,000	2,000	
Taxable income	3,000	3,000	3,000	3,000	3,000	5,000
Taxes (Straight Line)	1,020	1,020	1,020	1,020	1,020	1,700

Note that under both methods of depreciation Datum pays $6,800 of taxes (within rounding error). The present value of the tax bill is $4,479 with the five-year class schedule, and $4,538 under straight line depreciation. Datum should select the accelerated depreciation schedule.

Solution 16

After three years, Datum has depreciated the computer $2,000 + $3,200 + $1,920 = $7,120 to a book value of $10,000 - $7,120 = $2,880. If the selling price is $5,000, Datum took too much depreciation, reduced taxable income too much, and paid too little taxes. Thus, the IRS must recapture the underpaid tax.

Datum owes taxes on the difference between the selling price and book value: .34($5,000 - $2,880) = $721. If the selling price is only $2,000, then Datum took too little depreciation, reduced taxable income too little, and paid too much tax. Datum should get a refund of the tax on the difference between book value and selling price: .34($2,880 - $2,000) = $299. If we applied the half-year convention, depreciation for the third year would be $1,920/2 = $960, and the tax paid or refund received would adjust accordingly.

Solution 17

The following table illustrates the working capital requirements for the project.

Year	0	1	2	3	4	5
Revenues		$12,000	$13,200	$14,520	$15,972	$0
Inventory	1,080	1,188	1,307	1,437	0	0
Net receivables		600	660	726	799	0
Net working capital	1,080	1,788	1,967	2,163	799	0

Revenues increase at the 10% inflation rate, as do inventory and net receivables. Note that following the algorithm that inventory equals 5% of next year's revenues produces zero inventory in year 4. This is unrealistic since some inventory will be required to support $15,972 sales in year 4. A common procedure used to avoid this problem is to let inventory in year 4 be 9% of what revenues would have been in year 5 if they continued the same trend. That is, assume that inventory in year 4 is .09($15,972)(1.1) = $1,581.

Solution 18

The following table illustrates the cash flows associated with NWC requirements in question 17.

Year	0	1	2	3	4	5
Revenues		$12,000	$13,200	$14,520	$15,972	$0
Inventory	1,080	1,188	1,307	1,437	0	0
Net receivables		600	660	726	799	0
Net working capital	1,080	1,788	1,967	2,163	799	0
Change in NWC	1,080	708	179	196	(1,364)	(799)
Cash flow	(1,080)	(708)	(179)	(196)	1,364	799

Note that increases in net working capital represent a cash outflow while decreases in NWC represent a cash inflow. If inventory in year 4 is assumed to be $1,581 (see solution 17), then NWC for year 4 is $2,380. The change in NWC depends on when inventory is recovered. If we assume inventory, like receivables net of payables, is recovered in year 5, then the change in NWC for year 4 is a ($1,581 + $799) – $2,163 = $217 increase, and for year 5 is a ($0 – $2,380) = – $2,380 decrease.

Solution 19

Note that without competitive pressures nominal prices will increase by 5% per year; with competitive pressures the net increase in nominal prices is $(1.05)(.98) - 1 = .0290$ or 2.90%. For example, from time zero to time one competitive pressures cause real prices to decline from $400 to $392, while inflation causes the nominal price to be $392(1.05) = 411.60. The percentage increase is ($411.60 – $400)/$400 = .0290 or 2.9%. In year 2 real prices are $400(.98)(.98) = 384.16, while nominal prices are $384.16(1.05)(1.05) = 423.54. Depreciation is in nominal terms to begin with, so no adjustments are required. The table is in nominal terms.

Year	1	2	3
Unit sales (000)	5.0	7.5	6.0
Unit prices ($)	411.60	423.54	435.82
Revenues ($000)	2,058.0	3,176.6	2,614.9
Unit cost ($)	157.50	165.38	173.64
Costs ($000)	787.5	1,240.4	1,041.8
Net Revenues ($000)	1,270.5	1,936.2	1,573.1
Depreciation ($000)	50.0	50.0	50.0
Taxable Income ($000)	1,220.5	1,886.2	1,523.1
Taxes ($000)	415.0	641.3	517.8
Cash flow ($000)	855.5	1,294.9	1,055.3

Solution 20

We need the discount rate in nominal terms to discount the nominal cash flows in Problem 19. Given an inflation rate of 5% and a real discount rate of 6%, the nominal discount rate is $(1.05)(1.06) - 1 = .1130$ or 11.30%. The present value of the cash flows is

$$PV = \frac{\$855.5}{(1.113)} + \frac{\$1294.9}{(1.113)^2} + \frac{\$1055.3}{(1.113)^3}$$

$$PV = \$2,579.36$$

Solution 21

To find the answer we need to calculate the depreciation tax shield and after-tax net revenues for each year. The depreciation tax shield is the tax rate times the amount of depreciation. After-tax net revenues are discounted at 11.3% and the depreciation tax shields are discounted at 6%. Results are presented in the following table.

Year	1	2	3
Unit sales ($000)	5.00	7.50	6.00
Unit price ($)	411.60	423.54	435.82
Revenues ($000)	2,058.00	3,176.60	2,614.90
Unit cost ($)	157.50	165.38	173.64
Costs ($000)	787.50	1,240.40	1,041.80
Net revenues ($000)	1,270.50	1,936.20	1,573.10
After-tax net ($000)	838.50	1,277.90	1,038.20
Present Value (@11.3%) after-tax net revenues ($000)	753.40	1,031.60	753.00
Depreciation ($000)	50.00	50.00	50.00
Tax shield ($000)	17.00	17.00	17.00
Present value (@6.0%) depreciation tax shield ($000)	16.00	15.10	14.30
Total present value ($000)	769.40	1,046.70	767.30

For the three years, the total present value equals $2,583,400. This present value exceeds the value from problem 20 because the depreciation tax shield cash flows are now less risky and therefore more valuable.

CHAPTER 8

STRATEGY AND ANALYSIS
IN USING NET PRESENT VALUE

CHAPTER MISSION STATEMENT

Chapter 8 provides the student a sense of how corporate strategy and positive net present values are related. The chapter discusses the sources of positive net present values, and how stock market values can be used by managers to avoid making short-sighted decisions. The chapter shows how decision trees, sensitivity analysis, and scenario analysis are used to deal with uncertainty in incremental cash flow forecasts. Finally, the chapter discusses and provides examples of the importance of managerial options in project analysis.

The key concepts presented in Chapter 8 are outlined below.

- ♦Corporate strategy and positive NPV
    - ●creating positive NPVs
    - ●competition and positive NPVs
    - ●corporate strategy and the stock market
- ♦Decision trees
- ♦Sensitivity analysis
- ♦Scenario analysis
- ♦Break-even analysis
    - ●accounting profit break-even
    - ●present value break-even
- ♦Managerial options
    - ●option to expand
    - ●option to abandon

CONCEPT TEST

1. Positive NPV projects should be hard to find in a _____ economy.

2. Two important ways to create positive NPVs are to _____, or to _____.

3. Competition forces NPV to equal _____.

4. The available evidence is _____ with the notion that markets and managers are myopic toward capital budgeting decisions.

5. To help managers avoid making short-sighted decisions, they should use the information contained in _____ whenever possible.

6. One device for identifying uncertain future cash flows is a _____.

7. Decision trees are useful up to a point, but it is hard for decision trees to capture all of the _____ in a changing environment.

8.   Decision trees highlight, but do not necessarily deal with how _____ changes over the life of the project.

9.   A _____ is useful for determining the impact of assumptions made about critical variables in calculating NPV.

10.   Sensitivity analysis is useful because it shows where more _____ is needed.

11.   A drawback to sensitivity analysis, however, is that it deals with variables in _____.

12.   A variant of sensitivity analysis which deals with a number of factors at the same time is _____.

13.   The sales level at which net income is zero is called the _____ sales level.

14.   The sales level at which NPV is zero is called the _____ break-even level.

15.   The problem with accounting profit break-even analysis is that it ignores the _____.

16.   The standard NPV analysis is static because it ignores _____.

17.   The value of a project should be its NPV and the value of any _____.

CONCEPT TEST ANSWERS

1.	competitive	9.	sensitivity analysis
2.	introduce a new product; develop a new technology	10.	information
		11.	isolation
3.	zero	12.	scenario analysis
4.	inconsistent	13.	accounting profit break-even
5.	market prices	14.	present value
6.	decision tree	15.	opportunity cost of the investment
7.	managerial options	16.	options to expand or abandon
8.	risk	17.	managerial options

PROBLEMS

Problem 1

The Eureka Company is going to introduce a new consumer product, but Janeen Wilson its VP for Marketing wants to do consumer surveys or test marketing first. If brought to market without research about consumer tastes Eureka believes that there is a sixty-forty chance that the product will be successful. If successful, the project has a NPV = $450,000. If the product is a failure and withdrawn from the market, then NPV = -$100,000. A consumer survey will cost $50,000 and delay the introduction by two years. If the survey is successful, then there is an 80% chance of consumer acceptance, in which case the NPV = $450,000. If, on the other hand the survey is a failure, then NPV = -$100,000. The discount rate is 12%. Should Eureka proceed with the survey?

Problem 2

Eureka has a second new product to introduce. This time the firm will test-market the product for one year before full scale operations begin. The one-year test will require an investment of $250,000 at time zero. There is a 70% chance that the test will be a success. In this event, the firm will proceed with investing $500,000 at time 1 which will return $235,000 per year for five years. If the test is a failure, Eureka will salvage its initial investment for $75,000. The appropriate discount rate for the project is 12%. However, the initial test marketing period is considered riskier and Eureka believes a 20% rate should be used. Should Eureka go ahead with the test marketing phase of the project?

Problem 3

A financial analyst is evaluating a project that is expected to produce annual sales of 200 units at $2 cash flow per unit for the foreseeable future. After one year, the expected demand will be revised to either 100 units or 300 units, depending on the success of the project. Success and failure are equally likely. The cost of the project is $2,200, while the discount rate is 20%. The project can be dismantled and sold in one year for $1,600. Should the project be accepted?

The following two problems refer to information provided in Chapter 7, Problems 1-5.

Problem 4

Eduardo Salinas, Datum's newest accountant, has objected to your recommendation that the "DataScan" (Chapter 7, Problems 1-5) project be rejected, and has stated: "At 10,000 units per year, we are way above the break-even point on this project." What is the accounting break-even unit volume? Is he correct?

Problem 5

Datums's financial analyst suggests that the present value break-even point is more important. How many units must be sold to break-even on a present value basis?

Problem 6

You are wondering how much you should pay for a frozen yogurt machine for your fast food restaurant. You expect the machine to last 5 years and have no salvage value. Depreciation would be straight line over 5 years. Fixed costs are $1,800 per year, while variable costs are 50 cents per serving. You expect to sell 100 servings per day at $1.25 per serving. The tax rate is 34%, the discount rate is 10%. What is the maximum you should pay for the machine just to break-even?

Problem 7

Evergreen Amalgamated Inc. is introducing a new line of sump pumps. The firm wants to know if it should proceed with the new pumps. Use the information in the following table to calculate the expected NPV of the new line of pumps. Assume that the project lasts 5 years, depreciation is straight line over the life of the project, the tax rate is 34%, and the discount rate is 20%

	Pessimistic	Expected	Optimistic
Market Size	5,000	10,000	20,000
Market Share	20%	30%	50%
Price	$1,750	$2,250	$2,500
Variable costs	$1000	$900	$700
Fixed Costs (000)	$2,000	$1,700	$1,500
Investment (000)	$1,750	$1,500	$1,250

Problem 8

The CEO of Evergreen Amalgamated wants to get a feeling about the robustness of the expected NPV. That is, she wants to know how sensitive the NPV is to assumptions about the underlying marketing and cost data? Perform a sensitivity analysis on the above table.

Problem 9

Evergreen Amalgamated (Problem 7) wants to conduct a scenario analysis of the sump pump project. Evergreen wants to know what effect increased competition will have on the expected NPV. Competition will likely reduce market share to 20% and the selling price to $1,750 per pump. Under this scenario, what is the project's NPV?

Problem 10

Evergreen Amalgamated has created a technological breakthrough which allows the firm to manufacture a highly efficient pump at low cost. This unique pump will allow Evergreen to capture 50% of the sump pump market. Variable costs for the new pump are only $700 per unit. What is the project's NPV under this scenario?

Problem 11

Excelsior Products is analyzing a new consumer product that requires an initial investment of $110,000 and will generate an expected cash flow of $12,000 per year forever. Consumer acceptance, however, is uncertain. The company believes that product "newness" will generate the first year's cash flow. After the first year, however, the firm will have a better understanding of consumer demand. If demand is high, the product will generate $14,500 per year. But there is a 20% chance that demand will be low, in which case cash flow will be $2,000 per year. After the first year, the firm could terminate the project and sell the assets for $82,500. The discount rate is 12%. What is the expected net present value of the project ignoring the option to terminate the project.

Problem 12

Continuing the previous problem, what is the net present value of Excelsior's project if the analysis includes the option to terminate the project?

SOLUTIONS

Solution 1

If no consumer survey takes place, the project commences immediately, and the expected NPV is

$$E(NPV) = .60(\$450,000) + .4(-\$100,000) = \$230,000.$$

If the marketing survey takes place, the project starts at time 2 and has the same NPVs as before. However, if the survey is successful, there is now an 80% chance that consumers will find the product appealing. The expected NPV at time 2 is, therefore,

$$E(NPV(2)) = .80(\$450,000) + .20(-\$100,000) = \$340,000.$$

Discounting back to time zero, and subtracting the cost of the survey, the expected NPV of this strategy equals

$$E(NPV) = -\$50,000 + \$340,000/(1.12)^2 = \$221,046.$$

The expected NPV is less with the marketing survey than without. Thus, on a strictly NPV basis, no survey should be done. Realistically, however, given the closeness of the two values, the firm is likely to undertake the survey in order to reduce some of the uncertainty associated with new product introductions. Of course, if the survey is a failure, the firm will abandon the project and be out the $50,000 cost of the survey.

Solution 2

As in all decision tree problems, the solution starts at the end of the project. If the test-marketing is successful, Eureka will invest $500,000 at t=1. The net present value (at t=1) of this investment is

$$NPV(t=1) = -\$500,000 + \$235,000 \, A^5_{.12} = \$347,122.$$

There is a 70% chance that Eureka will make the investment and receive this NPV. There is a 30%

change that Eureka will salvage existing assets and receive $75,000. Thus, at time t=1 the expected NPV equals

$$E(NPV(t=1)) = .70(\$347,122) + .30(\$75,000) = \$265,485.$$

Because the test market period is considered risky, this expected NPV is discounted back to time zero at 20%. Then, the expected net present value at time zero, net of the initial cost of test-marketing is

$$E(NPV) = -\$250,000 + \$265,485/(1.20) = -\$28,762.$$

Therefore, because the NPV is negative, Eureka should not proceed with test-marketing the new product.

Solution 3

The expected cash flow is a perpetuity of $400 per year and the discount rate is 20%. The present value of the cash flows is ($400/.20) = $2,000, so the net present value is ($2,000 - $2,200) = -$200. Therefore, it appears that the project should not be accepted. However, this analysis is static.

One year from now, the opportunity cost of staying in business is the $1,600 we give up by not selling. If the expected cash flows are revised to $200 (=$2×100) at that time, then the present value of the cash flows, as of year one, is ($200/.20) = $1,000, and the net present value is ($1,000 - $1,600) = -$600. Thus, if we accept the project now, we will abandon it in one year if it is unsuccessful. Our cash flow at year one is then ($1,600 + $200) = $1,800 in this case. On the other hand, if the demand is revised upward to 300 units, then the present value of the future cash flows at year 1 is ($600/.20) = $3,000, and the year 1 net present value is $1,400 (=$3,000 - $1,600). With high demand, the year 1 value is $3,600 (=$600 from year 1 sales+ $3,000 present value of future sales). Thus, at year 1, we have equal chances of $1,800 (low demand) and $3,600 (high demand). The expected value is therefore [.5($1,800) + .5($3,600)] = $2,700. The present value of this year 1 expected value is $2,250, so the net present value is $50 (=$2,250 - $2,200).

Recognizing the value of the option to abandon the unsuccessful project has increased the NPV by $250. Where did this increase in value come from? Our original analysis assumed we would continue the project even if it was a failure. At year 1, the NPV of the project was -$600 in the event of a failure. The option to abandon saves us this $600. There is a 50% probability of this outcome, so the expected saving is $300. The present value of this expected saving (the value of the option to abandon) is ($300/1.20) = $250.

Solution 4

The accounting break-even is the ratio of fixed costs plus depreciation to unit price less unit variable cost, or (in millions) [(12 + 5)/(.0021)] = 8,095 units. The "DataScan" project is projected to more than break-even on an accounting basis, so the above statement is correct, but misleading. The project will still lose money when we consider the time value of money (see Problem 5 below).

Solution 5

To calculate the present value break-even point, we must first calculate the equivalent annual cost for the capital investment. In this case, the capital requirements occur at different points in time. The capital requirements consist of $(-\$40 - \$2.4 - \$8 - \$1.4(.66)) = -\$51.324$ million in year zero and $(\$8 + \$2.4 + \$3.96)$ million $= \$14.36$ million in year 8. The present value of the year 8 capital requirement is $6.70 million, so the effective capital investment is $(-\$51.324 + \$6.70)$ million $= -\$44.625$ million.

The annuity factor for 8 years at a 10% discount rate is 5.3349. The equivalent annual cost (EAC) is $[(\$44.625 \text{ million})/5.3349] = \$8.365$ million. The break-even point is the after-tax costs divided by the after-tax contribution margin. In the numerator we have

$$\text{EAC} + \text{Fixed Costs } (1 - T_c) - \text{Depreciation } (T_c)$$

$$= \$8.365 + \$12 \,(.66) - \$5(.34) = \$14.585 \text{ million}$$

In the denominator we have

$$(\text{Sales price} - \text{Variable costs}) \,(1 - T_c)$$

$$= (\$9500 - \$7400) \,(.66) = \$1,386$$

The present value break-even point is

$$\$14,585,000/\$1,386 = 10,523 \text{ units}$$

The break-even point is slightly higher than the anticipated sales of 10,000 units per year.

Solution 6

The maximum that you should pay for the machine is the price that makes NPV equal zero. The solution involves setting your annual sales to the present value break-even point, and solving for the equivalent annual cost of the investment. Let EAC be the equivalent annual cost of the (unknown) investment, i.e., EAC = initial investment/annuity factor. The present value break-even point is defined as the ratio of the after-tax fixed costs (including EAC) to the after-tax contribution margin. The after tax costs are

$$\text{EAC} + \text{Fixed Costs } (1 - T_c) - \text{Depreciation } (T_c)$$

while the after-tax contribution margin is

$$(\text{Sales price} - \text{Variable costs}) \,(1 - T_c)$$

Depreciation is unknown, but may be expressed in terms of EAC. With straight line depreciation over 5 years, annual depreciation equals (initial investment)/5. The present value annuity factor for 5 years and 10% is 3.7908. Thus, depreciation = (initial investment)/5 = EAC(3.7908)/5, where investment is EAC(3.7908). Set the break-even point to annual unit sales = $100 \times 365 = 36,500$ servings. Then

$$[EAC + \$1800(.66) - EAC(3.7908)(1/5)(.34)]/[(\$1.25 - \$0.50)(.66)]$$

$$= 36,500 \text{ units}$$

Solving for EAC, we find EAC = \$22,742. Then, the most you should be willing to pay is \$22,742(3.7908) = \$86,209.

Solution 7

The information in the table indicates that Evergreen expects to capture 30% of the market for this type of sump pump. This translates into sales of 3,000 pumps per year at \$2,250 per pump. Variable costs per pump are \$900, while fixed costs per year are \$1,700 thousand. The expected \$1,500 thousand investment creates annual depreciation of \$1,500 thousand/5 yrs = \$300 thousand. The expected annual cash flow is (in thousands)

$$\text{units} \times \text{(after tax contribution margin)} + \text{depreciation tax shield} - \text{after tax fixed costs}$$

$$3 \times (\$2250 - \$900)(1 - .34) + \$300(.34) - \$1700(1 - .34) = \$1,653$$

The expected NPV is

$$NPV = -\$1500 + \$1653(2.9906) = \$3443 \text{ thousand}$$

where 2.9906 is the present value annuity factor for 5 years and 20%.

Solution 8

Sensitivity analysis consists of substituting, one at a time, alternate values of market size, market share, price, etc. while leaving all other values at their expected value and recalculating NPV. For example, the expected annual cash flow for a pessimistic forecast of price is (in thousands)

$$3 \times (\$1750 - \$900)(1 - .34) + \$300(.34) - \$1700(1 - .34) = \$663$$

The expected NPV is

$$NPV = -\$1500 + \$663(2.9906) = \$483 \text{ thousand}$$

where 2.9906 is the present value annuity factor for 5 years and 20%. Repeating these calculations for all pessimistic and optimistic values produces the following table of NPVs:

	Net Present Values ($ thousands)		
	Pessimistic	Expected	Optimistic
Market Size	−553	3,443	11,437
Market Share	779	3,443	8,773
Price	483	3,443	4,924
Variable costs	2,851	3,443	4,628
Fixed Costs (000)	2,851	3,443	3,838
Investment (000)	3,244	3,443	3,643

Clearly, the NPV is sensitive to the firm's forecast of market size, market share, and price. NPV is relatively insensitive to variable and fixed costs, and investment.

Solution 9

Scenario analysis is, essentially, sensitivity analysis with changes to two or more input values at one time. In this case, the pessimistic values of market share and price are used with the expected values of all other factors. Under this scenario, expected sales are .20(10,000) = 2,000 pumps selling at $1,750 each. The cash flow per year is (in thousands)

$$2 \times (\$1750 - \$900)(1 - .34) + \$300(.34) - \$1700(1 - .34) = \$102$$

The expected NPV is

$$NPV = -\$1500 + \$102(2.9906) = -\$1,195 \text{ thousand}$$

where 2.9906 is the present value annuity factor for 5 years and 20%. Under this scenario the project would not be worthwhile since the NPV is negative.

Solution 10

Under this very optimistic scenario, Evergreen expects to sell .50(10,000) = 5,000 pumps at $2,250 per pump. Variable costs are $700 per pump. The annual cash flow becomes (in thousands)

$$5 \times (\$2250 - \$700)(1 - .34) + \$300(.34) - \$1700(1 - .34) = \$4,095$$

The expected NPV is

$$NPV = -\$1500 + \$4095(2.9906) = \$10,747 \text{ thousand}$$

where 2.9906 is the present value annuity factor for 5 years and 20%. Under this scenario, Evergreen's ability to make a unique pump at low cost proves to be highly valuable. Evergreen's $1.5 million investment produces a $10.7 million NPV, but given the profitability of this pump, Evergreen should keep an eye open for competitors.

Solution 11

The net present value of Excelsior's project is

$$NPV = -\$110,000 + \$12,000/.12 = -\$10,000$$

Note that after the first year, ignoring the option to terminate, the expected cash flow is

$$E(CF) = .80 \times \$14,500 + .20 \times \$2,000 = \$12,000.$$

Solution 12

After the first year, Excelsior can terminate the project and sell the assets for $82,500. The firm will do so if the present value at year 1 of future cash flows is less than $82,500. If after the first year demand is high, then Excelsior will continue with the project because the present value of future cash flows $120,833 (=$14,500/.12) exceeds the termination value. If demand is low, the present value of future cash flows is only $16,667 ($2,000/.12). Thus, if demand turns out low, Excelsior will terminate the project and sell the assets for $82,500.

The expected net present value at time 0, including the termination option is

$$NPV = -\$110,000 + \frac{\$12,000 + .80 \times \$120,833 + .20 \times \$82,500}{(1.12)}$$

$$= \$1,756.$$

Thus, the project becomes worthwhile to pursue once the option to terminate is included in the analysis. This option increases the NPV of the project by $11,756 = .20 \times (\$82,500 - \$16,667)/1.12$.

CHAPTER 9

CAPITAL MARKET THEORY:
AN OVERVIEW

CHAPTER MISSION STATEMENT

The purpose of Chapter 9 is to provide the student a brief overview of capital market history and the relationship between returns on assets and their risk. The chapter defines returns, both dollar and percentage, and shows how to calculate average returns and holding period returns. The distribution to returns is discussed, along with means and variances used to describe the distribution. The chapter introduces the concept of diversification, and finally the capital asset pricing model and beta.

The key concepts presented in Chapter 9 are outlined below.

> ♦Returns
>> ●dollar returns
>> ●percentage returns
>> ●dividend yield and capital gains
> ♦Holding period returns
>> ●capital market history
> ♦Return statistics
>> ●frequency distribution
>> ●arithmetic average
>> ●risk premium
> ♦Risk statistics
>> ●variance
>> ●standard deviation
> ♦Risky discount rate
>> ●market portfolio
>> ●risk premium
> ♦Risk and Beta
>> ●diversification
>> ●capital asset pricing model
>> ●beta

CONCEPT TEST

1. The cash or income component from owning a share of stock is called the _____.

2. The portion of an investor's return that comes from changes in value is called the _____ component of the return.

3. You own a share of stock which has a total return of 26% for the last four years. The 26% return is your four-year _____.

4. If you add the returns for an asset during the four previous years and then divide the total by four, you have computed the _____ return.

5. The Treasury bill rate is commonly referred to as the _____.

6. The excess above the T-bill return earned on a share of stock is called the _____ on the stock's return.

7. The return on a share of stock or other risky asset is composed of two parts, the _____ and the _____.

8. The most common measures of risk for assets such as stocks and bonds are the _____ and the _____.

9. The 'bell-shaped curve' is called the _____.

10. If an asset's return is normally distributed, the probability that a given return will be within one standard deviation of the mean is _____. The probability that a given return is within two standard deviations of the mean is _____.

11. The commonly used measures of the tendency for the prices of two assets to move up and down together are the _____ and the _____.

12. If the returns on two assets change in the same direction and are directly proportional, then the returns have _____.

13. If the returns on two assets change in the opposite direction and are directly proportional, then the returns have _____.

14. If there is no relationship between the returns on two risky assets, then their returns have _____.

15. In general, the returns on risky assets are _____ correlated.

16. The variance of a portfolio of stocks is less than the variance of an individual stock because of _____.

17. The tendency of an individual stock's returns to covary with the market is measured by the stock's _____.

ANSWERS TO CONCEPT TEST

1.   dividend
2.   capital gains
3.   holding-period return
4.   mean or arithmetic average
5.   risk-free rate
6.   risk premium
7.   risk-free return; risk premium
8.   variance; standard deviation
9.   normal distribution

10. 68%; 95%
11. covariance; correlation
12. perfect positive correlation
13. perfect negative correlation
14. zero correlation
15. positively
16. diversification
17. beta

PROBLEMS

Problem 1

Exactly one year ago you purchased 100 shares of Wendy's International Inc. for $21 5/16 per share. Today's stock price is $24 15/16, and over the past year you received dividends of $0.24 per share. What is the percentage increase in price? What is the percentage return from dividends? What is your total return for the year?

Problem 2

Two years ago you purchased a share of stock for $24 3/8. The first year that you owned the stock you received an 80% return; over the second year, however, the stock fell by 51%. What is your share of stock worth today? What was your average rate of return? What was your holding period return?

Problem 3

Suppose that you are considering investing in one of two stocks. Both cost $100 per share. Share A promises a $3.60 dividend and should be worth $108.40 next year. Share B, on the other hand promises a $4.80 dividend and will be worth $107.20 next year. Which stock is the better investment.

Problem 4

Suppose that, one year ago, you bought 100 shares of Bradley Corporation common stock for $32 per share. During the year, you have received total dividends of $250. Bradley common stock is currently selling for $33.50 per share. How much did you earn in capital gains? What was your total dollar return? Calculate your capital gains yield, dividend yield and total percentage return.

Problem 5

Suppose that, one year from today, you expect the Bradley Corporation common stock described in Problem 4 to be selling for $33 per share, and that during the coming year, you expect to receive dividends of $2 per share. Calculate your expected capital gains yield, dividend yield and total percentage return for the coming year. Calculate your holding period return for the two year period.

Use the following information to solve Problems 6-10:

	Returns (%)	
Year	X	Y
1	15	18
2	4	-3
3	-9	-10
4	8	12
5	9	5

Problem 6

What is the mean return for asset X? For asset Y?

Problem 7

What is the five-year holding period return for asset X? For asset Y?

Problem 8

What is the variance of the return for asset X? For asset Y?

Problem 9

What is the standard deviation of the return for asset X? For asset Y?

Problem 10

Suppose that the returns for assets X and Y each have a normal distribution with means and standard deviations calculated in Problems 6 and 9, respectively. For each asset, determine the range of returns within one standard deviation of the mean, and the range of returns within two standard deviations of the mean. Interpret these results.

Problem 11

The returns to common stocks and T-Bills during World War II are presented below. Calculate the holding period return over this period. Calculate the risk premium for each year and the total period.

	Returns (%)	
Year	Common Stocks	T-Bills
1942	20.34	0.27
1943	25.90	0.35
1944	19.75	0.33
1945	36.44	0.33

Problem 12

Calculate the holding period returns to common stocks and T-Bills over the five-year period shown in the following table. Calculate the risk premium for each year and the five-year average premium.

	Returns (%)	
Year	Common Stocks	T-Bills
1970	4.01	6.52
1971	14.31	4.39
1972	18.98	3.84
1973	−14.66	6.93
1974	−26.47	8.00

Problem 13

The Ectoplasto Drug Company's common stock is considered highly speculative. Security analysts believe that over the next year four possible outcomes are possible for the company's research program. There is a 60% chance that their new drug will be successful, in which case the stock will be worth $240 per share. The is a 5% chance that the drug will be a complete failure, in which case the stock will be worthless. There are two mid-range outcomes: a 15% chance of a good but not spectacular drug, and a 20% chance of an average selling drug. With a good drug the stock will be worth $180 per share, while an average drug will produce a stock price of $75 per share. If the appropriate discount rate is 25%, how much should you be willing to pay for the stock today?

Problem 14

Given the prices and probabilities in the previous problem, determine the returns expected under each outcome.

Problem 15

The probability that the economy will experience a recession next year is .2, while the probabilities of moderate growth or rapid expansion are .6 and .2, respectively. The common stock of Firm A is expected to return -5%, 15% or 30% depending on whether the economy experiences a recession, moderate growth or rapid expansion, respectively. The rates of return for Firm B are expected to be 0%, 16% or 22%, respectively. Calculate the expected rate of return for each firm's common stock.

Problem 16

What is the variance of the expected return for Firm A's common stock? For Firm B's common stock?

Problem 17

What is the standard deviation of the expected rate of return for Firm A's common stock? For Firm B's common stock?

Problem 18

The Erie Electroplating Company's stock has a beta of 1.60. The market risk premium is 8.5% and the risk free rate is 3.7%. What is Erie's expected return?

Problem 19

The expected return on Chambersburg Forging Company's stock is 12%. At the same time, the risk free rate is 4%, and the market risk premium is 8.5%. What is the beta of Chambersburg's stock?

SOLUTIONS

Solution 1

Your investment in Wendy's stock increased from $2,131.25 (=$21 5/16 × 100) to $2,493.75 (=$24 15/16 × 100), which is an increase of 17.01%. You received $24.00 in dividends on your $2,131.25 investment, which is a 1.13% return. Your total return is 18.14% =[($2,493.75 + $24.00 - $2,2131.25)/ $2,131.25].

Solution 2

Two years ago you paid $24 3/8 = $24.375 for the share, after the first year it was worth $24.375(1.80) = $43.875 or $43 7/8, after the second year the stock is worth $43.875(.49) = $21.50 or $21 1/2. Your average rate of return was (80% - 51%)/2 = 14.5%; your holding period return was (1.80)(.49) - 1 = -.1180 or -11.8%. Note that, although you end up with less money than you started with, your average rate of return was positive! The holding period return correctly describes your wealth position after two years.

Solution 3

Holding all other factors constant, such as risk, taxes, etc., the stock which provides the higher return should be the better investment. Total return is the combination of dividends and capital gains. For share A, the dividend yield is \$3.60/\$100 = .036 or 3.6%, while capital gains provide a (\$108.40 – \$100.00)/\$100 = .084 or 8.4% return. Thus, total return for A is 3.6% + 8.4% = 12.0%. For share B, the dividend yield is 4.8% while the capital gain yield is 7.2%, and total return is 12.0%. Both A and B offer the same return and, therefore, you should be indifferent between them (all other considerations held constant).

Solution 4

Capital gains are equal to [(\$33.50 – \$32)(100)] = \$150 and total dollar return is (\$150 + \$250) = \$400. Capital gains yield is [\$150/(\$32)(100)] = .0469 or 4.69%. Dividend yield is [\$250/(\$32)(100)] = .0781 or 7.81%. Total percentage return is [(\$150 + \$250)/(\$32)(100)] = .1250 or 12.50% = (4.69% + 7.81%).

Solution 5

The capital gains yield for the coming year is [(–\$.50)(100)/(\$33.50)(100)] = –.0149 or –1.49%. The dividend yield is [(\$2)(100)/(\$33.50)(100)] = .0597 or 5.97%. The total percentage return is (–.0149 + .0597) = .0448 or 4.48%. The holding period return can be determined from the general formula for the T-period holding period return:

$$[(1 + R_1) \times (1 + R_2) .... \times (1 + R_T)] - 1$$

Therefore, we can calculate the two-year holding period return as follows:

$$[(1.1250)(1.0448)] - 1 = .1754 \text{ or } 17.54\%$$

Note that the holding period return can also be determined directly from the capital gains and dividend payments for each of the two years. Capital gains are [\$150 + (–\$50)] = \$100 for the two year period. Dividends are (\$250 + \$200) = \$450. However, the calculation of the holding period return is based on the assumption that dividends received during the first year are reinvested in Bradley common stock during the second year; that is, we assume that the \$250 dividend received at the end of year 1 is invested at a 4.48% rate during year 2. Therefore, for the purposes of calculating the holding period return, we assume returns from dividends at the end of the two-year period equal to [(\$250)(1.0448) + (\$200)] = \$461.20. The two-year holding period return is:

$$[(\$100 + \$461.20)/\$3200] = .1754 \text{ or } 17.54\%.$$

Solution 6

	Returns (%)	
Year	X	Y
1	15	18
2	4	-3
3	-9	-10
4	8	12
5	9	5
Totals	27%	22%

The mean returns are, for X: $\overline{R} = E(R) = (27\%/5) = 5.4\%$, for Y: $\overline{R} = E(R) = (22\%/5) = 4.4\%$.

Solution 7

In general, the T-period holding period return can be calculated as:

$$[(1 + R_1) \times (1 + R_2) \ldots \times (1 + R_T)] - 1.$$

Therefore, for asset X, we can calculate the five-year holding period return as follows:

$$[(1.15)(1.04)(.91)(1.08)(1.09)] - 1 = .2812 \text{ or } 28.12\%$$

Similarly, the five-year holding period return for asset Y is 21.14%.

Solution 8

	Returns		Deviations		Squared deviations	
Year	X	Y	X	Y	X	Y
1	.15	.18	.096	.136	.009216	.018496
2	.04	-.03	-.014	-.074	.000196	.005476
3	-.09	-.10	-.144	-.144	.020736	.020736
4	.08	.12	.026	.076	.000676	.005776
5	.09	.05	.036	.006	.001296	.000036
Totals	.27	.22	.000	.000	.032120	.050520

Thus, Var(X) = σ^2(X) = (.032120/4) = .008030 and var(Y) = σ^2(Y) = .012630. Note that you divide the sum of the squared deviations by T–1 = 4; this gives you the sample variance, while dividing by T=5 gives you the population variance.

Solution 9

The standard deviation is the square root of the variance. Therefore, the standard deviation for asset X is SD(X) = σ(X) = $\sqrt{(.008030)}$ = .089610 or 8.961%, and SD(Y) = σ(Y) = $\sqrt{(.012630)}$ = .112383 or 11.2383%.

Solution 10

For asset X, the range of returns within one standard deviation of the mean is from [.054 – (1)(.089610)] to [.054 + (1)(.089610)], or –3.56% to 14.36%. The range of returns within two standard deviations of the mean is from [.054 – (2)(.089610)] to [.054 + (2)(.089610)], or –12.52% to 23.32%. These results indicate that there is approximately a 68% probability that, in any given year, the return for asset X will be between –3.56% and 14.36%, and approximately a 95% probability that the return will be between –12.52% and 23.32%. For asset Y, the probability is approximately 68% that the return will be between –6.84% and 15.64%, and approximately 95% that the return will be between –18.08% and 26.88%.

Solution 11

	Returns (%)		
Year	Common Stocks	T-Bills	Risk Premium
1942	20.34	0.27	20.07
1943	25.90	0.35	25.55
1944	19.75	0.33	19.42
1945	36.44	0.33	36.11

The holding period return for common stocks over the four years is (1.2034)(1.2590)(1.1975)(1.3644) – 1 = 1.4754 or 147.54%. For T-Bills, the four year holding period return is 1.29% The arithmetic average returns are 25.61% for common stocks and 0.32% for T-Bills. The average risk premium is 25.29%.

Solution 12

	Returns (%)		
Year	Common Stocks	T-Bills	Risk Premium
1970	4.01	6.52	-2.51
1971	14.31	4.39	9.92
1972	18.98	3.84	15.13
1973	-14.66	6.93	-21.59
1974	-26.47	8.00	-34.47

The holding period returns for common stocks and T-Bills are -11.23% and 33.34%. This means that if you invested $100 in common stock and $100 in T-Bills at the start of 1970, by the end of 1974 these investments would be worth $88.77 and $133.34, respectively. The average annual returns are -0.77% and 5.94%. The average risk premium is -6.70%. Although we expect to receive a positive risk premium when we invest in common stocks, sometimes, after the fact, we end up receiving a negative risk premium.

Solution 13

The expected price next year is

$$.60 \times \$240 + .05 \times \$0 + .15 \times \$180 + .20 \times \$75 = \$186$$

Discounting back one year at 25% produces a price of $148.80. Thus, you should be will to pay no more than $148.80 for a share of Ectoplasto's stock.

Solution 14

Initial Price	Outcome Price	Return
$148.80	$240	61.3%
148.80	0	-100.0
148.80	180	21.0
148.80	75	-49.6

Note that the expected return equals

$$25\% = .60 \times 61.3\% + .05 \times -100.0\% + .15 \times 21.0\% + .20 \times -49.6\%.$$

Solution 15

The expected rates of return for Firms A and B common stock are:

$$E(R_A) = (.20)(-.05) + (.60)(.15) + (.20)(.30) = .14 = 14\%$$

$$E(R_B) = (.20)(.00) + (.60)(.16) + (.20)(.22) = .14 = 14\%$$

Solution 16

The variance for Firm A is calculated using values in the following table where Deviation is deviation from the expected return found in the previous problem.

State of the economy	Probability	Return	Deviation	Squared deviation	Probability × squared deviation
Recession	.20	−.05	−.19	.0361	.00722
Mod Gwth	.60	.15	.01	.0001	.00006
Rapid Exp	.20	.30	.16	.0256	.00512

The variance is determined by first calculating the deviation from the expected return for each state; these deviations are then squared and multiplied by the respective probabilities of each state. The sum of the weighted squared deviations is the variance. Therefore, Var(A) = σ^2 = .01240. The comparable calculations for Firm B indicate that Var(B) = .00544.

Solution 17

The standard deviation is the square root of the variance. The standard deviation for Firm A's common stock is SD(A) = σ = $\sqrt{(.01240)}$ = .11136 or 11.14%, and SD(B) = $\sqrt{(.00544)}$ = .07376 or 7.38%.

Solution 18

From the capital asset pricing model, the expected return on Erie's stock is

$$E(R) = 3.7\% + 1.60(8.5\%) = 17.3\%$$

Solution 19

Using the rates of return provided, we can use the capital asset pricing model to solve for the stock's beta.

$$E(R) = 12\% = 4\% + \beta(8.5\%)$$

solving for beta

$$\beta = .94.$$

CHAPTER 10

RETURN AND RISK:
THE CAPITAL ASSET PRICING MODEL (CAPM)

CHAPTER MISSION STATEMENT

The purpose of Chapter 10 is to more formally explain the relationship between return and risk that was first introduced in Chapter 9. This relationship is the capital asset pricing model (CAPM). Chapter 10 discusses how individuals may view a security's variance as an appropriate measure of risk. For a portfolio of assets, however, investors should view a security's contribution to the risk of the portfolio as the appropriate measure of risk. This contribution is indicated by the security's beta, which is a measure of a security's covariance risk with respect to the market portfolio. The chapter provides the necessary mathematics to calculate the expected return and variance of a portfolio containing many risky assets.

The major concepts discussed in Chapter 10 are outlined below.

♦Individual securities
- ●returns
- ●variances
- ●covariances

♦Portfolios
- ●returns
- ●variances
- ●covariances

♦Efficient set for two assets

♦Efficient set for many assets
- ●variance
- ●diversification

♦Riskless borrowing and lending
- ●optimal portfolio
- ●capital market line

♦Market equilibrium
- ●homogeneous expectations
- ●beta
- ●characteristic line

♦Capital Asset Pricing Model
- ●security market line

CONCEPT TEST

1. The expected return on a portfolio is computed as a _____ of the individual security expected returns.

2. If the correlation between two securities is less than 1, then the portfolio standard deviation is less than the _____ of the individual security standard deviations.

3. By combining two securities whose returns are negatively correlated, you are achieving what we call a _____.

4. The set of all feasible portfolios which can be formed by combining risky securities is called the _____ set or the _____ set.

5. The set of feasible portfolios that investors should only consider is the _____.

6. The portfolio in the opportunity set which has the lowest standard deviation is called the _____ portfolio.

7. The formula for the variance of a portfolio has two kinds of terms: _____ terms and _____ terms.

8. The formula for the variance of a portfolio has as many _____ terms as there are securities in the portfolio.

9. The formula for the variance of a portfolio has as many _____ terms as there are pairs of securities in the portfolio.

10. The standard deviation of a portfolio is almost always less than a weighted average of the standard deviations of the individual securities; this effect is known as _____.

11. For a very highly diversified portfolio, the portfolio variance approaches the _____ as the number of assets grows large.

12. Studies have shown that the number of stocks that you should have in your portfolio to achieve diversification is about _____.

13. The opportunity set for a portfolio comprised of the risk-free asset and a risky asset is a _____ line, whereas the opportunity set for a portfolio comprised of two risky assets is a _____ line.

14. The _____ is the efficient set for all assets.

15. The _____ principle refers to the fact that the portfolio selection process can be thought of as two steps, one involving objective data and the other involving personal preferences.

16. The assumption of _____ states that all investors have the same information regarding security returns, variances and covariances.

17. The contribution of a security to the risk of the portfolio is measured by the _____ between the return for the security and the market portfolio.

18. With riskless borrowing and lending and _____ expectations, all investors would hold the same portfolio of risky assets call the _____ portfolio.

19. The algebraic representation of the security market line is called the _____.

20. The y-intercept, corresponding to a zero beta, on the SML is _____.

21. The slope of the SML is equal to the _____.

22. The beta of the market portfolio is _____.

23. The y-axis of the SML measures _____.

24. The x-axis of the SML measures _____.

25. Total risk consists of _____ and _____.

26. To an individual forming a diversified portfolio, only _____ risk is important.

ANSWERS TO CONCEPT TEST

1. weighted average
2. weighted average
3. hedge
4. opportunity; feasible
5. efficient set
6. minimum variance
7. variance; covariance
8. variance
9. covariance
10. diversification
11. average covariance
12. thirty
13. straight; curved
14. capital market line

15. separation
16. homogeneous expectations
17. covariance
18. homogeneous; market
19. capital asset pricing model
20. the risk free rate
21. market risk premium
22. one
23. expected return
24. beta
25. systematic risk; diversifiable risk
26. systematic

PROBLEMS

Problem 1

Calculate the covariance between the returns for assets X and Y using the following historical returns?

	Returns (%)	
Year	X	Y
1	15	18
2	4	-3
3	-9	-10
4	8	12
5	9	5

Problem 2

What is the correlation between the returns for assets X and Y?

Problem 3

What is the covariance between the returns for Firm A stock and Firm B stock? The expected returns and variances were calculated in Chapter 9, Problems 15 and 16.

State of the economy	Probability of state	Return on A	Return on B
Rapid growth	.20	.30	.22
Moderate growth	.60	.15	.16
Recession	.20	-.05	.00

Problem 4

What is the correlation between the returns for Firm A stock and Firm B stock?

Use the following information for Stock C and for the market portfolio to solve Problems 5-10.

State of the economy	Probability of state	Return on C	Return on market
Rapid growth	.10	.25	.18
Moderate growth	.20	.10	.20
Normal growth	.50	.15	.04
Recession	.20	-.12	.00

Problem 5

What is the expected return for Stock C? For the market?

Problem 6

What is the standard deviation for Stock C? For the market?

Problem 7

What is the covariance between Stock C and the market? What is the correlation?

Problem 8

Calculate the value of beta, ß, for Stock C.

Problem 9

What is the expected return for a portfolio of Stock C and the market portfolio where 20% is invested in Stock C?

Problem 10

What is the variance of a portfolio that is invested 60% in Stock C and 40% in the market portfolio?

Problem 11

An individual plans to invest in Stock A and/or Stock B. The expected returns are 12% and 18% for Stocks A and B, respectively. The standard deviations are 6% and 12% for Stocks A and B. The correlation between A and B is .15. Find the expected return and the standard deviation of a portfolio with 80% of the investor's funds in Stock A.

Problem 12

Suppose that the investor in Problem 11 wants to construct a portfolio with expected return equal to 14.4%. What proportion of the investor's portfolio should be invested in each asset? What is the standard deviation for the portfolio?

Problem 13

Suppose that the investor described in Problem 11 decides to form a portfolio consisting of three assets, as follows: 10% invested in Stock A, 30% invested in Stock B, and 60% invested in a risk free asset with a return of 6%. What is the expected return for this portfolio? What is the portfolio's standard deviation of returns?

Problem 14

Harry starts with $100, lends $50 to Sally at the risk free rate, and invests the rest in the market portfolio. Sally, meanwhile, starts with $100, borrows $50 from Harry at the risk free rate, and invests in the market portfolio. The market portfolio's expected return is 12% and the risk free rate is 4%. What returns should Harry and Sally receive on their individual portfolios?

Problem 15

If the standard deviation of the market portfolio is 20%, what are the standard deviations of Harry's and Sally's portfolios?

Problem 16

Stocks A and B have perfect negative correlation. Define x as the percentage invested in Stock A and (1 − x) as the percentage invested in Stock B. The standard deviations for A and B are .40 and .20, respectively. If a portfolio of A and B has zero variance, what is x?

For Problems 17-20 assume that the risk free rate is 4% and the market risk premium is 8%.

Problem 17

Falcon Semiconductor Corporation has a beta of 2.25. What is its expected return?

Problem 18

If we form a portfolio that is invested 60% in Falcon Semiconductor stock and 40% in the risk-free asset, what is the expected return for the portfolio? The beta for the portfolio?

Problem 19

Fenway Corporation common stock has a beta of 1.5. A security analyst forecasts an expected return of 15% over the next year. In a CAPM framework, is Fenway common stock a good buy?

Problem 20

Construct a portfolio of Falcon Semiconductor common stock and the risk-free asset such that the portfolio's beta is equal to 1.5. What is the expected return on this portfolio?

Problem 21

Assume that the three stocks listed below plot on the SML. The standard deviation for the market is 22%. What is the equation for the SML? Fill in the missing correlations and betas in the table.

Security	$E(R_i)$	$Var(R_i)$	$Corr(R_i,R_m)$	$Beta_i$
1	.07	.0225		
2	.14	.0400		0.80
3	.10	.1225	.60	
4	.07	.0000		

Problem 22

The stock of the Fargo Corporation goes up 12% when the market portfolio increases by 8%, and Fargo goes down by 8% when the market goes down by 8%. What is Fargo's beta?

Problem 23

A stock has a beta of .45 and a standard deviation of 30%. The market portfolio has a standard deviation of 20%. What is the correlation between returns on the stock and returns on the market portfolio?

Problem 24

The market portfolio consists of two stocks, U and V, whose returns are independent of each other. Stock U is worth $60 and stock V is worth $40. The expected returns on U and V are 7.90% and 18.15%, respectively. The standard deviation of U is 18% and the standard deviation of V is 42%. Calculate the return and standard deviation of the market portfolio.

Problem 25

The risk free rate is 4%. Calculate the beta for U and the correlation between U and the market portfolio. Do the same for V.

SOLUTIONS

Solution 1

Year	Returns X	Returns Y	Deviations X	Deviations Y	Product of deviations $(x-\bar{x})(y-\bar{y})$
1	.15	.18	.096	.136	.013056
2	.04	-.03	-.014	-.074	.001036
3	-.09	-.10	-.144	-.144	.020736
4	.08	.12	.026	.076	.001976
5	.09	.05	.036	.006	.000216
Totals	.27	.22	.000	.000	.037020

Thus, $\text{Cov}(R_X, R_Y) = \sigma_{XY} = (.030720/4) = .009255$. Notice that since we are using historical data, we must divide by T-1 = 4 to obtain the sample covariance.

Solution 2

The correlation is equal to the covariance divided by the product of the standard deviations. The standard deviations were calculated in Chapter 9, Problem 8. The covariance is:

$$\text{Corr}(R_X, R_Y) = \text{Cov}(R_X, R_Y)/(\sigma_X \sigma_Y) = .009255/(.08961)(.112383) = .9190$$

Note that when calculating variance and covariance using historical returns, we must divide by T-1 =4.

Solution 3

The covariance is determined from the data in the following table, where Prob is the probability of each state of the economy, Difference A and Difference B are the differences between the return in the given state of the economy and the expected return. The expected return of A is 14%, and B's expected return is 14%.

State of the economy	Probability of state	$(A-\bar{A})$	$(B-\bar{B})$	$(A-\bar{A})(B-\bar{B})$	$\text{Prob} \times (A-\bar{A})(B-\bar{B})$
Rapid gwth	.20	.16	.08	.0128	.00256
Mod. gwth	.60	.01	.02	.0002	.00012
Recession	.20	-.19	-.14	.0266	.00532

The covariance is determined by first calculating the deviation from the expected return for each stock under each state of the economy; next, the deviations for the two stocks in each state are multiplied, and these products are then multiplied by the respective probabilities of each state. The sum of the weighted squared products is the covariance. Therefore, $Cov(R_A,R_B) = \sigma_{AB} = (.00256 + .00012 + .00532) = .00800$.

Solution 4

The correlation is equal to the covariance divided by the product of the standard deviations. From Chapter 9, Problem 17 the standard deviation of A is .11136 and the standard deviation of B is .07376, thus:

$$Corr(R_A,R_B) = Cov(R_A,R_B)/(\sigma_A\sigma_B) = .00800/(.11136)(.07376) = .9740$$

Solution 5

Stock C's expected return is

$$E(R_C) = .10(.25) + .20(.10) + .50(.15) + .20(-.12) = .096 \text{ or } 9.6\%$$

The market's expected return is

$$E(R_M) = .10(.18) + .20(.20) + .50(.04) + .20(.00) = .078 \text{ or } 7.8\%$$

Solution 6

For Stock C:

State of the economy	Probability of state	R	$(R-\bar{R})$	$(R-\bar{R})^2$	$Prob\times(R-\bar{R})^2$
Rapid gwth.	.10	.25	.154	.02372	.00237
Moderate	.20	.10	.004	.00002	.00000
Normal	.50	.15	.054	.00292	.00145
Recession	.20	-.12	-.216	.04666	.00933

The variance of stock C's returns is the sum of the last column:

$$Var\ (C) = \sigma^2 = .01315$$

The standard deviation is Std Dev (C) $= \sigma = \sqrt{(.01315)} = .11467$ or 11.467%. Similar calculations for the market show:

$$\text{Var (Mkt)} = \sigma^2 = .00596$$

$$\text{Std Dev (Mkt)} = \sigma = \sqrt{(.00596)} = .07720 \text{ or } 7.720\%$$

Solution 7

State of the economy	Probability of state	Stk C $(R-\bar{R})$	Mkt $(M-\bar{M})$	Prob$\times(R-\bar{R})(M-\bar{M})$
Rapid gwth.	.10	.154	.102	.001571
Moderate	.20	.004	.122	.000098
Normal	.50	.054	-.038	-.001026
Recession	.20	-.216	-.078	.003370

The covariance between the returns on stock C and the market returns is the sum of the last column:

$$\text{Cov (C, Mkt)} = \sigma_{C,Mkt} = .004013$$

The correlation is the covariance divided by the product of the two standard deviations

$$\text{Corr (C, Mkt)} = .004013/(.11467)(.07720) = .45332$$

Solution 8

Beta is calculated as follows:

$$\beta_C = \text{Cov(C, Mkt)/Var (Mkt)}$$

$$= \sigma_{C,Mkt}/\sigma^2_{Mkt} = .004013/.00596 = .6733$$

Solution 9

The expected return is:

$$E(R_p) = .20(.096) + .80(.078) = .0816 \text{ or } 8.16\%$$

Solution 10

The portfolio variance can be determined as follows:

$$Var(p) = \sigma^2 = X^2_C \, \sigma^2_C + X^2_M \, \sigma^2_M + 2X_C X_M \, \sigma_{C,M}$$

$$= (.60)^2(.01315) + (.40)^2(.00596) + 2(.60)(.40)(.004013)$$

$$= .007614$$

Solution 11

The expected return for the portfolio is .132 or 13.2% and the variance is .0032256. The standard deviation is the square root of the variance: $\sigma = .056794$ or 5.6794%. Note that in calculating the variance we could use the covariance between A and B rather than the correlation. The covariance is equal to the correlation times the product of the standard deviations:

$$Cov(A,B) = \sigma_{AB} = corr(A,B) \times \sigma_A, \times \sigma_B = [(.15)(.06)(.12)] = .00108, \text{ then}$$

$$Var = (.80)^2(.06)^2 + (.20)^2(.12)^2 + 2(.80)(.20)(.00108) = .056794$$

Solution 12

In order to form a portfolio with expected return equal to 14.4%, the investor must solve the following equation for x:

$$.12x + (.18)(1 - x) = .144.$$

where x is the proportion of the portfolio invested in Stock A and $(1 - x)$ is the proportion invested in Stock B. The solution for x is .60, so that the portfolio will have 60% invested in stock A. The variance for this portfolio is .0041184 and the standard deviation is .064175 or 6.4175%.

Solution 13

The expected return for the portfolio is:

$$(.10)(.12) + (.30)(.18) + (.60)(.06) = .138 = 10.2\%.$$

For a portfolio comprised of these three assets, the variance of the portfolio is found as follows:

$$Var(p) = \sigma^2 = X^2_A \, \sigma^2_A + X^2_B \, \sigma^2_B + X^2_{rf} \, \sigma^2_{rf}$$

$$+ 2X_A X_B \, \sigma_{A,B} + 2X_A X_{rf} \, \sigma_{A,rf} + 2X_B X_{rf} \, \sigma_{B,rf}$$

Since the risk-free asset pays a guaranteed return, its variance equals zero, as does its covariance with other securities. Thus, all terms involving the risk free asset's variance and covariance equal zero. The portfolio variance simplifies to just three terms:

$$\text{Var(p)} = \sigma^2 = X^2_A\,\sigma^2_A + X^2_B\,\sigma^2_B + 2X_AX_B\,\sigma_{A,B}$$

Therefore, the variance of the portfolio is equal to:

$$(.1)^2(.06)^2 + (.3)^2(.12)^2 + (2)(.1)(.3)(.00108) = .001397$$

and the standard deviation is .03737 or 3.737%. Note that the covariance is .00108, as indicated earlier in Problem 11.

Solution 14

Harry invests $50 at the market return and $50 at the risk free rate. His expected return is

$$E(R_{Harry}) = .50(12\%) + .50(4\%) = 8\%$$

Sally invests $150 in the market portfolio at 12%, but must pay back $50 plus 4% interest to Harry. Her expected return is

$$E(R_{Sally}) = 1.50(12\%) - .50(4\%) = 16\%$$

Notice that since Sally borrows at the risk free rate, the appropriate weight is minus one-half (-.50). The minus sign indicates borrowing, and the one-half indicates that she borrows one-half of her initial wealth. The sum of the weights must equal one (1.50 − 0.50 = 1.0).

Solution 15

The formula for the variance of a two-asset portfolios is:

$$\text{Var(p)} = \sigma^2 = X^2_1\,\sigma^2_1 + X^2_2\,\sigma^2_2 + 2X_1X_2\,\sigma_{1,2}$$

In this problem, since one asset is risk free, the second and third terms in the formula are equal to zero. Thus, the standard deviations are:

$$\sigma_{Harry} = .50(20\%) = 10\%$$

$$\sigma_{Sally} = 1.50(20\%) = 30\%$$

Solution 16

The percentage invested in A, x, must be one-third.

Solution 17

The expected return on Falcon Semiconductor, from the SML, is 4% + 8%(2.25) = 22%.

Solution 18

The expected return is .60(22%) + .40(4%) = 14.8%. The beta is .60(2.25) + .40(0) = 1.35. Notice that if we substitute this portfolio beta of 1.35 into the SML equation, we get the same expected return of 14.8%.

Solution 19

From the SML, the expected return for Fenway, given its beta of 1.5, should be 16%; A 15% return is not sufficient for the risk involved, therefore, Fenway is not a good buy.

Solution 20

Let x represent the proportion of the portfolio invested in Falcon Semiconductor stock. Since a portfolio's beta is the weighted average of the individual security betas, the required portfolio is determined by solving the following equation for x:

$$1.5 = 2.25x + (0)(1 - x)$$

$$x = 2/3$$

Since the portfolio has the same beta as the Fenway stock, the expected return is 16%. Thus, if we short sell Fenway Corporation's stock and invest the proceeds in a portfolio composed of 2/3 Falcon Semiconductor and 1/3 risk-free lending, we have created a risk-free arbitrage opportunity (if Fenway provides a 15% return as expected). Essentially, we would be borrowing at 15% and lending at 16%.

Solution 21

Stock 4 has a 7% expected return and zero variance; thus the risk-free rate is 7%. The correlation of Security 4 with the market is zero since the return for Security 4 does not vary. The beta for Security 4 is also zero. Security 1 has the same 7% return, so Security 1 must have a zero beta and thus zero correlation with the market. Security 2 has a beta of .8. A portfolio invested 80% in the market and 20% in the risk-free asset also has a beta of .8 and must have a return of 14%. This implies a market return of $.8[E(R_m)] + .2(7\%) = 14\%$, so the market expected return must be 15.75%. Based on these numbers, the SML equation is:

$$E(R_i) = 7\% + 8.75\% \; ß_i$$

Security 3 has an expected return of 10%, so its beta must be [(.10 - .07)/.0875] = .343. For Security 2, the beta is .8. Since the market standard deviation is .22, the covariance of Security 2 with the market must satisfy the following equation:

$$.8 = [Cov(R_2, R_M)]/(.0484)$$

Therefore, $Cov(R_2, R_M) = .03872$. The correlation is [.038721(.20 × .22)] = .88. The filled in table is shown below:

Security	$E(R_i)$	$Var(R_i)$	$Corr(R_i, R_m)$	$Beta_i$
1	.07	.0225	.00	0.0
2	.14	.0400	.88	0.8
3	.10	.1225	.60	0.343
4	.07	.0000	.00	0.0

Solution 22

Fargo's beta measures the firm's sensitivity to changes in the market portfolio. Graphically, this is measured by the characteristic line. The problem presents sufficient information to plot the two points required to draw the characteristic line. With Fargo's return on the y-axis and the market return on the x-axis, the two points (x,y) are (8%, 12%) and (-8%, -8%). Beta is the slope of the line:

$$Beta = \text{ß} = \text{(change in y)/(change in x)} =$$

$$(12\% - (-8\%))/(8\% - (-8\%)) = 20\%/16\% = 1.25$$

Solution 23

To solve this problem we need to know the definition of beta in terms of the correlation between the stock and the market. Beta of stock S is defined as:

$$\text{ß} = cov(S,M)/Var(M) = \sigma_{S,M}/\sigma^2_M$$

$$\text{ß} = \sigma_S \sigma_M corr(S,M)/\sigma^2_M$$

Substituting values and solving for the correlation:

$$\text{ß} = .45 = (30\%)(20\%) corr(S,M)/(20\%)^2$$

$$corr(S,M) = .30$$

Solution 24

The market portfolio is a value weighted average of the two stocks. The weight of U in the market portfolio is $60/($60 + $40) = .60, and the weight of V is .40. The expected return on the market is:

$$E(R_M) = .60(7.90\%) + .40(18.15\%) = 12.00\%$$

The variance of the market portfolio is:

$$\text{Var(m)} = \sigma^2_M = .60^2(18\%)^2 + .40^2(42\%)^2 + 2(.60)(.40)(0)$$

$$= 116.64 + 282.24 = 398.88$$

The market portfolio's standard deviation is 19.97%.

Note that since U and V are independent, the third term equals zero.

Solution 25

The expected return on U is 7.90%, the risk free rate is 4%, and the market portfolio's return is 12%. Thus, using the SML and solving for beta, we find:

$$E(R_U) = 7.90\% = 4\% + \beta(12\% - 4\%)$$

$$\beta = .488$$

Since beta is the covariance between the stock and the market divided by the variance of the market portfolio, we can write the covariance in terms of correlation and solve for the correlation:

$$\beta = \text{cov(U,M)/Var(M)} = \sigma_{U,M}/\sigma^2_M$$

$$\beta = \sigma_U \sigma_M \text{corr(U,M)}/\sigma^2_M$$

$$\beta = (18\%)(19.97) \text{corr(U,M)}/398.88 = .488$$

$$\text{corr(U,M)} = .542$$

Similar calculations for V show that $\beta = 1.769$ and corr (V,M) = .841.

CHAPTER 11

AN ALTERNATIVE VIEW OF RISK AND RETURN:
THE ARBITRAGE PRICING THEORY

CHAPTER MISSION STATEMENT

Chapter 11 introduces the arbitrage pricing theory (APT), an asset pricing model that is an alternative to the capital asset pricing model (CAPM). The chapter starts by characterizing actual returns as the combination of an asset's expected return and an unexpected component. The unexpected component is influenced by economic factors common to all assets and by idiosyncratic events. The sensitivity of each asset to the common economic factors is described by beta coefficients. Diversified portfolios eliminate idiosyncratic returns. Similar to the CAPM, a linear relationship exists between expected returns and an asset's risk as measured by its sensitivity to the different economic factors.

The key concepts addressed in Chapter 11 are outlined below.

- ◆Factor models
  - ●announcements
  - ●expected returns
  - ●unexpected returns
- ◆Risk
  - ●systematic
  - ●unsystematic
- ◆Betas
  - ●beta coefficient
  - ●factor model
  - ●market model
- ◆Portfolios and Factor models
  - ●diversification
  - ●expected return
  - ●linear relationship
  - ●market portfolio
  - ●zero beta asset
- ◆CAPM and the APT

CONCEPT TEST

1. The actual return for a risky security has two parts: the _____ return and the _____ return.

2. Security prices sometimes change following announcements, while other times, they do not. This is because an announcement has two parts: the _____ component and the _____ component.

3. Of the two components described in Question 2, security prices react only to the _____ component.

4. A new discovery that affects only a single company, or a small group of companies, is an example of an _____ or an _____ risk.

5. Risks that affect all companies to some degree are called _____ or _____ risks.

6. The covariance between the unsystematic risks of two companies is, by definition, equal to _____.

7. A _____ indicates the response of a stock's return to a systematic risk.

8. Security returns are often written as:

$$R = E(R) + \beta_1 (F_1) + \beta_2(F_2) + ... + \beta_k(F_k) + \epsilon$$

    This model is called a _____.

9. If security returns are written as:

$$R = E(R) + \beta_{GNP} (F_{GNP}) + \beta_1(F_1) + \epsilon$$

    then F_{GNP} is the _____.

10. If security returns are written as:

$$R = E(R) + \beta_{GNP} (F_{GNP}) + \beta_1(F_1) + \epsilon$$

    then the expected value of F_{GNP} is _____.

11. If security returns are written as:

$$R = E(R) + \beta_{GNP} (F_{GNP}) + \beta_1(F_1) + \epsilon$$

    then ϵ is the _____.

12. A factor model which has an index such as the S&P 500 as the only factor is often called a _____.

13. Individual securities have both unsystematic and systematic risk. In a large, well-diversified portfolio, the _____ risks are diversified away.

14. The riskiness of a large, well-diversified portfolio depends on only its _____.

15. The total return for a security has three components: the _____, the _____, and the _____.

16. Expected return depends only on _____.

17.   For the market model, the line that relates expected returns to betas for the single factor is called the
      _____.

18   Suppose that, for a market model, the expected market return is 14% and the risk-free rate is 5%.
      What is the return for an asset with a beta of 2?

19.   For the model described in Question 18, what is the expected return for an asset with a beta of 0?
      An asset with a beta of 1?

20.   For all practical purposes, the CAPM is indistinguishable from the _____.

21.   Empirical models do a _____ job explaining returns, but they are unsatisfactory because they
      are not based on economic _____.

ANSWERS TO CONCEPT TEST

1.	expected; unexpected or surprise	12.	market model
2.	expected; unexpected	13.	unsystematic
3.	unexpected	14.	beta coefficient(s)
4.	unsystematic; idiosyncratic	15.	expected return; systematic return; unsystematic return
5.	systematic; market		
6.	zero	16.	systematic risk
7.	beta coefficient	17.	security market line (SML)
8.	k-factor model	18.	23%
9.	unexpected change in GNP	19.	5%; 14%
10.	zero	20.	one factor APT
11.	unsystematic return	21.	good; theory

PROBLEMS

Use the information below to solve Problems 1-3.

Suppose a three-factor model is appropriate to describe the returns for a stock. The relevant data regarding these factors are presented here:

	Beta of factor	Expected value	Actual value
Inflation	-1.0	4%	2.5%
Change in:			
Interest rates	-0.5	1%	-3.0%
GNP	2.0	3%	4.5%
Stock return		15%	

Problem 1

What is the effect of the systematic risk on the stock return?

Problem 2

Suppose that an unanticipated development contributes −2.5% to the return for the stock. What is the total effect of risk on the return for the stock?

Problem 3

What is the total return for the stock?

Use the information below to solve Problems 4-6.

You are working with a two-factor model that is based on the growth rate in GNP and interest rates. For Georgio Corporation, a major producer of zucchini, the GNP beta is 2 and the interest rate beta is .65. The expected return on Georgio stock is 16%, the expected growth in GNP is 2%, and interest rates are expected to be 8%. One year later, GNP growth turns out to have been 4%, and interest rates, 7%. Also, the company experienced a 3% increase in share value as the result of a patented cost-saving technology.

Problem 4

What is the effect of the systematic risk on the return for Georgio stock?

Problem 5

What is the total effect of risk on the return for Georgio stock?

Problem 6

What is the actual return on the Georgio stock?

Use the information below to solve Problems 7-10.

Assume the one-factor market model and the following information for Stocks X, Y and Z, and the market portfolio:

	Expected return	Beta
Stock A	9.5%	0.90
Stock B	13.0%	1.15
Stock C	11.0%	1.20
Market	12.0%	1.00

Problem 7

Write the market model equation for each stock.

Problem 8

Write the market model equation for a portfolio with the following proportions: $X_A = .20$, $X_B = .30$, and $X_C = .50$.

Problem 9

Suppose the actual return for the market is 11% and there are no unsystematic surprises in the returns for each stock. Calculate the return for each stock.

Problem 10

Given the information in Problem 9, calculate the return for the portfolio described in Problem 8.

Problem 11

Consider the following two models:

$$R_A = E(R_A) + \beta_A(F_m) + \epsilon_A$$

$$R_A = \alpha_A + \beta_A(R_m) + \mu_A$$

where R_m is the total return (expected plus unexpected) on a market index, F_m is the unexpected return on the same index, α_A is a constant, and ϵ and μ are the diversifiable components of the return. Both of these equations are refereed to as market models. What is α_A if the two models are equivalent?

Problem 12

Assume that returns for security i are described by the following single factor model:

$$R_i = .20 + \beta_i F + \epsilon_i$$

What are the return and variance of a portfolio consisting of N securities like security i?

Problem 13

Assume that the market model describes returns to risky asset X whose beta equals 0.8. The variance of the unsystematic component of X's return is 225, and the variance of the market portfolio is 144. What is the variance of X?

Problem 14

What is the variance of a portfolio consisting of a very large number of securities like X whose idiosyncratic risks are independent.

Problem 15

The following one factor model is appropriate to describe stock returns to the Glacier Corporation. The factor is the change in gross domestic product (GDP). Glacier's beta equals 1.5, and its expected return is 18%.

$$R_G = E(R_G) + \beta_G F + \epsilon_G$$

Last year, Glacier's stock return was only 7%, while the change in GDP was 2.0%. During the year Glacier unexpectedly announced that its dynamic CEO was killed in a mountain climbing accident, which caused a 8% decline in its stock price. What expected change in GDP was incorporated in Glacier's stock price at the start of last year?

Problem 16

Assume that stock returns to the Isberg Corporation follows the same one factor model which describes returns to the Glacier Corporation. Isberg's beta is 2.0 and its expected return is 22%. Form a portfolio of Glacier and Isberg such that portfolio returns are independent of changes in GDP.

SOLUTIONS

Solution 1

The effect of the systematic risk (m) on the stock return is given by:

$$m = ß_I (F_I) + ß_r(F_r) + ß_{GNP}(F_{GNP})$$

where the subscripts I, r, and GNP refer to inflation, interest rates, and GNP, respectively.

Substituting values, where F = Actual value – Expected value,

$$m = [(-1)(.025 - .04)] + [(-.5)(-.03 - .01)] + [(2)(.045 - .03)]$$

$$m = .065$$

Solution 2

The unanticipated surprise represents an unsystematic risk. Therefore, $\epsilon = -2.5\%$ and the total effect of risk is:

$$m + \epsilon = .065 + -.025 = .04 \text{ or } 4\%$$

where m is calculated in Problem 1.

Solution 3

Total return is expected return plus the risky portion of the return, as calculated in Problem 2:

$$R = .15 + .065 + -.025 = .19 \text{ or } 19\%.$$

Solution 4

The effect of the systematic risk (m) is given by:

$$(2)(.04 - .02) + (.65)(.07 - .08) = .0335 \text{ or } 3.35\%$$

Solution 5

The total effect of risk is:

$$m + \epsilon = .0335 + .03 = .0665 \text{ or } 6.65\%$$

Solution 6

The actual return is $R = .16 + .0335 + .03 = .2235$ or 22.35%.

Solution 7

For Stock A, the market model equation is:

$$R_A = .095 + [.90(R_m - .12)] + \epsilon_A$$

The market model equations for B and C are:

$$R_B = .130 + [1.15(R_m - .12)] + \epsilon_B$$

$$R_C = .110 + [1.20(R_m - .12)] + \epsilon_C$$

Solution 8

Portfolio returns can be written as:

$$R_P = X_A [R_A + \beta_A (R_m - .12) + \epsilon_A] +$$

$$X_B [R_B + \beta_B (R_m - .12) + \epsilon_B] +$$

$$X_C [R_C + \beta_C (R_m - .12) + \epsilon_C]$$

$$= (.20)[.095 + (0.90)(R_m - .12) + \epsilon_A] +$$

$$(.30)[.130 + (1.15)(R_m - .12) + \epsilon_B] +$$

$$(.50)[.110 + (1.20)(R_m - .12) + \epsilon_C]$$

Rearranging these terms, we can express the return on the portfolio as follows:

$$R_p = X_A R_A + X_B R_B + X_C R_C +$$

$$(X_A \beta_A + X_B \beta_B + X_B \beta_B)(R_m - .12) +$$

$$X_A \epsilon_A] + X_B \epsilon_B + X_C \epsilon_C$$

$$= (.20)(.095) + (.30)(.130) + (.50)(.110) +$$

$$[(.20)(.90) + (.30)(1.15) + (.50)(1.20)](R_m - .12) +$$

$$(.20)\epsilon_A + (.30)\epsilon_B + (.50)\epsilon_C$$

$$= .113 + 1.125(R_m - .12) +$$

$$(.20)\epsilon_A + (.30)\epsilon_B + (.50)\epsilon_C$$

In this last expression, .113 is the expected return for the portfolio and 1.125 is the beta for the portfolio. Each of these portfolio characteristics is a weighted average of the corresponding characteristics for the individual securities.

Solution 9

The return for Stock A is:

$$R_A = .095 + [.90(R_m - .12)] + \epsilon_A$$

$$= .095 + [.90(.11 - .12)] + 0 = .086 \text{ or } 8.60\%.$$

The return for Stock B is:

$$R_B = .130 + [1.15(.11 - .12)] + 0 = .1185 \text{ or } 11.85\%.$$

The return for Stock C is:

$$R_C = .110 + [1.20(.11 - .12)] + 0 = .098 = 9.8\%$$

Solution 10

The return for the portfolio can be determined as follows:

$$R_p = .113 + 1.125(R_m - .12) + (.20)\epsilon_A + (.30)\epsilon_B + (.50)\epsilon_C$$

$$= .113 + (1.125)(.11 - .12) + 0 = .10175 \text{ or } 10.175\%$$

Note that this result is equal to the weighted average of the security returns from Problem 9:

$$(.20)(.086) + (.30)(.1185) + (.50)(.098) = .10175$$

Solution 11

The unexpected return on the market index is the actual return, R_m minus the expected return, $E(R_m)$. If we substitute $[R_m - E(R_m)]$ for F_m, we get:

$$R_A = E(R_A) + \beta_A[(R_m) - E(R_m)] + \epsilon_A$$

$$= E(R_A) + \beta_A(R_m) - \beta_A[E(R_m)] + \epsilon_A$$

$$= [E(R_A) - \beta_A E(R_m)] + \beta_A(R_m) + \epsilon_A$$

Thus α_A must be equal to $[E(R_A) - \beta_A E(R_m)]$, which is a constant.

Solution 12

Assume that the portfolio is equally weighted with weights 1/N. The return on the portfolio is

$$R_p = (1/N) \Sigma R_i = (1/N) \Sigma(.20 + \beta_i F + \epsilon_i)$$

$$= .20 + \beta_p F + (1/N)\Sigma\epsilon_i$$

Note that Σ represents the summation over i from 1 to N. If β_i is the same for all securities, then $\beta_p = \Sigma(1/N)\beta_i = (1/N)N\beta_i = \beta$.

The variance of the portfolio is found by finding $Var(R_p)$, where R_p is essentially the sum of a constant plus two random variables. Using the discussion of variance in Chapter 10, particularly equation 10.10, the variance of the portfolio is

$$Var(R_p) = \sigma^2_p = \beta^2 Var(F) + (1/N)Var(\epsilon_i) + (1 - 1/N)Cov(\epsilon_i, \epsilon_j)$$

Note that the second and third terms on the right hand side represent the $Var[(1/N)\Sigma\epsilon] = (1/N)^2 Var(\Sigma\epsilon)$, and follows from equation 10.10 in the text. Generally, we assume that the unsystematic risk of one firm is unrelated to the unsystematic risk of another firm, thus $Cov(\epsilon_i, \epsilon_j) = 0$. If the portfolio consists of a large number of securities, then (1/N) approaches zero and the second term vanishes. Thus, the risk of a well diversified portfolio is just the first term $\beta^2 Var(F)$.

Solution 13

The market model is

$$R_x = \alpha_x + \beta_x(R_m) + \epsilon_x$$

and $\beta_x = .8$, $Var(R_m) = 144$, and $Var(\epsilon_x) = 225$. Following the solution to Problem 12, and letting $N=1$, the variance of X is

$$Var(R_x) = \sigma^2_x = \beta^2 Var(R_m) + Var(\epsilon_x)$$

$$= (.8)^2(144) + 225 = 317.16$$

Note that $Var(R_x)$, which represents the total risk of X, consists of market risk $\beta^2 Var(R_m)$ and unsystematic risk $Var(\epsilon_x)$.

Solution 14

We can use the solution to Problem 12 to answer this question. The portfolio variance is given by

$$Var(R_p) = \sigma^2_p = \beta^2 Var(R_m) + (1/N)Var(\epsilon) + (1 - 1/N)Cov(\epsilon_i, \epsilon_j)$$

Since $Cov(\epsilon_i, \epsilon_j) = 0$ and $N >>> 1$, the variance simplifies to

$$Var(R_p) = \sigma^2_p = \beta^2 Var(R_m)$$

$$= (.8)^2 (144) = 92.16$$

Solution 15

The factor F equals the difference between the actual change in GDP and the expected change in GDP, $F = (\Delta GDP - E(\Delta GDP))$. Substituting this into the model and solving for $E(\Delta GDP)$, we find

$$R_G = E(R_G) + \beta_G (\Delta GDP - E(\Delta GDP)) + \epsilon_G$$

$$7\% = 18\% + 1.5(2.0\% - E(\Delta GDP)) - 8\%$$

$$E(\Delta GDP) = - (2/3) (7\% - 18\% + 8\%) + 2.0\%$$

$$E(\Delta GDP) = 4.0\%$$

Thus, at the start of last year the market expected GDP to increase by 4% and built this estimate into Glacier's stock price. However, as it turned out, GDP grew by only 2.0%, thus causing an unexpected systematic return of - 3%. Combined with an unsystematic component of -8%, Glacier's return fell 11% below the expected 18%.

Solution 16

The one factor models for Glacier and Isberg are:

$$R_G = E(R_G) + \beta_G F + \epsilon_G$$

$$= 18\% + 1.5F + \epsilon_G$$

$$R_I = E(R_I) + \beta_I F + \epsilon_I$$

$$= 22\% + 2.0F + \epsilon_I$$

Let x be the amount invested in Glacier and (1 − x) the amount invested in Isberg. The portfolio return is:

$$R_p = x[18\% + 1.5F + \epsilon_G] + (1 - x)[22\% + 2.0F + \epsilon_I]$$

$$= 22\% - x4\% - (.5x - 2.0)F + x(\epsilon_G - \epsilon_I) + \epsilon_I$$

For the portfolio return to be independent of F, then (.5x − 2.0) must equal zero, or x = 4.0. Thus, you should sell Isberg and invest the proceeds in Glacier. Starting with $100, you should sell short $300 worth of Isberg stock and invest $400 (=$100 + $300) in Glacier. Assuming idiosyncratic returns are zero, the portfolio return would be 6.0%. To see this, assume that F = (2.0% − 4%), then Glacier's return is 18% + 1.5(2.0 − 4) = 15%, and Isberg's return is 22% + 2.0(2.0 − 4) = 18%. The portfolio return is (−3.0)(18%) + (4.0)(15%) = −54.0% + 60% = 6.0%.

CHAPTER 12

RISK, RETURN, AND CAPITAL BUDGETING

CHAPTER MISSION STATEMENT

The purpose of Chapter 12 is to apply the risk and return concepts discussed in the previous two chapters to capital budgeting. The chapter describes how to estimate beta using the returns on an asset and the market portfolio. On a qualitative level, the chapter describes how a firms operating leverage, financial leverage, and the cyclical nature of its revenues help determine the systematic risk, beta, of the firm. The notion of an asset beta is introduced, and how financial leverage affects the firm's equity beta. Firm versus project discount, or hurdle, rates is discussed, and finally the firm's weighted average cost of capital is defined.

The key concepts presented in Chapter 12 are outlined below.

- ♦Cost of equity capital
- ♦Estimating beta
  - ●real world betas
  - ●stability of beta
  - ●using an industry beta
- ♦Determinants of beta
  - ●cyclicality of revenues
  - ●operating leverage
  - ●financial leverage
- ♦Asset beta
- ♦Firm versus project hurdle rates
- ♦Weighted average cost of capital

CONCEPT TEST

1. A firm with extra cash available has two alternatives: pay the cash to stockholders in the form of _____, or _____.

2. The appropriate discount rate for capital budgeting projects with risky cash flows is the _____ for financial assets with risk level comparable to that of the project under consideration.

3. A security's _____ is equal to the slope of the characteristic line relating the security's expected return with that of the market.

4. Beta is determined using the statistical technique called _____.

5. Regression analysis is required in order to determine the slope of the so-called _____ for a given stock.

6. _____ data must be used for regression analysis; the resulting beta is then an estimate of the value of beta in the future.

7.   The statistic _____ measures the proportion of a stock's total risk that is systematic risk.

8.   If the project's risk is different from that of the firm as a whole, the appropriate value for beta is the beta for the _____, not the beta for the _____.

9.   Beta is equal to the _____ of a security with the market, divided by the _____ of the market.

10. If a company is developing a new product, the risk of the project will generally be _____ than for the industry as a whole.

11. Firms that are financed with both equity and debt are termed _____.

12. The existence of debt in a firm's capital structure _____ the riskiness of the firm's common stock.

13. A firm financed entirely with equity is said to be subject to _____, while the stockholders of a levered firm are also subject to _____.

14. Beta for the common stock of a levered firm is _____ than beta for an otherwise identical unlevered firm.

15. Three factors which determine beta are: _____, _____, and _____.

16. Cyclical stocks have _____ beta values.

17. A firm with a high degree of operating leverage tends to have a _____ value of beta.

18. A firm with a high degree of financial leverage tends to have a _____ value of beta.

ANSWERS TO CONCEPT TEST

1.   dividends; invest in a project
2.   expected return
3.   beta
4.   regression analysis
5.   line of beat fit
6.   historical
7.   R-squared
8.   project; firm
9.   covariance; variance
10. higher

11. levered firms
12. increases
13. business risk; financial risk
14. greater
15. revenues; operating leverage; financial leverage
16. high
17. high
18. high

PROBLEMS

Use the following information to solve Problems 1-5.

The returns for the Hudson River Corporation and the New York Stock Exchange Composite Index (NYSE) during the past five years are listed below:

Year	Hudson River	NYSE
1	.12	.06
2	.15	.14
3	.04	.07
4	-.05	.00
5	.09	.13

Problem 1

Calculate the average return and standard deviation for HRC and for the NYSE.

Problem 2

Calculate the value of the covariance between the returns for Hudson River and the returns for the NYSE Composite Index.

Problem 3

Calculate the value of beta for Hudson River Corporation.

Problem 4

The risk-free rate is 6% and the market risk-premium is 8.5%. Assume that HRC is an all-equity firm. What is the appropriate discount rate for new projects which have a risk level equal to that of the firm?

Problem 5

In a regression model with one independent variable, the value of R^2 is equal to the correlation squared. Calculate R^2 and interpret its meaning in terms of the risk of HRC.

Use the following information to solve Problems 6-10.

The possible rates of return for assets K and M for five possible states of the economy are listed in the table below, along with the probability (Pr) of occurrence:

State	Pr	R_K	R_M
1	.20	.010	.115
2	.20	.150	.155
3	.30	.260	.235
4	.20	.030	.085
5	.10	-.060	.035

Problem 6

Calculate the expected return for asset K. Calculate the expected return for asset M.

Problem 7

What is the standard deviation for asset K? For asset M?

Problem 8

What is the covariance between the returns for asset K and the returns for asset M?

Problem 9

Assume that M is the market portfolio. Calculate the value of ß for asset K.

Problem 10

Assume that K is an all-equity firm. Use the risk free rate and the market risk-premium from Problem 4 to determine the appropriate discount rate for new projects that have a risk level equal to that of the firm.

Problem 11

Consider a firm which can use either Technology X or Technology Y when producing a particular product. The characteristics of the two technologies are indicated in the following table:

	Technology X	Technology Y
Fixed costs (per year)	$100,000	$150,000
Variable cost (per unit)	$180	$170
Selling price (per unit)	$200	$200

Technology X has lower fixed costs than Technology Y, but it has higher variable costs because X is more labor intensive while Y is more highly automated. Calculate the contribution margin for each technology.

Problem 12

Calculate Earnings before Interest and Taxes (EBIT) for each technology at sales levels of 4,000 units, 5,000 units, 6,000 units, 10,000 units, and 20,000 units. Interpret the results in terms of operating leverage and beta.

Problem 13

Suppose that Technology Y in Problem 12 had fixed costs of $200,000. Calculate EBIT for Technology Y at the sales levels indicated in Problem 12. Interpret the results in terms of operating leverage and beta.

Problem 14

Helper Industries has an asset beta of 1.20 and wants to know what its equity beta will be at different debt ratios. Assume that the firm can issue risk free debt at 6%, the market risk premium is 8%, and that there are no taxes. Calculate the firm's equity beta and cost of equity at debt ratios from 30% to 60% in 10% increments.

Problem 15

Calculate Helper Industries' weighted average cost of capital at each of the debt ratios from the previous problem.

Problem 16

The Hoosic Company has $285 million of risk free debt outstanding at the same time its common stock is worth $665 million. Analysis indicates that the firm's equity has a beta of 1.25. What is the firm's asset beta?

Problem 17

Hoosic's cost of debt is 6%, the same as the risk free rate. The return on the market is 14%. What is Hoosic's weighted average cost of capital (WACC)? Assume that there are no taxes.

Problem 18

Now suppose that Hoosic pays corporate taxes at a 35% rate. Assume that the before tax cost of debt is still 6%, and that the cost of equity is now 14.95%. What is Hoosic's weighted average cost of capital (WACC)?

Problem 19

Hoosic has an investment project which will expand the size of its existing business. The project costs $275,000 and will generate an after tax cash flow of $34,905 per year forever. Hoosic intends on keeping its debt ratio constant. What is the net present value of this project?

Problem 20

The Hustings Company is evaluating two independent investment projects. Project A is a new process to manufacture methane. Project A requires an investment of $1,000 and produces $600 per year for two years. Project B involves an innovative means of transporting methane at low cost. This project also requires and investment of $1,000, but generates $620 per year for two years. The risk free rate is 6% and the market risk premium is 8.5%. What are the NPVs of these projects, and should Hustings accept or reject them? The following table provides additional information about the projects and Hustings (* indicates firm's cost of capital).

Project	Beta	IRR(%)
A	0.8	13.07
B	1.2	15.62
Firm	1.0	14.50*

SOLUTIONS

Solution 1

The required calculations are summarized in the table below:

Year	Returns		Deviations		Squared deviations	
	HRC	NYSE	HRC	NYSE	HRC	NYSE
1	.12	.06	.05	−.02	.0025	.0004
2	.15	.14	.08	.06	.0064	.0036
3	.04	.07	−.03	−.01	.0009	.0001
4	−.05	.00	−.12	−.08	.0144	.0064
5	.09	.13	.02	.05	.0004	.0025
Total	.35	.40	.00	.00	.0246	.0130

The average returns for Hudson River and for the NYSE are (.35/5) = .07 or 7%, and (.40/5) = .08 or 8%, respectively. The variances are: Var(HRC) = (.0246/4) = .00615 and Var(NYSE) = (.0130/4) = .00325. Note that since we are using historical data, we divide by T− 1 = 4. The standard deviations are: Std Dev(HRC) = $\sqrt{(.00615)}$ = .07842, and Std Dev(NYSE) = $\sqrt{(.00325)}$ = .05701.

Solution 2

The required calculations are summed in the following table:

Year	Returns		Deviations		Product of deviations
	HRC	NYSE	HRC	NYSE	
1	.12	.06	.05	−.02	−.0010
2	.15	.14	.08	.06	.0048
3	.04	.07	−.03	−.01	.0003
4	−.05	.00	−.12	−.08	.0096
5	.09	.13	.02	.05	.0010
Total	.35	.40	.00	.00	.0147

The covariance between Hudson River and the NYSE is (.0147/4) = .00368.

Solution 3

Beta is equal to the covariance between returns for HRC and the returns for the market, divided by the variance of the market returns:

$$ß = Cov(HRC,NYSE)/Var(NYSE) = \sigma_{HRC,NYSE}/\sigma^2_{NYSE}$$

$$= .00368/.00325 = 1.132$$

Solution 4

The appropriate discount rate is determined from the capital-asset pricing model as follows:

$$E(R) = .06 + (.085)ß = .06 + (.085)(1.132) = .156 \text{ or } 15.6\%$$

Solution 5

The correlation is equal to the covariance divided by the product of the standard deviations:

$$[.00368/(.07842)(.05701)] = .8231$$

Therefore, R^2 is equal to $[(.8231)^2] = .6775$. This result indicates that 67.75% of the total risk of HRC's stock is systematic risk, and 32.25% is unsystematic risk which cannot be explained by the market index.

Solution 6

State	Pr	R_K	R_M	$Pr \times R_K$	$Pr \times R_M$
1	.20	.010	.115	.0020	.0230
2	.20	.150	.155	.0300	.0310
3	.30	.260	.235	.0780	.0705
4	.20	.030	.085	.0060	.0170
5	.10	−.060	.035	−.0060	.0035
E(R)				.1100	.1450

The expected returns for K = .110 or 11% and for M = .145 or 14.5%.

Solution 7

For asset K we have:

State	Pr	R_K	$(R_K - .11)^2$	$Pr \times (R_K - .11)^2$
1	.20	.010	.01000	.00200
2	.20	.150	.01610	.00032
3	.30	.260	.02250	.00675
4	.20	.030	.00640	.00128
5	.10	−.060	.02890	.00289
				.01324

The variance for asset K is: $\sigma^2_K = .01324$. The standard deviation is the square root of .01324: $\sigma_K = .11507$ or 11.507%. Similar calculations show that the variance and standard deviation for asset M are: $\sigma^2_M = .00456$ and $\sigma_M = .06753$ or 6.753%.

Solution 8

State	Pr	$(R_K - .11)$	$(R_M - .145)$	$Pr \times (R_K - .11)(R_M - .145)$
1	.20	-.100	-.030	.00060
2	.20	.040	.010	.00008
3	.30	.150	.090	.00405
4	.20	-.080	-.060	.00096
5	.10	-.170	-.110	.00187

.00756

The covariance between the returns for K and the returns for M is: .00756.

Solution 9

$$ß \text{ is equal to } Cov(K,M) / Var(M) = (.00756/.00456) = 1.658$$

Solution 10

The appropriate discount rate is determined from the capital-asset pricing model as follows:

$$E(R_K) = .06 + (.085)ß_K = .06 + (.085)(1.658) = .2009 \text{ or } 20.09\%$$

Solution 11

The contribution margin is the difference between selling price and variable cost per unit. For Technology X, the contribution margin is ($200 - $180) = $20. For Technology Y, the contribution margin is $30.

Solution 12

For sales equal to 4,000 units, revenues are [(4,000)($200)] = $800,000 for each technology. For Technology X, total variable costs are [(4,000)($180)] = $720,000 and EBIT is equal to:

$$\$800,000 - \$100,000 - \$720,000 = - \$20,000.$$

For Technology Y, EBIT is -$30,000 for sales of 4,000 units. At sales of 5,000 units, EBIT is zero for each technology. The remaining results are summarized in the table below:

Sales (units)	EBIT Technology X	EBIT Technology Y
4,000	($ 20,000)	($ 30,000)
5,000	0	0
6,000	$ 20,000	$ 30,000
10,000	$100,000	$150,000
20,000	$300,000	$450,000

Note that the technology with the higher contribution margin (i.e., Technology Y) has the larger changes in EBIT for a given change in sales. As a result, for Technology Y, EBIT increases more quickly as sales increase. In other words, operating leverage is greater for Technology Y than for Technology X. We would expect that the beta value for Technology Y would be greater than for Technology X. (Note that a firm choosing between these two technologies would not have a very difficult choice to make since Technology Y provides greater profitability for all sales levels above the break-even level of 5,000 units.)

Solution 13

EBIT is now $50,000 lower at each sales level for Technology Y. The results are summarized below:

Sales (units)	EBIT Technology X	EBIT Technology Y
4,000	($ 20,000)	($ 80,000)
5,000	0	($ 50,000)
6,000	$ 20,000	($ 20,000)
10,000	$100,000	$100,000
20,000	$300,000	$400,000

The conclusions regarding operating leverage and beta are essentially the same as described in Problem 12. That is, Technology Y still has the higher operating leverage because EBIT increases more quickly for any given increase in sales. In addition, we would still expect that Technology Y has the higher beta value. However, the choice between the two technologies is not as clear cut as in the previous problem. For sales levels below 10,000 units, Technology X has the higher level of EBIT; at sales levels above 10,000 units, Technology Y has the higher EBIT because the larger contribution margin has compensated for the higher fixed costs at these sales levels.

Solution 14

The following table shows Helper Industries' equity betas and cost of equity calculated from

$$\beta_{equity} = [(Debt + Equity)/Equity]\, \beta_{asset}$$

and the CAPM $R_s = R_{rf} + \beta(R_{rf} - R_m)$

Debt Ratio	Equity Beta	Cost of Equity
0.00	1.20	15.60%
.30	1.71	19.68
.40	2.00	22.00
.50	2.40	25.20
.60	3.00	30.00

Solution 15

Without taxes, the weighted average cost of capital (WACC) will remain constant at 15.6% as the debt ratio changes.

Solution 16

In a world without corporate taxes, a firm's asset beta is a weighted average of the firm's equity beta and its debt beta. In Hoosic's case, the debt is risk free, thus the debt beta is zero. Hoosic's asset beta is:

$$\beta_{asset} = [Equity/(Debt + Equity)]\, \beta_{equity} =$$

$$[\$665/(\$285 + \$665)](1.25) = .875$$

Solution 17

The weighted average cost of capital is an average of the firms cost of debt and cost of equity where the weights are the debt ratio (Debt/Value) and the equity multiplier (Equity/Value). The firm's cost of equity is determined using the CAPM: $R_s = R_{rf} + \beta(R_{rf} - R_m) = 6\% + 1.25(14\% - 6\%) = 16.0\%$. Thus, Hoosic's WACC is:

$$WACC = R_B\, B/(B + S) + R_s\, S/(B + S) =$$

$$6\% (\$285/\$950) + 16.0\% (\$665/\$950) = 13.00\%$$

Solution 18

The WACC formula is similar to the one used in the previous problem, but now the after tax cost of debt is used (assumes interest is a tax deductible expense). With corporate taxes, the WACC is:

$$WACC = R_B(1 - T_c) B/(B + S) + R_s S/(B + S) =$$

$$6\%(1 - .35)(\$285/\$950) + 14.95\% (\$665/\$950) = 11.635\%$$

Solution 19

Since the project is a scale expansion project, it has the same risk as the firm. In this case, the WACC is the appropriate discount rate. From Problem 16 the WACC = 13.15%. Thus, the NPV of the investment is:

$$NPV = -\$275,000 + \$34,905/.11635 = \$25,000.$$

Solution 20

To calculate each project's NPV we must know the appropriate discount rate. Since the risk of each project differs from the firm's risk, the average cost of capital is not the appropriate discount rate. Using the CAPM, however, we can calculate the appropriate discount rate for each project.

Project A

$$R_A = 6\% + (8.5\%)0.8 = 12.8\%$$

$$NPV_A = -\$1,000 + \$600/(1.128) + \$600/(1.128)^2$$

$$= \$3.47$$

Project B

$$R_B = 6\% + (8.5\%)1.2 = 16.2\%$$

$$NPV_B = -\$1,000 + \$620/(1.162) + \$620/(1.162)^2$$

$$= -\$7.26$$

Project A should be accepted since its NPV is positive (its IRR is greater than its required rate of return). Project B should be rejected since its NPV is negative (its required return is more than its IRR). Note that the firm's cost of capital, 14.5%, is not relevant in evaluating the merits of Projects A and B since their risk is different than the firm's. If we did use 14.5% as a bench mark, we would have accepted B and rejected A!

CHAPTER 13

CORPORATE-FINANCING DECISIONS
AND EFFICIENT CAPITAL MARKETS

CHAPTER MISSION STATEMENT

The purpose of this chapter is to introduce the student to the concept of an efficient capital market and its implications for corporate financing decisions. Managers should seek positive net present value financing opportunities, but these opportunities are rare because of the efficiency of the capital markets. An efficient capital market is a market where prices fully and quickly reflect all available relevant information. Investors should expect a normal return based on the level of risk, and should expect to buy and sell securities at a fair price. If markets are efficient, then corporate managers cannot fool investors by manipulating financial statements to make earnings look better than they are, managers cannot time security sales based in public information, and managers can sell large blocks of stock without affecting the stock price.

The major concepts presented in Chapter 13 are outlined below.

- ◆Value creating financing decisions
    - ●fooling investors
    - ●reducing costs
    - ●increasing subsidies
    - ●creating new securities
- ◆Efficient capital markets
    - ●competition for information
    - ●normal returns
    - ●fair prices
    - ●no excess returns
- ◆Types of efficiency
    - ●weak form
    - ●semistrong form
    - ●strong form
- ◆Common misconceptions about the EMH
- ◆Evidence
    - ●random price changes
    - ●event studies
    - ●professional investor performance
    - ●contrary views
- ◆Implications for corporate finance
    - ●accounting practices
    - ●timing of new issues
    - ●price pressure effects

CONCEPT TEST

1. The three basic ways in which to create valuable financing opportunities are: _____, _____, and _____.

2. A market in which prices reflect available information is called an _____.

3. In an efficient market, all sales or purchases of assets are _____ transactions.

4. The _____ asserts that the prices of widely traded stocks and bonds reflect their true values.

5. If markets are efficient, then investors should receive a _____ rate of return.

6. If markets are efficient, then firms should be able to sell securities for a _____ price.

7. If the past history of stock prices is not useful in earning abnormal returns, then the market is at least _____ efficient.

8. If publicly available information is not useful in earning abnormal returns, then the market is at least _____ efficient.

9. If no information of any kind is useful in earning abnormal returns, then the market is _____ efficient.

10. Stock price changes have very low serial correlations. This fact is consistent with the _____ form of the efficient markets hypothesis.

11. Professional money managers, as a group, cannot outperform market indexes. This fact is consistent with the _____ form of the efficient markets hypothesis.

12. The difference between a security's actual return in a given period and the return on a market index is called the _____ for that period.

13. The _____ is the sum of the abnormal returns over a given period of time.

14. In the absence of any new information, the cumulative abnormal return for a stock should be _____.

15. If stock price changes are independent and come from the same probability distribution, then stock price changes are said to follow a _____.

16. Does the efficient markets hypothesis imply that stock prices are random?

17. Does the efficient markets hypothesis suggest that all stocks have the same expected return?

18. Does the efficient markets hypothesis imply that stock prices do not have an upward trend?

19. If you are a firm believer in the EMH, should you select your stock portfolio by throwing darts at the *Wall Street Journal* stock listings?

20. Investors who examine the past history of stock prices in order to identify patterns are called _____.

21. An examination of the behavior of security returns following an announcement of new information is called an _____.

22. The presence of seasonalities is _____ with market efficiency.

23. Some believe that the stock market crashes of 1929 and 1987 are evidence consistent with the _____.

24. If managers have private information about the value of their firm's stock, then they may try to sell stock when it is _____. As a result, announcements of new stock sales may lead to stock price _____.

25. Accounting choice should not affect stock prices if _____, and _____.

26. If the market is inefficient, then selling large blocks of stock will cause the stock price to _____, an example of the _____.

27. If managers are able to time security issues, they would issue equity when they believe that their stock is _____, and repurchase stock when they believe that the stock is _____.

28. Recent studies of IPOs and seasoned equity issues suggest that managers issue stock when it is _____.

For Questions 29 through 33, answer using one of the responses A through D below. In evaluating the hypothetical scenarios, pay particular attention to the word 'necessary' in response D.

A.   Strong-form efficiency is violated.
B.   Semistrong-form and strong-form efficiency are violated.
C.   All forms are violated.
D.   There is no necessary violation of any form.

29. You look up insider trading activities in SEC publications at your local law library. You are consistently able to beat the market by basing your trades on this information.

30. The Genius-is-a-Bull-Market mutual fund has outperformed the market for five consecutive years.

31. Your uncle Joe got extremely rich in a short period of time buying stocks based on his charting of their historical price movements and buying whenever the pattern looked like Mount Everest.

32. Whenever a stock reaches a 52-week high, its subsequent performance is abnormally poor.

33.   A finance professor can predict with greater than 60% accuracy whether the market will be up or
      down in a given month.

ANSWERS TO CONCEPT TEST

1.   fool investors; reduce costs or increase
     subsidies; create a new security
2.   efficient market
3.   zero NPV
4.   efficient market hypothesis
5.   normal
6.   fair
7.   weak-form
8.   semistrong form
9.   strong form
10. weak
11. semistrong
12. abnormal return
13. cumulative abnormal return
14. zero
15. random walk
16. no
17. no
18. no
19. no
20. technical analysts
21. event study
22. inconsistent
23. bubble theory
24. overvalued; decreases
25. annual reports contain sufficient
     information; markets are semistrong
     efficient
26. decline; price pressure effect
27. overvalued; undervalued
28. overpriced
29. B; it's public information
30. D; after the fact, some funds have done
     this well
31. D; some will get rich in spite of
     themselves
32. C
33. D

PROBLEMS

Use the following information to solve Problems 1-3:

Isinglass Company common stock has a daily standard deviation of return of 80 basis points (.80%). The
expected return on the market is 2 basis points (.02%) per day. On a particular day, designated day 0,
Isinglass announced a major new product.

You have been asked to perform an event study. An abnormal return (AR) is considered statistically
significant if it is larger than 2 standard deviations [2(.80%) = 1.60%] in absolute value.

Problem 1

The returns on Isinglass around the announcement are shown below. Interpret the results in terms of the market's opinion of the new product. Are the observed returns consistent with market efficiency?

Day relative to announcement	Actual return
−3	1.1%
−2	0.5
−1	−0.6
0	3.0
1	1.0
2	−0.8
3	−0.4

Problem 2

A different set of returns is shown below. Answer the question posed in Problem 1 based on these returns.

Day relative to announcement	Actual return
−3	1.1%
−2	0.5
−1	2.0
0	3.0
1	1.0
2	−0.8
3	−0.4

Problem 3

A third set of returns is given below. Answer the question posed in Problem 1 based on these returns.

Day relative to announcement	Actual return
-3	1.1%
-2	0.5
-1	-0.6
0	-3.0
1	-2.0
2	-3.8
3	-2.4

SOLUTIONS

Solution 1

The abnormal returns are calculated as the actual returns minus the expected market return:

Day relative to announcement	Actual return	Abnormal return
-3	1.1%	1.08%
-2	0.5	0.48
-1	-0.6	-0.62
0	3.0	2.98
1	1.0	0.98
2	-0.8	-0.82
3	-0.4	-0.42

Inspecting the abnormal returns, we see that only the AR on day 0 is significant, i.e., 2.98%/.80% > 2.0. This result is consistent with market efficiency because the price adjusts quickly to the new information. Apparently, the market views the new product as a good investment because the price increased significantly following the announcement.

Solution 2

The abnormal returns are:

Day relative to announcement	Actual return	Abnormal return
−3	1.1%	1.08%
−2	0.5	0.48
−1	2.0	1.98
0	3.0	2.98
1	1.0	0.98
2	−0.8	−0.82
3	−0.4	−0.42

In this case, the abnormal return on day −1 is significant. This suggests that the information was 'leaked.' If the information was not public knowledge until day 0, then this result is not inconsistent with semistrong-form efficiency. However, since the abnormal return is positive for day 0, strong-form efficiency appears to have been violated. If the market were strong-form efficient, all of the adjustment should have occurred on day −1.

Solution 3

The abnormal returns are:

Day relative to announcement	Actual return	Abnormal return
−3	1.1%	1.08%
−2	0.5	0.48
−1	−0.6	−0.62
0	−3.0	−3.02
1	−2.0	−2.02
2	−3.8	−3.82
3	−2.4	−2.42

The market's reaction is significantly negative. In addition, the negative abnormal returns are significant for the three days following the announcement. This violates the notion of semistrong-form market efficiency.

CHAPTER 14

LONG TERM FINANCING: AN INTRODUCTION

CHAPTER MISSION STATEMENT

The purpose of Chapter 14 is to acquaint the student with the sources of long term financing: common stock, preferred stock, and long term debt. The chapter describes how common stock is treated on the firm's balance sheet and some of the various features of common stock. The basics of long-term debt and preferred stock are covered. Finally, the chapter reviews the patterns of long-term financing.

The key concepts are outlined below.

♦Common stock
- par value
- authorized versus issues
- capital surplus
- retained earnings
- market/book/replacement values
- shareholder rights
- dividends
- classes of stock

♦Long-term debt
- interest versus dividends
- notes/debentures/bonds
- repayment
- seniority
- security
- indenture

♦Preferred stock
- cumulative/noncumulative dividends
- tax treatment of dividends versus interest
- preferred stock puzzle

♦Patterns of financing
- internal versus external financing
- financial deficit
- pecking order
- recent trends

CONCEPT TEST

1. The stated value of a share of stock is often $1.00. This value is called the _____ of the stock.

2. If a share of common stock has no stated value, then the stock is _____ stock.

3. The number of shares issued by a corporation multiplied by the par value of each share is called the _____ of the corporation.

4.   At any point in time, the amount of stock that can be sold without shareholder approval is limited to the number of _____ shares.

5.   The amount of directly contributed equity capital in excess of par value is called the _____.

6.   The portion of net income not paid as dividends is called _____.

7.   Total common equity or _____ of a firm is the sum of _____, _____, and _____.

8.   For a given corporation, the number of shares outstanding is equal to the number of shares _____ less the number _____.

9.   Shares that have been repurchased by the issuing firm are called _____.

10. The most important distinction in the corporate voting mechanism concerns whether elections feature _____ voting or _____ voting.

11. If you own 100 shares of stock and you can cast 100 votes in the election for a member of the board of directors, the stock features _____ voting.

12. If you own 100 shares of stock and you can cast 400 votes in the election for a member of the board of directors, the stock features _____ voting.

13. The information in question 12 indicates that the number of directors to be elected is _____.

14. A grant of authority allowing another party to vote your shares is called a _____.

15. When a group other than management solicits authority to vote shares in order to replace management, a _____ occurs.

16. The payment of dividends is at the discretion of a corporation's _____.

17. Dividends received by individuals are, for the most part, taxed as _____.

18. Of the dividends received by a corporation, _____% are not taxed.

19. The thee distinctive features of debt are: debt does not represent an _____, interest paid is _____, and unpaid debt is a _____ of the firm.

20. Long-term corporate debt is usually denominated in units of $_____ called the _____ value or _____ value.

21. Long-term debt prices and interest payments are usually quoted as percentages of _____.

22. Interest payments on long-term debt are usually paid _____.

23. Typical debt securities are called _____, _____, and _____.

24. Strictly speaking, a _____ is secured by property, whereas a _____ is not, but the term _____ is used for both.

25. Long-term debt, by definition, is payable more than _____ from the date it is issued.

26. Long-term debt is sometimes called _____ debt.

27. The process of repaying a long-term debt by making installment payments is called _____.

28. When the last installment is made on a long-term debt, the debt is said to be _____.

29. A typical arrangement for installment payments on long-term debt requires the corporation to make annual deposits in a _____.

30. The corporation usually has the right to repurchase debt prior to maturity, at a specified price. Such debt is said to be _____ and the price the corporation must pay is called the _____.

31. Preference in position among lenders regarding repayment is called _____.

32. In the event of default, holders of _____ debt are generally not paid until other specified creditors are paid.

33. If a debt involves a specific attachment to property, it is called _____ debt.

34. The written agreement between the debt issuer and the lender is called the _____.

35. The written agreement between the debt issuer and the lender generally contains _____ that restrict certain activities of the corporation.

36. Holders of preferred stock must be paid their _____ before any cash can be paid to _____.

37. Preferred shares typically have a stated _____ of $100.

38. Dividends payable on preferred stock are either _____ or _____.

39. The major issuers of preferred stock are _____.

40. The major purchasers of preferred stock are _____.

41. The major source of long-term financing for U.S. corporations is _____.

42. The major use of long-term financing for U.S. corporations is _____.

43. The difference between the uses of financing and internally generated sources is called the _____.

44. The primary source of external financing used to cover the financial deficit is _____.

45. In the United States during the late 1980s, net new equity issues were _____.

46. Corporate financing strategy exhibits a _____ in which internally generated cash flow is the first form of financing, and issuing common stock is the last form.

ANSWERS TO CONCEPT TEST

1. par value
2. no par
3. dedicated capital
4. authorized
5. capital surplus
6. retained earnings
7. book value; dedicated capital; capital surplus; cumulative retained earnings
8. issued; repurchased
9. treasury stock
10. straight; cumulative
11. straight
12. cumulative
13. four
14. proxy
15. proxy fight
16. board of directors
17. ordinary income
18. 80
19. ownership interest; tax-deductible; liability
20. 1000; face; par
21. par value
22. semiannually
23. notes; bonds; debentures
24. bond; debenture; bond
25. one year
26. funded
27. amortization
28. extinguished
29. sinking fund
30. callable; call price
31. seniority
32. subordinated
33. secured
34. indenture
35. restrictive covenants
36. stated dividend; common shareholders
37. liquidating value
38. cumulative; noncumulative
39. regulated public utilities
40. corporations
41. internal cash flow
42. capital expenditures
43. financial deficit
44. borrowing
45. significantly negative
46. pecking order

PROBLEMS

The December 31, 1996 shareholders' equity accounts for Kellogg Company are shown below (dollars in millions). Use this information to solve Problems 1-5.

Shareholders' equity (millions)	1996
Common stock	$ 77.9
Capital in excess of par value	123.9
Retained earnings	4,150.3
Treasury stock, at cost (101,876,325 shares)	(2,903.4)
Currency translation adjustment	(166.3)
Total shareholders' equity	$1,282.4

Problem 1

Kellogg has 500,000,000 shares authorized and 311,524,437 shares issued in 1996. What is the par value of Kellogg's common stock?

Problem 2

How many shares does Kellogg have outstanding on December 31, 1996?

Problem 3

On December 31, 1995 Kellogg reported treasury stock as $(2,361.2). During 1996 the firm repurchased 7,453,055 shares for treasury stock. What price per share, on average, did Kellogg pay for the repurchased shares?

Problem 4

What is Kellogg's book value per share at the end of 1996?

Problem 5

Suppose that you forecast that in 1997 Kellogg's net income will be $564.0 million. You expect Kellogg to pay dividends of $360.1 million in 1997, and to repurchase another 4.8 million shares during 1997 at an average cost of $82.00 per share. Assume that the currency translation adjustment remains constant. What will the year-end 1997 shareholders' equity accounts look like?

Problem 6

The Ottumwa Maize Company expects to earn $200 million in 1998, and pay $210 million in dividends. Furthermore, Ottumwa expects to buy back 1/2 million shares at $20 per share. Half the shares will become treasury stock, while the other half will be retired and become authorized but unissued stock. Par value is $1.00 per share. Use the following information for 1997 to develop a pro forma 1998 Shareholders' equity account. No other changes are expected. (Dollars in thousands)

Shareholders' equity (thousands)	1997
Common stock	$ 69,490
Additional paid in capital	611,062
Retained earnings	1,358,271
Treasury stock, at cost	(0)
Total shareholders' equity	$2,038,823

Problem 7

Calculate Ottumwa's book value per share for 1997 and 1998.

Problem 8

On March 17, 1995 Hubbell Incorporated had outstanding 5,874,164 shares of Class A Common Stock and 27,094,539 shares of Class B Common Stock. Each share of Class A stock is entitled to twenty votes and each share of Class B stock is entitled to one vote. How many shares of Class A stock must you own to control a simple majority of the votes?

Problem 9

Banc One Corporation's Series C convertible preferred stock pays dividends at an annual rate of $3.50 and has a $50 stated value. The shares are selling for $105 1/8. What dividend yield would you receive if you purchased this stock?

Problem 10

Banc One Corporation's Series C convertible preferred stock is convertible into 1.928982 shares of Banc One's common stock. If the preferred shares could be converted at any time, and they are selling for $105 1/8, what is your estimate for the price of the firm's common stock.

Problem 11

You wish to become a director of Ottumwa Maize Company. There are 1000 shares outstanding and five directors. What is the minimum number of shares you must have to insure being elected if Ottumwa Maize has straight voting? Cumulative voting?

SOLUTIONS

Solution 1

The par value of Kellogg's common stock is the book value of $77.9 million divided by the 311,524,437 shares issued. Thus, par value equals $.25 = $77.9/311.5 per share.

Solution 2

The number of shares outstanding equals the number issued less the number repurchased as treasury stock: 209,648,112 = 311,524,437 – 101,876,325.

Solution 3

The change in treasury stock represents the cost of the repurchased shares. Kellogg spent $542.2 million = $2,903.4 – $2,361.2 million to repurchase 7,453,055 shares. On average, Kellogg paid $72.75 = $542.2/ 7.453 per share.

Solution 4

Book value per share is the total value of shareholders' equity divided by the number of shares outstanding. Thus, book value per share is

$$\$1,282.4 \text{ million}/209.648 \text{ million shares} = \$6.12 \text{ per share}$$

Solution 5

Kellogg pays out some of its net income as dividends and retains the rest. Thus, $564.0 – $360.1 = $203.9 million goes into retained earnings. The estimated 1997 retained earnings account is $4,150.3 + $203.9 = $4,354.2 million. The common stock and capital in excess of par accounts remain the same since no new stock was issued. The cost of additional treasury stock equals 4.8 million shares times $82 per share or $393.6 million. The pro forma account would appear as follows:

Shareholders' equity (millions)	E1997	1996
Common stock	$ 77.9	$ 77.9
Capital in excess of par value	123.9	123.9
Retained earnings	4,354.2	4,150.3
Treasury stock, at cost	(3,297.0)	(2,903.4)
Currency translation adjustment	(166.3)	(166.3)
Total shareholders' equity	$1,092.7	$1,282.4

Solution 6

Retained earnings for 1998 is 1997's retained earnings plus net income less cash dividends: $1,358,271 + ($200,000 − $210,000) = $1,348,271 thousand. Notice that dividends exceed net income, which reduces retained earnings. It is not unusual for firms with temporarily low earnings or even losses to continue paying dividends. Cash dividends will be paid from cash flow, which likely exceeds reported earnings, or the firm will borrow to maintain the dividend at the current level. The firm spent $20 per share × 500 thousand shares = $10,000 thousand to buy back stock. Half of this goes into the treasury stock account, while the other half is accounted for in the common stock and additional paid in capital accounts. Since 250 thousand $1 par shares were retired, common stock decreases by $250 thousand. The remaining $5,000 thousand − $250 thousand = $4,750 thousand is subtracted from additional paid-in capital.

Shareholders' equity (thousands)	E1998	1997
Common stock	$69,240	$ 69,490
Additional paid in capital	606,312	611,062
Retained earnings	1,348,271	1,358,271
Treasury stock, at cost	(5,000)	(0)
Total shareholders' equity	$2,018,823	$2,038,823

Solution 7

In 1997 Ottumwa had 69,490 thousand shares outstanding with a total book value of $2,038,823 thousand. Book value per share is $29.34 per share. In 1998 the book value per share is estimated at $2,018,823/68,990 = $29.26 per share.

Solution 8

The total number of votes outstanding is 5,874,164 shares × 20 votes/share + 27,094,539 shares × 1 vote/share = 144,577,819 votes. A simple majority equals 50 percent plus one. The number of votes you must control equals .50 × 144,577,819 + 1 = 72,288,911. At twenty votes per share, this is equivalent to 3,614,446 Class A shares. You could gain voting control of the firm by owning just 10.96 percent of the outstanding shares.

Solution 9

Banc One's Series C preferred stock costs $105.125 per share and pays a $3.508 annual dividend. Thus, your dividend yield is $3.50/$105.125 = .0333 or 3.33%.

Solution 10

Absent transaction costs, Banc One's preferred shares would be converted into common shares if the common stock was worth more than $105.125/1.928982 = $54.50. Thus, the common shares must be priced below this value. Actually, the common stock was valued at $54.25 per share.

Solution 11

If the Firm uses straight voting, the directors are elected one at a time, so you will need $(1,000/2) + 1 = 501$ shares to insure becoming a director. If you have fewer than 500 shares, you can not be assured of being elected.

If the firm uses cumulative voting, then there is a total of $[5(1,000)] = 5,000$ votes to be cast, and the directors are elected simultaneously. Since there are five directors, 1,000 votes is certainly sufficient to guarantee that you will win 1 of the 5 positions. You actually need only $[(5,000/6) + 1] = 834$ votes, however, so that 167 shares are sufficient. In general, if n directors are being elected, the necessary minimum you must have is $[1/(n + 1)]\%$ of the shares. This example illustrates how cumulative voting encourages minority participation; it takes fewer shares to get a minority director elected when a firm uses cumulative, rather than straight, voting.

CHAPTER 15

CAPITAL STRUCTURE: BASIC CONCEPTS

CHAPTER MISSION STATEMENT

The purpose of this chapter is to introduce the student to the foundations of capital structure concepts. The chapter first discusses capital structure decisions in an ideal world without taxes or transaction costs. This discussion leads to the famous Modigliani-Miller Propositions I and II that show that a firm's capital structure is a matter of indifference. The discussion next adds corporate taxes and the tax deductibility of interest. Under these conditions, the MM Propositions are modified to show that capital structure does matter, and that the firm's value depends directly on its level of debt. The deductibility of interest creates a debt tax shield whose value accrues to stockholders.

The key concepts presented in Chapter 15 are outlined below.

- ◆Financing objective
    - ●maximizing firm value
    - ●maximizing shareholder value
- ◆MM Proposition I (no tax)
    - ●leverage and firm value
    - ●choice between debt and equity
    - ●key assumptions
- ◆MM Proposition II (no tax)
    - ●cost of equity
    - ●weighted average cost of capital
    - ●market value balance sheet
- ◆Capital structure irrelevance
- ◆MM Proposition I (corporate tax)
    - ●deductibility of interest
    - ●interest tax shield
- ◆MM Proposition II (corporate tax)
    - ●cost of equity
    - ●weighted average cost of capital
- ◆Stock prices and leverage

CONCEPT TEST

1. Stockholders benefit from a financial restructuring of the firm only if the value of the firm _____.

2. An all-equity company is referred to as an _____ firm, while a company with debt in its financial structure is referred to as a _____ firm.

3. The mixture of debt and equity that a company chooses to employ is called its _____ or _____.

4. A firm's overall cost of capital is a weighted average of the cost of _____ and the cost of _____.

For Questions 5-9, assume that there are no taxes or bankruptcy costs.

5. The value of the firm is unaffected by its debt/equity ratio. This is a statement of _____.

6. The cost of equity capital is linearly related to the debt/equity ratio with a slope of _____ and a y-intercept of _____.

7. The conclusion stated in Question 6 is a statement of _____.

8. The overall cost of capital _____ as the debt/equity ratio increases.

9. The required return on equity _____ with an increase in the debt-equity ratio because additional debt _____ the risk of the firm's equity.

10. An individual investor can often borrow at a rate equal to, or lower than, the rate at which a corporation can borrow by establishing a _____ with a securities broker.

For Questions 11-15, assume that corporate taxes exist but that there are no bankruptcy costs.

11. The value of a levered firm exceeds the value of an unlevered firm with the same assets. This is a statement of _____.

12. A gain from leverage exists because interest payments generate a _____.

13. The amount by which the value of a levered firm exceeds the value of an unlevered firm with the same assets is equal to the _____.

14. The overall cost of capital _____ as the debt/equity ratio increases.

15. MM Proposition II (Corporate Taxes) states that there is a _____ relationship between expected return on equity and the debt-equity ratio.

ANSWERS TO CONCEPT TEST

1. increases
2. unlevered; levered
3. capital structure; financial structure
4. debt; equity
5. MM Proposition I
6. $r_o - r_B$; r_o
7. MM Proposition II
8. stays the same

9. increases; increases
10. margin account
11. MM Proposition I (Corporate Taxes)
12. tax shield
13. PV tax shield
14. decreases
15. positive

PROBLEMS

Use the information below to solve Problems 1-6.

Maxlever and Nolever are identical firms in all ways except that Maxlever employs debt in its capital structure and Nolever does not. The EBIT for each firm is $100. The total value of the equity in Maxlever is $400, and the total value of the equity in Nolever is $700. Maxlever's bonds have a market value and a face value of $400. The interest rate is 10% and there are no taxes.

Problem 1

Suppose that an investor purchases 20% of the equity of Maxlever. What is the cost and the return for this investment?

Problem 2

Explain how the investor can duplicate the cash flow from the investment described in Problem 1 by borrowing and investing in the equity of Nolever.

Problem 3

Describe the arbitrage opportunity which exists as a result of the fact that the value of Maxlever is greater than the value of Nolever.

Problem 4

Suppose that the total value of Nolever's equity is $900, rather than $700, and that an investor purchases 20% of the equity of Nolever. What is the cost and the return for this investment?

Problem 5

Explain how the investor can duplicate the cash flow from the investment described in Problem 4 by lending and investing in the equity of Maxlever.

Problem 6

Describe the arbitrage opportunity which exists as a result of the fact that the value of Maxlever is greater than the value of Nolever.

Use the information below to solve Problems 7-10.

The Fulcrum Company, a major manufacturer of telephone switching equipment, has a perpetual expected EBIT of $200. The interest rate is 12%.

Problem 7

Assuming that there are no taxes or other market imperfections, what is the value of Fulcrum if its debt/equity ratio is .25 and its overall cost of capital is 16%? What is the value of the equity? What is the value of the debt?

Problem 8

What is the cost of equity capital for Fulcrum?

Problem 9

Suppose the corporate tax rate is 30%, there are no personal taxes or other imperfections, and Fulcrum has $400 in debt outstanding. If the unlevered cost of equity is 20%, what is Fulcrum's value? What is the value of the equity?

Problem 10

In Problem 9, what is the overall cost of capital?

Use the following information to solve Problems 11-15.

Michelson-Morley Incorporated is an all-equity firm with earnings expected to be $800,000 in perpetuity. The firm has 100,000 shares outstanding. The cost of capital is 20%. M-M is considering a major expansion of its facilities which will require an initial outlay of $750,000 and which is expected to produce additional annual earnings of $250,000 per year in perpetuity. Management considers the expansion to have the same risk as the firm's existing assets. Assume throughout that there are no taxes and no costs of bankruptcy.

Problem 11

What is the value of the firm's assets prior to undertaking the proposed expansion? What is the value of the firm's equity? What is the price per share of the firm's stock?

Problem 12

Suppose M-M plans to finance the expansion by issuing common stock. How many shares of stock must be issued? What is the value of the firm's equity after the new stock issue? What is the price per share of the firm's stock?

Problem 13

Suppose M-M plans to finance the expansion by issuing bonds with an interest rate of 10%. What is the value of the firm after the new bond issue? What is the value of the firm's equity? What is the price per share of the firm's stock?

Problem 14

Calculate the expected yearly income after interest for the equity holders. Use the expected yearly income to calculate the expected return for the equity holders.

Problem 15

Use MM Proposition II (no taxes) to determine the expected return for Michelson-Morley's equity holders.

The following information applies to Problems 16-20.

The Monongahela Valley Manufacturing Company has $750 debt outstanding with pretax cost of 6% and its common stock has a value of $1,250. The required return on equity is 14.34%. MVM faces a corporate tax rate of 35%.

Problem 16

Calculate Monongahela's equivalent unlevered cost of equity, r_o, and the firm's weighted average cost of capital.

Problem 17

What is Monongahela's EBIT?

Problem 18

Monongahela Valley Manufacturing is recapitalizing by issuing $250 in debt and using the proceeds to buy back stock. What is MVM's new value of B, S, and V?

Problem 19

After the recapitalization, what are MVM's required return on equity and WACC?

Problem 20

Find the values of S and V using the values of r_s and WACC from Problem 19 and the EBIT from Problem 17, respectively.

Problem 21

Monongahela Valley Manufacturing now announces that instead of issuing $250 of debt, the firm will reduce leverage by issuing $250 of stock and buy back $250 in debt, thus reducing debt to $500. What is MVM's value of B, S, and V under this scenario?

SOLUTIONS

Solution 1

The investment is:

$$(.20)(S_L) = (.20)(V_L - B_L) = (.20)(\$400) = \$80$$

where the subscript L stands for the levered firm, Maxlever. The return for this investment is:

$$(.20)(Earn - r_B B_L) = (.20)[\$100 - (.10)(\$400)] = \$12$$

where *Earn* is the firm's EBIT and r_B is the interest rate on the firm's debt.

Solution 2

First, borrow $[(.20)B_L)] = [(.20)(\$400)] = \$80$ at an interest rate of 10%. Then purchase 20% of the equity in Nolever, at a cost of $[(.20)(V_U)] = [(.20)(\$700)] = \$140$, where the subscript U represents the unlevered firm Nolever. The return from this strategy is

$$(.20)(Earn - r_B B_L) = (.20)[\$100 - (.10)(\$400)] = \$12$$

which is the same as the cash flow for Problem 1.

Solution 3

The investor's cash flow is the same for the strategy in Problem 2 as it is for the strategy in Problem 1. The two strategies differ only in the amount invested; in Problem 1, $80 is invested for a cash flow of $12, while in Problem 2, only ($140 − $80) = $60 is invested for the same cash flow. Consequently, a rational investor would pursue the second strategy, thereby increasing the value of Nolever and decreasing the value of Maxlever. Prices will adjust until V_L is equal to V_U. Note that the investor could be more aggressive about his investment strategy by selling short the equity of Maxlever for $80 at the same time that he borrows and invests in the equity of Nolever. This strategy provides a certain $20 profit since, in equilibrium, the values of the two firms must be equal.

Solution 4

The cost of purchasing 20% of the equity in Nolever is $[(.20)(V_U)] = [(.20)(\$900)] = \$180$. The cash flow from this investment would be $[(.20)(Earn)] = [(.20)(\$100)] = \$20$.

Solution 5

We can reproduce the cash flow by first lending $[(.20)(B_L)] = [(.20)(\$400)] = \$80$ at a 10% interest rate. Next, purchase 20% of the equity in Maxlever:

$$(.20)(S_L) = (.20)(V_L - B_L) = (.20)(\$400) = \$80$$

The cash flow from this strategy is:

$$(.20)(Earn - r_BB_L) + (.20)(r_BB_L) =$$

$$(.20)[\$100 - (.10)(\$400)] + (.10)(\$80) = \$20.$$

Solution 6

The investor's cash flow is $20 for each of the investment strategies described in Problems 4 and 5. However, the size of the investment is $180 in Problem 4 and only $160 in Problem 5. All rational investors would choose the strategy described in Problem 5, thereby resulting in an increase in the value of Maxlever and a decrease in the value of Nolever. Equilibrium is reached when the values of the two firms are equal. As in Problem 3, the investor can use short selling to produce an arbitrage profit; he can sell short the equity of Nolever for $180 and adopt the strategy of lending and buying Maxlever, as described in Problem 5.

Solution 7

If there are no taxes, then MM Proposition I holds and Fulcrum's capital structure is irrelevant, so the value of the firm is ($200/.16) = $1,250.

If the debt/equity ratio is .25, then for every $5 in capital, there is $4 in equity. Thus, Fulcrum is 80% equity, and the value of the equity is $1,000. The value of the debt is $250.

Solution 8

The cost of equity capital can be computed using MM Proposition II as:

$$r_S = r_o + (B/S)(r_o - r_B)$$

$$=.16 + (.25)(.16 - .12) = .17 \text{ or } 17\%$$

Alternatively, we can compute the equity cash flow as [$200 - 12($250)] = $170, and divide by the value of equity. Since the equity is worth $1,000, the cost of capital is ($170/$1,000) = .17 or 17%.

Solution 9

We can use MM Proposition I with taxes to value Fulcrum. The value of Fulcrum as an unlevered firm is:

$$EBIT(1 - T_c)/r_o = (\$200)(.70)/.20 = \$700$$

The present value of the tax shield is $T_cB = [.30(\$400)] = \$120$. The total value is therefore $820. The value of the equity is ($820 - $400) = $420.

Solution 10

The debt to equity ratio for Fulcrum is ($400/$420). Using MM Proposition II with taxes, the cost of equity is:

$$.20 + (1 - .30)(.20 - .12)(400/420) = .2533 \text{ or } 25.33\%$$

Alternatively, the cash flow to equity is:

$$[\$200 - .12(\$400)](1 - .30) = \$106.40$$

Thus, the return on equity is ($106.40/$420) = .2533 or 25.33%, as previously calculated.
The overall cost of capital is:

$$(\$420/\$820)(.2533) + (\$400/\$820)(.12)(1 - .30) = .1707 \text{ or } 17.07\%$$

Solution 11

The value of the firm is ($800,000/.20) = $4,000,000. Since M-M is an all-equity firm, the value of the firm's equity is also $4,000,000. Price per share is ($4,000,000/100,000) = $40.00.

Solution 12

The net present value of the expansion is:

$$-\$750,000 + (\$250,000/.20) = \$500,000$$

Therefore, when Michelson-Morley announces the expansion, the value of the firm increases to ($4,000,000 + $500,000) = $4,500,000. That is, the value of the firm's assets and the value of the equity each increase to $4,500,000. Therefore, price per share increases to ($4,500,000/100,000) = $45. Note that this increase in value occurs immediately following the announcement of the expansion, but before the financing is obtained. In order to obtain $750,000 in equity financing, the firm sells ($750,000/$45) = 16,667 shares of stock. The proceeds of the stock issue are used to acquire the new assets, so that the value of the firm becomes ($4,000,000 + $500,000 + $750,000) = $5,250,000, which is the value of the firm's equity. The price per share is still $45 after the financing; that is, ($5,250,000/116,667 shares) = $45.00 per share.

Solution 13

As in Problem 12, the value of the firm increases to $4,500,000 after the announcement of the positive NPV expansion. When the firm issues $750,000 of new debt, the value of the firm's assets increases to $5,250,000, but the value of the firm's equity remains at $4,500,000. The value of the firm is the same as under the equity financing arrangement, as indicated by MM Proposition I (No Taxes). The price per share of the firm's stock is $45 after the announcement and before the financing is obtained, and remains at $45 after the financing is obtained.

standard188 Capital Structure

Solution 14

Expected yearly income is:

$$\$800{,}000 + \$250{,}000 - (.10)(\$750{,}000) = \$975{,}000.$$

The expected return for the equity holders is ($975,000/$4,500,000) = .21667 or 21.67%.

Solution 15

MM Proposition II (no taxes) indicates that the return to equity holders (r_s) is:

$$r_S = r_o + (B/S)(r_o - r_B)$$

$$r_s = .20 + (\$750{,}000/\$4{,}500{,}000)(.20 - .10) = .21667 \text{ or } 21.67\%$$

Solution 16

The unlevered cost of equity can be found using MM Proposition II (with taxes).

$$r_S = r_o + (B/S)(r_o - r_B)(1 - T_c)$$

$$1434 = r_o + (\$750/\$1{,}250)(r_o - .06)(1 - .35)$$

$$r_o = .1200 \text{ or } 12.0\%$$

The firm's WACC is

$$WACC = (B/V) \, r_B \, (1 - T_c) + (S/V) \, r_s$$

$$= (\$750/\$2{,}000) \, .06 \, (1 - .35) + (\$1{,}250/\$2{,}000) \, .1434$$

$$= .10425 \text{ or } 10.425\%.$$

Solution 17

We can derive EBIT two ways: from V using the WACC, or from S.

The value of the firm is the cash flow going to all investors capitalized at the WACC:

$$V = B + S = EBIT(1 - T_c)/WACC$$

$$\$2{,}000 = \$750 + \$1{,}250 = EBIT(.65)/.10425$$

$$EBIT = \$320.769$$

Alternatively, the value of equity is the cash flow going to shareholders capitalized at the cost of equity:

$$S = (EBIT - r_B B)(1 - T_c)/r_s$$

$$\$1,250 = [EBIT - (.06)\$750](.65)/.1434$$

$$EBIT = \$320.769.$$

Solution 18

MVM's debt is now B = $750 + $250 = $1,000. The new debt creates an additional interest tax shield equal to $T_c \Delta B$ = .35($250) = $87.50. Thus, the new value of the firm is V = $2,000 + $87.50 = $2,087.50, and the value of equity is S = $2,087.50 − $1,000 = $1,087.50.

Solution 19

MM's Proposition II (with taxes) is used to find the required return on equity.

$$r_S = r_o + (B/S)(r_o - r_B)(1 - T_c)$$

$$r_S = .12 + (\$1,000/\$1,087.50)(.12 - .06)(1 - .35)$$

$$r_s = .15586 \text{ or } 15.586\%$$

where r_o = .12 is from Problem 16.

The WACC is:

$$WACC = (B/V)\, r_B\, (1 - T_c) + (S/V)\, r_s$$

$$= (\$1,000/\$2,087.50)\, .06\, (1 - .35) + (\$1,087.50/\$2,087.50)\, (.15586)$$

$$= .099879 \text{ or } 9.988\%$$

Note that under MM Propositions I and II (with taxes) the WACC becomes lower as more debt is added to the capital structure. For a fixed level of EBIT, this must be true if the value of the firm is to increase without limit under Proposition I (with taxes).

Solution 20

The value of equity in the recapitalized firm is the cash flow going to stockholders, EBIT net of interest and taxes, discounted at r_s.

$$S = (EBIT - r_B B)(1 - T_c)/r_s$$

$$= [\$320.769 - (.06)\$1,000](.65)/.15586$$

$$= \$1,087.51.$$

The value of the firm is EBIT less taxes discounted at the WACC.

$$V = EBIT (1 - T_c)/WACC$$

$$= \$320.769(.65)/.099879$$

$$= \$2,087.52$$

These are the same values (within rounding error) obtained in Problem 18.

Solution 21

Following the solution to problem 18, less debt will change the interest tax shield by $T_c \Delta B = .35(-\$250)$ $=- \$87.50$. Thus, the new value of the firm is $V = \$2,000 - \$87.50 = \$1,912.50$, and the value of equity is $S = \$1,912.50 - \$500 = \$1,412.50$. Notice that the original equity of $\$1,250$ was reduced by the $\$87.50$ lost tax shield to $\$1,162.50$. An additional $\$250$ in equity brings the total to $\$1,412.50$.

CHAPTER 16

CAPITAL STRUCTURE:
LIMITS TO THE USE OF DEBT

CHAPTER MISSION STATEMENT

The purpose of Chapter 16 is to extend the discussion of capital structure concepts in Chapter 15 by introducing real-world factors that offset the value of the debt tax shield. The cost of financial distress, including the direct and indirect costs of bankruptcy, agency costs, and the effect of personal taxes tend to limit the use of debt. Furthermore, growth opportunities or inflation will reduce the incentive to use debt. The discussion posits how these limiting factors lead to an optimal capital structure. Finally, the chapter discusses the evidence on how firms establish capital structure. An appendix describes in more detail Miller's model and the effect of a graduated personal income taxes on capital structure.

The key concepts presented in Chapter 16 are outlined below.

- ♦ Costs of financial distress
    - bankruptcy risk
    - bankruptcy cost
    - direct costs
    - indirect costs
- ♦ Agency costs of debt
    - taking risks
    - underinvestment
    - milking the property
- ♦ Reducing the costs of financial distress
    - protective covenants
    - consolidation of debt
- ♦ Integrating tax effects and financial distress costs
    - MM perspective
    - marketed versus nonmarketed claims
- ♦ Shirking, perquisites, and bad investments
    - agency costs of equity
    - free cash flow hypothesis
- ♦ Growth and the debt-equity ratio
- ♦ Personal taxes
    - Miller's model
- ♦ How firms establish capital structure

CONCEPT TEST

1. The _____ costs of financial distress include attorneys' fees, administrative and accounting fees, and fees to expert witnesses.

2. If a firm is close to bankruptcy, the incentive to _____ may result in the acceptance of a high-risk project with a relatively low expected value.

3. A firm close to bankruptcy may chose not to undertake a positive NPV project because of the incentive toward _____.

4. Stockholders have an incentive to _____ in times of financial distress, which means that it is in the stockholders' best interest to pay extra dividends.

5. The indirect costs of financial distress are paid by _____.

6. Two ways to reduce the costs of financial distress are the inclusion of _____ in the bond indenture and _____.

7. _____ covenants limit or prohibit certain actions, while _____ covenants require certain actions on the part of the company.

8. One often discussed limitation to the amount of debt that a firm can employ is _____.

9. If we consider the impact of corporate taxes and the possibility of bankruptcy, the optimum capital structure is the point where the gain from additional _____ is offset by _____.

10. In Question 9, the value of a levered firm is equal to the value of an unlevered firm with the same assets, plus the PV of the _____ less the PV of the _____.

11. The pie model slices the firm's cash flow into _____ claims such as stocks and bonds, and _____ claims such as taxes, the cost of bankruptcy, and potential lawsuits.

12. The costs associated with an entrepreneur's incentive to shirk and to acquire perquisites when new equity is issued are referred to as the _____ of equity.

13. The free cash flow hypothesis suggests that debt reduces the _____ for managers to _____ resources.

14. A key feature of the U.S. tax code is that payments to bondholders, relative to shareholders, are taxed _____ at the personal level.

15. Suppose that corporations are not taxed at all and that there are personal taxes on interest but not on capital gains. In this case, the optimum capital structure is _____.

16. If the firm is viewed as a pie. then the value of the pie can be decomposed into two types of claims: _____ claims and _____ claims.

17. When firms announce increases in leverage, firm value typically _____ and when firms announce decreases in leverage, firm value typically _____.

18. In a world with taxes but without the cost of financial distress, _____ and/or _____ may help explain debt ratios below 100%.

19. Growth opportunities suggest an optimal debt ratio less than 100%, thus high-growth firms should have _____ debt ratios than low-growth firms.

ANSWERS TO CONCEPT TEST

1.	direct	10.	tax shield; bankruptcy costs
2.	take large risks	11.	marketed; nonmarketed
3.	underinvestment	12.	agency costs
4.	milk the property	13.	opportunity; waste
5.	stockholders	14.	unfavorably
6.	protective covenants; consolidation of debt	15.	100% equity
		16.	marketed; nonmarketed
7.	negative; positive	17.	increases; decreases
8.	financial distress costs	18.	growth opportunities; inflation
9.	tax savings; increased risk of bankruptcy	19.	lower

PROBLEMS

Use the following information to solve Problems 1-3.

Firms X, Y, and Z each expect to be in business for one year and each forecasts cash flows of either $200 or $700 for the year. The probability of each cash flow is .50. Bondholders and stockholders of each firm are risk-neutral and the interest rate is 20 percent. Firm X is an all-equity firm. Firms Y and Z have debt obligations of $100 and $300, respectively, due at the end of the year.

Problem 1

Calculate the values of equity, debt, and the firm for X, Y and Z.

Problem 2

What are the expected return and the promised return for the bondholders of Firm Y? What are these returns for the bondholders of Firm Z?

Problem 3

Suppose that, in the event of bankruptcy, financial distress costs for Firm Z will total $60. What is the value of the debt, the equity, and the firm for Z?

Use the following information to solve Problems 4-6.

Nevada Nuggets, Inc. is considering two mutually exclusive projects to expand manufacturing capacity. Nevada is obligated to make a $700 payment to bondholders next year. The projects will determine the value of the firm as follows:

Project	Probability	Value of firm	Value of stock	Value of bonds
A	.5	$3,000	$2,300	$700
	.5	$4,500	$3,800	$700
B	.5	$ 100	$ 0	$100
	.5	$6,900	$6,200	$700

Problem 4

Calculate the expected value of the firm, the stock, and the bonds if Nevada Nuggets selects Project A.

Problem 5

Calculate the expected value of the firm, the stock, and the bonds if Nevada selects Project B.

Problem 6

Which project will Nevada Nuggets accept? If NN were an all-equity firm, which project would be accepted?

Use the following information to answer questions 7-9.

Assume a risk-neutral world with a discount rate of 25%. You are evaluating two mutually exclusive one-year investment projects of different risks, but similar expected payoffs. Each project requires an initial investment of $300, the payoffs are described in the following tables.

Project	Probability	Payoff t = +1
X	.25	$200
	.50	$400
	.25	$600
Y	.50	$300
	.50	$500

Problem 7

Calculate the expected payoff at t = 1 and the NPV of each project. Assume all equity financing.

Problem 8

Your bank will lend you 70% of the project's cost, i.e., $210. If you finance the project with 30% equity and 70% debt, determine the payoffs to stockholders and bondholders.

Problem 9

If you are the only stockholder, which project would you choose if it had to be financed with equity? Which project would you choose if you put up $90 and the bank put up the remaining $210?

Use the following information to solve Problems 10-11.

A firm forecasts that next year's cash flow will be either $7,000 or $3,000, each with probability .50. Since the firm's obligation to bondholders is $5,000, there is a .50 probability of bankruptcy. The firm is considering a project which is certain to increase cash flows by $2,000, thus allowing the firm to avoid bankruptcy. The cost of the project is $1,200, which will be paid by the firm's existing stockholders.

Problem 10

Will the firm adopt the project?

Problem 11

If the firm were an all equity firm, would the project be accepted?

Problem 12

Ms. Kristy is the owner-entrepreneur of a publishing company. The firm is currently valued at $5 million and Kristy plans to expand the firm. Financing for the expansion will be obtained either by borrowing $5 million at a 10% interest rate or by issuing $5 million of stock. Total cash flow to the firm after the expansion will depend to a great extent on the intensity with which Kristy works at the firm. If she works five days per week and takes two months vacation, cash flow will be $1 million per year, but if she works six days per week and takes two weeks vacation, cash flow will be $1.5 million per year. What is the cash flow to Kristy for each alternative?

Use the information below to solve Problems 13-15. (These problems are a continuation of Problems 7-10 in Chapter 15)

The Fulcrum Company has a perpetual expected EBIT of $200 and the interest rate is 12%. If Fulcrum experiences financial distress in a given year, then EBIT is expected to be $100 in that year.

Problem 13

The probability of financial distress for Fulcrum depends on the amount of debt Fulcrum uses. Assuming that the corporate tax rate is 30%, complete the table below. Which of the four capital structures described below is optimal? Use the unlevered equity cost to discount any bankruptcy cost effects.

Amount of debt	Probability of distress	Expected EBIT	Cost of equity	Stock value	Total value
$ 0	.00				$800
200	.10				
400	.30				
600	.50				

Problem 14

Assume that the corporate tax rate is 30%, the effective tax rate on personal income from bonds is 40%, and the effective rate on equity income is zero. Fulcrum has $500 in debt outstanding. The unlevered cost of capital is 20%. What is the gain from leverage for Fulcrum?

Problem 15

Suppose that, in Problem 14, the effective tax rate on personal income from bonds is 20%. What is the gain from leverage for Fulcrum now?

Problem 16

You are considering whether to invest in bonds that provide a 10% yield or common stocks that provide a dividend yield of 5% and expected capital gain of 5% per year. Assume a risk-neutral world, that you are an inframarginal investor, that the tax rate on dividend and interest income is 28%, and the tax rate on capital gains (realized or unrealized) is 15%. Should you invest in bonds or stocks?

Problem 17

The Nimbus Corporation is all equity financed and generates $250 thousand per year pretax income. The corporate tax rate is 35%, while investors are taxed at 15% on stock income and 28% on bond interest. Stockholders discount earnings at 20% after corporate and personal taxes. What is the value of Nimbus Corporation.

Problem 18

Nimbus Corporation decides to borrow $200 thousand and use the proceeds to buy back stock. What is the value of Nimbus now?

Problem 19

Now assume that the personal tax rate on equity income, T_s, is 28%. What is the value of Nimbus? What is Nimbus's value if equity income is free from personal tax?

Problem 20

Consider an economy with the following four groups of investors and no others:

Group	Marginal tax rate on interest	Personal wealth (millions)
Doctors	50%	$2,000
Lawyers	40%	1,000
Corporate executives	20%	500
Accounting professors	10%	10

Assume that all investors are risk-neutral and that they can earn a 5% tax-free return by investing in foreign real estate. The tax rate on equity income is zero and the corporate tax rate is 40%. Corporations are expected to receive EBIT of $180 million in perpetuity. What is the maximum debt/value ratio in this economy? What is the total corporate tax bill? How much is invested in foreign real estate?

Problem 21

Try this one on your own. Based on the information in Problem 20, what is the economy's debt/value ratio if Lawyers all buy stock?

SOLUTIONS

Solution 1

The expected cash flow to the stockholders of Firm X is [(.5)($200) + (.5)($700)] = $450 and the value of the equity is ($450/1.20) = $375.00. Since there is no debt, the value of Firm X is also $375.00.

The cash flow to the stockholders of Firm Y will be either $100 or $600, and the expected cash flow is [(.5)($100) + (.5)($600)] = $350. The value of the equity is ($350/1.20) = $291.67. The value of the debt is ($100/1.20) = $83.33. (note: since investors are risk neutral, the same discount rate applies to both equity and debt) The value of the firm is ($291.67 + $83.33) = $375.00. The value of X is equal to the value of Y. These values must be equal because the two firms simply represent different allocations of the firms' cash flows. In both cases, the value of the firm is the present value of the expected cash flow of $450 that gets distributed to investors.

For Firm Z, with $300 of debt, the possible cash flows to the debt holders are $200 and $300. In the first case, the firm would be bankrupt because the $200 cash flow could not fully satisfy the $300 liability. The possible cash flows to the stockholders are $0 and $400. The expected values of the cash flows to the debt holders and the stockholders are $250 and $200, respectively. Note again that the total expected cash flow is still $450, so that the value of the firm must be the same as for Firms X and Y. For Firm Z, the value of the firm's debt is $208.33 and the value of the firm's equity is $166.67, so that the value of the firm is $375.00.

Solution 2

For each firm, the expected return for the bondholders is 20%. For Firm Y, the promised return is also 20%, because the bondholders are assured of receiving their $100 payment, and the present value of $83.33 is derived by discounting this payment at a 20% rate. For Firm Z, however, the promised return is greater than the expected return; the promised return is $[(\$300/\$208.33) - 1] = 44\%$, although bondholders know that there is a .50 probability that they will receive only $200.

Solution 3

The value of the firm's equity is unchanged because the expected cash flow and the discount rate are unaffected by the financial distress costs. (Note that the discount rate is unchanged throughout this problem because we assume that investors are risk-neutral) The expected cash flow to the bondholders is now $[(.5)(\$200 - \$60) + (.5)(\$300)] = \$220$ and the value of the bonds is $(\$220/1.20) = \$183.33$. The value of the firm is $(\$183.33 + \$166.67) = \$350.00$. The value of the debt and the value of the firm have each decreased by $25.00. This is equal to the present value of the expected value of the financial distress costs:

$$[(.5)(\$0) + (.5)(\$60)]/1.20 = \$25.00$$

This result indicates that financial distress costs reduce the total of the portions of the 'pie' which go to the stockholders and the bondholders.

Solution 4

The expected value of the firm if A is chosen is $[(.5)(\$3,000) + (.5)(\$4,500)] = \$3,750$. The expected value of the firm's stock is $[(.5)(\$2,300) + (.5)(\$3,800)] = \$3,050$. The value of the bonds is $700.

Solution 5

The expected value of the firm if B is chosen is $[(.5)(\$100) + (.5)(\$6,900)] = \$3,500$. The expected value of the firm's stock is $3,100 and the expected value of the bonds is $400.

Solution 6

The expected value of the firm's stock is greater with Project B ($3,100) than with Project A ($3,050). Consequently, Nevada Nuggets' shareholders will choose to undertake Project B. Project B is the high-risk project and, with Project B, there is a .50 probability that the firm will be bankrupt. The possibility of bankruptcy increases the firm's motivation to undertake the high-risk project because the loss in value in the event of bankruptcy is shared with the bondholders. The value of the firm is greater for

Project A ($3,750 vs. $3,500), so that if the firm were an all-equity firm, Nevada would accept Project A, the low-risk project.

Solution 7

The expected payoff to Project X is $(.25)(\$200) + (.50)(\$400) + (.25)(\$600) = \$400$. Project X's NPV is $\$400/(1.25) - \$300 = \$20$. The expected payoff to Project Y is $(.50)(\$300) + (.50)(\$500) = \$400$. Project Y's NPV is also $20.

Solution 8

The payoffs to stockholders and bondholders are described in the following tables. Note that the bank lends you $210 at t=0 and you must pay back $210(1.25) = \$262.5$ at t = 1. Stockholders, as residual claimants, get what remains after the bondholders are paid.

Project	Probability	Payoff t = +1	Value of stock	Value of bonds
X	.25	$200	$ 0	$200.00
	.50	$400	$137.50	$262.50
	.25	$600	$337.50	$262.50
Y	.5	$300	$ 37.50	$262.50
	.5	$500	$237.50	$262.50

The expected payoff to stockholders in Project X is

$$E(\text{stock}) = (.25)(\$0) + (.50)(\$137.5) + (.25)(\$337.5) = \$153.125$$

The expected payoff to bondholders in Project X is

$$E(\text{bond}) = .25(\$200) + (.50)(\$262.5) + (.25)(\$262.5) = \$246.875$$

The expected payoffs to stockholders and bondholders in Project Y are $137.5 and $262.5, respectively.

Solution 9

You would be indifferent between projects X and Y if they had to be all equity financed. Both provide the same expected payoffs and a NPV of $20. If 70% debt financed, the riskier Project X would be preferred. Here, you invest $90 and next year your stock has an expected value of $153.125. In present value terms, the stock is worth $153.125/(1.25) = \$122.50$. Thus, the NPV of your equity investment is $122.50 - $90 = $32.50. If you pick Project Y, the NPV of your equity investment is $20. Thus, with debt financing, you have shifted the extra risk of Project X to the bondholders.

Solution 10

Without the project, the expected value of the bondholders' claim to the firm's cash flows is [(.5)($5,000) + (.5)($3,000)] = $4,000 and the expected value of the stockholders' claim is [(.5)($2,000) + (.5)($0)] = $1,000. With the project, the bondholders are certain to receive $5,000, and the expected value of the stockholder's claim increases to [(.5)($4,000) + (.5)($0)] = $2,000. However, the stockholders must invest $1,200 in order to increase the expected value by only $1,000. Therefore, stockholders will not accept the project.

Solution 11

The project requires that the stockholders invest $1,200 in order to receive a certain $2,000 cash flow. Since this is a certain $800 return, in one year, on a $1,200 investment, this is clearly a positive NPV investment at any reasonable discount rate. Consequently, the stockholders of the firm would adopt the investment if the firm were an all equity firm. The results of Problem 10 indicate that there is an incentive toward underinvestment when a firm is close to bankruptcy.

Solution 12

If Kristy borrows $5 million the interest expense will be $500 thousand per year. Cash flow to Kristy, as 100% owner of the firm, will be ($1 million - $.500 million) = $.500 million per year if she works five days per week, or ($1.5 million - $.500 million) = $1.0 million if she works six days per week. If Kristy issues $5.0 million of stock in exchange for 50% ownership, her cash flow will be either ($1.0 million/2) = $.500 million or ($1.5 million/2) = $.750. If Kristy works more intensely, the entire benefit of her additional work accrues to her as long as she is 100% owner of the firm. If she is 50% owner, she derives only half of the benefit of her additional work. In this situation, the equity financing alternative reduces Kristy's incentive to work hard.

Solution 13

In the zero debt case, expected EBIT is $200, the cost of equity is ($140/$800) = .175 or 17.5%. and the stock value equals the total value. For the case of $200 debt, the expected EBIT is [.90($200) + .10($100)] = $190. The value of the firm is:

$$V_L = EBIT (1 - T_c)/r_o + T_c B$$

$$= \$190 (.70)/.175 + (.30) \$200$$

$$= \$760 + \$60 = \$820$$

The cost of equity (by MM Proposition II with taxes) is:

$$r_s = r_o + (B/S)(1 - T_c)(r_o - r_B)$$

$$= .175 + (\$200/\$620)(1 - .30)(.175 - .12) = .1874 \text{ or } 18.74\%$$

Using similar calculations for other debt levels, the complete table is:

Amount of debt	Probability of distress	Expected EBIT	Cost of equity	Stock value	Total value
$ 0	.00	$200	17.50%	$800	$800
200	.10	190	18.74	620	820
400	.30	170	21.35	400	800
600	.50	150	30.33	180	780

Fulcrum should borrow $200 since that level of debt maximizes firm value.

Solution 14

The Miller Model indicates that the value of the levered firm (V_L) is related to the value of the unlevered firm (V_U) according to the following:

$$V_L = V_U + [1 - (1 - T_c)(1 - T_s)/(1 - T_B)] \ B$$

where T_s, and T_B are the personal tax rates on equity and debt, respectively. Therefore, the gain from leverage is the second term in the above equation:

$$[1 - (1 - .30)(1 - 0)/(1 - .40)] \ \$500$$

$$= -\$83.33$$

In this case, leverage reduces the value of the firm because the corporation is in a lower tax bracket than its bondholders; therefore, it is not desirable to shield taxes at the corporate level. Fulcrum should have an all-equity capital structure.

Solution 15

The gain from leverage is:

$$[1 - (1 - T_c)(1 - T_s)/(1 - T_B)] \ B$$

$$[1 - (1 - .30)(1 - 0)/(1 - .20)] \ \$500$$

$$= \$62.50$$

Leverage increases the value of the firm because the corporation is in a higher tax bracket than its bondholders.

Solution 16

To determine which investment is better, calculate your after tax return from each investment. The after-tax return on bonds is $10\%(1 - .28) = 7.2\%$. By comparison, the after-tax dividend yield is $5\%(1 - .28) = 3.6\%$ and the after-tax capital gain is $5\%(1 - .15) = 4.25\%$. An investment in stocks will provide a return of $3.6\% + 4.25\% = 7.85\%$, which is higher than the return on bonds. Thus, stocks make a better investment.

Solution 17

The value of this unlevered firm in the presence of corporate and personal taxes is

$$V_U = EBIT(1 - T_c)(1 - T_s)/r_o$$

where r_o is after corporate and personal taxes. Thus, the value of Nimbus is

$$V = \$250 \ (1 - .35)(1 - .15)/.20 = \$690.625 \text{ thousand.}$$

Solution 18

We can use the valuation formula under both corporate and personal taxes. Thus,

$$V_L = V_U + [1 - (1 - T_c)(1 - T_s)/(1 - T_B)] \ B$$

The value $V_U = \$690.625$ thousand was found in Problem 17. Substituting values, we have

$$V_L = \$690.625 + [1 - (1 - .35)(1 - .15)/(1 - .28)] \ \$200$$

$$V_L = \$690.625 + \$46.528 = \$737.153 \text{ thousand.}$$

Solution 19

With a new tax rate on equity income, the discount rate r_o will change. Previously, the rate before personal taxes was $.20/(1 - .15) = .235294$. Now with the new tax rate, the after all taxes rate is $.235294(1 - .28) = .169412$. The value of the unlevered Nimbus is

$$V_U = \$250(1 - .35)(1 - .28)/.169412 = \$690.625.$$

The value of the levered Nimbus is

$$V_L = \$690.625 + [1 - (1 - .35)(1 - .28)/(1 - .28)] \ \$200$$

$$V_L = \$690.625 + \$70.00 = \$760.625 \text{ thousand.}$$

If the personal tax rate on equity income is zero, then the value of the levered Nimbus becomes $\$690.625 + \$19.444 = \$710.069$.

Solution 20

Since all investors are risk-neutral, the return on common stock, which is untaxed, must equal 5%. In a Miller-model equilibrium, the bonds must offer $[.05/(1 - .4)] = .08333$ or 8.333%. Given the personal tax rates, Doctors will hold stock or foreign real estate; Corporate Executives and Accounting Professors will hold corporate bonds; and Lawyers will be indifferent between stocks and corporate bonds since their after tax income will be 5% on either investment. The maximum debt/value ratio occurs when Lawyers hold all corporate bonds.

If the Lawyers all hold corporate bonds, the total amount of debt in the economy is $[\$1,000 + \$500 + \$10] = \$1,510$. The total interest bill is $[(\$1,510)(.08333)] = \$125.83$. Corporate equity is worth:

$$[(\$180 - \$125.83)(1 - .40)]/.05 = \$650$$

Total corporate value is $B + S = \$1,510 + \$650 = \$2,160$, and the debt/value ratio is $\$1,510/\$2,160 = .6991$ or 69.91%. The total corporate tax bill is $[(\$180 - \$125.83)(.40)] = \$21.67$ per year. Total wealth in the economy is \$3,510. Total corporate value is \$2,160, thus $\$3,510 - \$2,160 = \$1,350$ is invested by Doctors in foreign real estate.

Solution 21

The total amount of debt will be \$510. Total interest will be \$42.50. Total corporate value will be unchanged at \$2,160, because in equilibrium capital structure is irrelevant. The debt/value ratio is 23.6%.

CHAPTER 17

VALUATION AND CAPITAL BUDGETING
FOR THE LEVERED FIRM

CHAPTER MISSION STATEMENT

The purpose of this chapter is to integrate the firm's investment decision with its financing decision. Earlier treatment of capital budgeting assumed that projects were all equity financed. Now, the benefits and costs of debt financing are incorporated into our net present value calculations. There are three basic approaches. The adjusted present value approach retains the procedure of evaluating projects as if they were all equity financing, but now adds the value effects of the financing arrangements, e.g., interest tax shield, issue costs, subsidized loans, etc. The flow-to-equity approach focuses on the cash flow that accrues to the equity holders after interest and taxes are paid. In this approach, the present value of these equity cash flows is compared to the initial equity investment. The weighted average cost of capital approach adjusts the discount rate to reflect the after-tax cost of debt. The WACC is then used to discount the unlevered cash flows. The chapter also discusses the effect that the debt tax shield has on a firm's beta. Finally, an appendix illustrates the APV approach using the RJR Nabisco leverage buy-out.

The key concepts presented in the chapter are outlined below.

- ◆Adjusted-present value approach
- ◆Flow-to-equity approach
- ◆Weighted average cost of capital approach
- ◆Comparisons of the three approaches
  - ●debt levels versus debt ratios
  - ●financing side effects
- ◆Non-scale enhancing projects
- ◆Side effects
  - ●issue costs
  - ●subsidized financing
- ◆Beta and leverage
  - ●unlevered beta

CONCEPT QUESTIONS

1. The _____ approach is defined as the net present value of a project as if it were all equity financed plus the present value of the financing side effects.

2. Four financing side effects that might affect the value of a project are _____, _____, _____, and _____.

3. The most important financing side effect is the _____.

4. The _____ approach discounts the cash flow from the project going to shareholders at the levered cost of equity.

5. To calculate cash flow to equity holders you subtract _____ and _____ from the unlevered cash flow.

6. If a firm uses both debt and equity financing, then the cost of capital for the firm is called the _____.

7. The weighted average cost of capital approach discounts _____ cash flows.

8. The WACC formula uses the _____ cost of debt.

9. The weights in the WACC are based on _____ values of debt and equity.

10. The FTE and WACC approaches are recommended if the firm's _____ remains constant.

11. The APV approach is recommended if the firm's _____ remains constant or is known.

12. The correct unlevered rate on equity, r_o, is difficult to determine if the project is not _____.

13. Two additional effects of debt are _____ and _____.

14. Flotation costs are typically stated as a percentage of the _____.

15. Cash flows from a subsidized loan are discounted at the _____ and not the _____.

16. In the presence of corporate taxes, beta for an unlevered firm is _____ the equity beta for a levered firm.

17. Leverage increases the equity beta less rapidly under corporate taxes because of the _____.

18. Formulas relating beta and leverage usually, for convenience, assume that the beta of debt equals _____.

ANSWERS TO CONCEPT TEST

1. adjusted present value (APV)
2. tax subsidy; issue costs; cost of financial distress; subsidized financing
3. tax subsidy to debt
4. flow-to-equity (FTE)
5. interest; principal payments
6. weighted average cost of capital
7. unlevered
8. after-tax
9. market
10. debt-to-value ratio
11. level of debt
12. scale enhancing
13. flotation costs; non-market rate financing
14. gross proceeds
15. market rate; subsidized rate
16. less than
17. riskless tax shield
18. zero

PROBLEMS

Use the following information for Problems 1-16.

Oswego Corporation is a major producer of farm equipment. Oswego stock currently sells for $36 per share; there are 25 million shares outstanding. Oswego also has perpetual debt outstanding with an aggregate market value of $600 million and a yield of 6%. Assume that the CAPM applies. The risk free rate is 6%, and the market risk premium is 8%. Oswego's stock has a beta of 1.75. The corporate tax rate is 35%.

Problem 1

What is the cost of equity for Oswego?

Problem 2

Oswego is considering a scale-enhancing project. What discount rate should Oswego use in evaluating this project?

Problem 3

The project under consideration by Oswego requires an outlay of $1.5 million and will generate after tax cash flow $280,000 per year forever. Oswego will maintain its current debt ratio while financing the project. What is the project's net present value?

Problem 4

Suppose that Oswego decides to use the APV approach to analyze the capital budgeting project. Assume for the moment that the tax rate equals zero, what is the value of beta for Oswego if the firm was financed entirely with equity, i.e., what is the unlevered beta?

Problem 5

Now assume that the corporate tax rate is 35%, what is Oswego's unlevered beta?

Problem 6

Calculate the cost of equity capital for Oswego assuming that the firm is all equity financed.

Problem 7

Calculate the net present value of the project described in Problem 3 assuming, initially, that the project is all equity financed.

Problem 8

What does the all-equity NPV calculated in Problem 7 suggest about the value of the interest tax shield imbedded in the NPV found using the WACC in Problem 3?

Problem 9

Oswego finances the project with a mixture of debt and equity designed to keep the firm's debt ratio constant. The firm issue 6% perpetual debt equal to 40% of the project's value. How much debt is issued?

Problem 10

Calculate the present value of the interest tax shield assuming Oswego borrows 40% of the project's value.

Problem 11

Calculate the project's adjusted net present value using the results from Problems 7 and 10. Compare this value with the results of Problem 3.

Problem 12

Oswego is considering expanding into the barn building industry. Seneca Corporation is a construction operation that is similar to the one proposed by Oswego. Seneca has a required return on equity of 17% and a target debt ratio of 30%. Assume that Oswego's expansion into the barn building industry will be financed entirely with equity. What value of beta would Oswego use in evaluating this expansion?

Problem 13

Use the beta value from Problem 12 to determine the appropriate value of beta for Oswego to use in evaluating its expansion into the construction business.

Problem 14

Calculate the discount rate Oswego should use in its evaluation of the proposed construction operation.

Problem 15

If Oswego enters the construction business, it will have to raise $300 million (ignoring issue costs) to finance the operation. The present value of the future cash flows has been estimated at $340 million. Assuming that Oswego proceeds with the proposal and that its debt-to-equity ratio will not change, calculate Oswego's equity beta after the investment.

Problem 16

Suppose that Oswego can borrow $120 million of the $300 million required for entry into the construction business. The interest rate is 6% and flotation costs are 1% of gross proceeds. Calculate the net present value of the flotation costs.

Problem 17

The Sabine Corporation has 1.6 million shares outstanding with a current price of $25 per share. The firm also has $20 million face value long term debt and $6 million face value short term debt outstanding. The long term debt matures in 19 years, has a 10% coupon, and is presently priced at $1,089.50 per bond. The short term debt, meanwhile, matures in three years, has an 8% coupon, and each bond is priced at $1,053.46. When the debt matures, new similar maturity debt will be issued in such amounts to maintain the same proportions of debt-to-value. The firm pays a $5.00 dividend per share, and this is not expected to change in the foreseeable future. The tax rate is 34%. Calculate Sabine's weighted average cost of capital.

Problem 18

Using the information in Problem 17, calculate Sabine's unlevered cost of equity, r_o. Assume MM Proposition II with taxes applies.

Use the following information to answer Problems 19-22.

The Succotash Company is thinking of acquiring another company as a scale-expansion project. The target firm has a market value debt-to-equity ratio of 1.0, an equity beta of 1.50, and EBIT of $3,943,900 per year. Succotash's capital structure is 70% equity and 30% debt, and if it acquires the target firm, will keep the debt ratio at 30%. The risk free rate is 8%, the market risk premium is 8.5%, the tax rate is 34%. Assume that all debt is risk free and that both firms are no-growth firms.

Problem 19

What is the value of the target firm's debt and equity?

Problem 20

What is the target firm's unlevered beta and unlevered cost of equity?

Problem 21

What discount rate should Succotash use to calculate the NPV of this acquisition?

Problem 22

What is the most that Succotash should pay for the target firm?

Problem 23

Sawtooth Machinery is considering a 4-year project to manufacture a new line of chainsaws. The project requires an investment of $760,000 and will generate $380 per year earnings before interest, taxes, depreciation, and amortization (EBITDA). The investment will be depreciated straight line to zero value over four years. Sawtooth maintains a debt ratio of 40%, has a cost of levered equity of 20.00%, and a tax rate of 35%. Sawtooth will borrow 40% of the project value at 6% and will pay down the debt in a way that maintains a 40% debt ratio. Calculate the net present value of this project.

Problem 24

Calculate the net present value of Sawtooth Machinery's project using both the flow-to-equity (FTE) approach.

SOLUTIONS

Solution 1

The cost of equity can be determined from the security market line (SML).

$$E(R) = r_s = r_f + \beta[E(R_m) - r_f]$$

$$= 6\% + 1.75(8\%) = 20.0\%$$

Solution 2

The discount rate that Oswego should use depends on the firm's capital structure policy. We'll assume that the firm intends to maintain a constant debt-to-value ratio. With B/V constant, then the WACC is appropriate. To determine the appropriate weights, we need to know the value of equity and the total value of the firm. The value of equity is 25 million shares × $36 per share or $900 million. Since the Oswego's debt is valued at $600 million, the firm's value is $900 + $600 = $1,500 million = $1.5 billion. The debt-to-value ratio is $600/$1,500 = .40 or 40%. Thus, the WACC is:

$$WACC = (B/V) r_B (1 - T_c) + (S/V) r_s$$

$$= (.40) 6\% (.65) + (.60)(20\%) = 13.56\%$$

Solution 3

The net present value (NPV) of this project is found using the WACC to discount the perpetual after-tax cash flows

210   **Valuation and Capital Budgeting**

$$NPV = -\$1,500,000 + \frac{\$280,000}{.1356}$$
$$= \$564,896.76$$

Solution 4

If the corporate tax rate is zero, and Oswego's debt has a beta equal to zero (since it has the same yield as the risk free rate), then the unlevered beta is:

$$\beta_U = [S/(S+B)]\ \beta_{equity}$$

$$= [\$900/\$1,500]\ 1.75 = 1.050.$$

Note: Technically the value of S should be different without taxes since the $900 value for S includes the interest tax shield. But we can assume that S/V remains at .70 even without taxes.

Solution 5

Now assuming a tax rate of 35% and a debt beta of zero, then

$$\beta_U = [S/(S + (1 - T_c)B)]\ \beta_{equity}$$

$$= [\$900/(\$900 + (.65)\$600)]\ 1.75 = 1.22093.$$

Beta is calculated to five decimal places to avoid rounding error in later calculations. Note that the unlevered beta is higher here than in Problem 4. This follows because with taxes the equity beta incorporates the risk free interest tax shield. Thus, by holding the equity beta constant at 1.75, the unlevered beta must be higher in the with-tax case.

Solution 6

The cost of unlevered equity is determined from the SML using beta from Problem 5.

$$E(R) = r_0 = r_f + \beta[E(R_m) - r_f]$$

$$= 6\% + 1.22093(8\%) = 15.76744\%$$

Solution 7

The after-tax cash flow is $280,000 per year forever. The present value at the all equity rate of 15.76774% is $1,775,811. Thus, NPV equals

$$NPV = -\$1,500,000 + \frac{\$280,000}{.1576774}$$

$$= \$275,811$$

Solution 8

Comparing the all equity NPV of $275,811 from Problem 7 to the $564,897 NPV found in Solution 3 suggests that, given a constant debt ratio, the value of the interest tax shield is $289,086 (=$564,897 − $275,811).

Solution 9

The total amount borrowed is 40% of the project's value. Thus,

$$B = .4 \times V_L = .4 \times [V_U + T_cB]$$

$$B = .4 \times V_U /(1 - .4 \times T_c).$$

From Problem 7 $V_U = \$1,775,811$, thus B = $825,959.

Solution 10

The present value of the interest tax shield is merely $T_c \times B$

$$PV \text{ (interest tax shield)} = .35 \times \$825,959 = \$289,086.$$

This is equal to the value suggested in Solution 8. An alternate way to find the present value of the interest tax shield is to find the NPV of the loan. Using exact values, B = $825,958.70, pre-tax interest is $49,557.52, after-tax interest is $32,212.39, the present value of after-tax interest is $536,873.16. Thus, the NPV of the loan is $825,958.70 − $536,873.16 = $289,085.54.

Solution 11

The adjusted present value of the project is:

$$APV = \text{all equity NPV} + \text{NPV of loan}$$

$$APV = \$275,811 + \$289,086 = \$564,897.$$

This value agrees with the NPV found in Problem 3.

Solution 12

Seneca is a 'pure play' firm, and we can use information about Seneca to determine the appropriate cost of capital for Oswego's construction business. We first determine the equity beta for Seneca. Seneca's required return on equity is 17%, the risk-free rate is 6%, and the market risk premium is 8%. Therefore, using the SML from Problem 1, and solving for ß, the equity beta is $[(.17 - .06)/.08] = 1.375$. Since this value of beta applies to Seneca, with a debt ratio of .30, we next determine $ß_U$ using the following:

$$ß_U = [S/(S + (1 - T_c)B)] \, ß_{equity}$$

$$= [\$.70/(\$.70 + (.65)\$.30)] \, 1.375 = 0.6039.$$

Where a debt ratio of .30 implies that for every $.30 in debt, Seneca has $.70 in equity.

Solution 13

The appropriate value of beta reflects both the risk of the construction business, as indicated by the beta value from Problem 12, and Oswego's capital structure. Solve for $ß_{equity}$ in the following equation:

$$ß_U = [S/(S + (1 - T_c)B)] \, ß_{equity}$$

where S = $900, B = $600, T_c = 35 and $ß_U$ = .6039. The value of $ß_{equity}$ is .8656.

Solution 14

Using $ß_{equity}$ = .8656 from Problem 13 and the SML from Problem 1, the cost of equity is 12.925%. The appropriate WACC for Oswego to use is:

$$WACC = .40(6\%)(.65) + .60(12.925\%) = 9.315\%$$

Solution 15

The new equity beta will be a weighted average of the old equity beta and the equity beta of the construction project. Before the project, Oswego's equity was worth $900 million. The value of the new project is $340 million, so the equity will increase by 60% of the $340 million, or $204 million. The total equity value will be ($900 million + $204 million) = $1.104 billion. The beta on the original $900 million is 1.75 and, on the new equity beta is .8656. The weighted average beta is:

$$(\$900/\$1,104)1.75 + (\$204/\$1,104).8656 = 1.5866$$

Solution 16

The total amount borrowed is $120,000,000/.99 = $121,212,121 and flotation costs are $1,212,121. These costs are amortized over the five-year life of the loan. The tax shield generated by these amortized costs produces a net cash flow of $[(\$1,212,121/5)(.35)] = \$84,848$ per year for five years. These payments are considered essentially risk free. The present value of this annuity at the 6% risk free rate is $357,411. The net present value of the flotation costs is $1,212,121 - $357,411 = $854,710.

Solution 17

The firm's WACC is simply a weighted average of the after-tax market determined cost of each source of capital, where the weights are based on market values. First, we must determine the cost of each source of capital. The cost of equity is the cash dividend divided by the current stock price: $r_s = \$5.00/\$25.00 = .20$ or 20%. The cost of long term debt is its yield to maturity: $r_{ltd} = 9.0\%$, the cost of the short term debt is its yield to maturity: $r_{std} = 6.0\%$. Next, we must determine the market value weights. The firm's capital structure in market value terms is:

Security	Book value	Market value	Weight
Stock ($1 par) (s)	$ 1,600,000	$40,000,000	.5873
Long term debt (ltd)	20,000,000	21,790,000	.3199
Short term debt (std)	6,000,000	6,320,000	.0928
Total	$27,600,000	$68,110,800	1.0000

Sabine's weighted average cost of capital is:

$$WACC = .5873(20\%) + .3199(9\%)(.66) + .0928(6\%)(.66) = 14.01\%$$

Solution 18

MM Proposition II with taxes is

$$r_s = r_o + B/S\ (r_o - r_B)(1 - T_c)$$

For Sabine, B is the total amount of debt $21,790,000 + $6,320,800 = $28,110,800, and S is $40 million. The rate on debt, r_B, is a weighted average of the rates on long term and short term debt:

$$r_B = (\$21.790/\$28.111)(9\%) + (\$6.321/\$28,111)(6\%) = 8.33\%$$

Substituting and solving for r_o, we find

$$20\% = r_o + (.7027)\ (r_o - 8.33\%)(1 - .34)$$

$$r_o = 16.30\%$$

Solution 19

The total value of the target firm can be found by discounting the after-tax earnings at the weighted average cost of capital. Then, given the debt-to-equity ratio, we can find the value of the firm's debt and the firm's equity. The firm's cost of equity is determined from the CAPM, $r_s = 8\% + 1.5(8.5\%) = 20.75\%$. The firm's debt is risk free, thus $r_B = 8\%$. The WACC is:

$$WACC = .5(8\%)(1 - .34) + .5(20.75\%) = 13.015\%$$

The target firm's value is

$$V = \$3,943,900(1 - .34)/.13015 = \$20 \text{ million}$$

Thus, given $D/S = 1$, then $D = \$10$ million and $S = \$10$ million.

Solution 20

The firm's unlevered beta and equity beta are related by the following expression (assuming risk free debt):

$$\beta_U = [S/(S + (1 - T_c)B)] \beta_{equity}$$

$$= [\$10/(\$10 + (.66)\$10)]1.50 = .9036$$

Then,

$$r_o = 8\% + .9036(8.5\%) = 15.68\%$$

Also, note that we can find r_o from MM Proposition II with taxes:

$$r_s = r_o + B/S (r_o - r_B)(1 - T_c)$$

$$20.75\% = r_o + 1.0(r_o - 8\%)(.66)$$

$$r_o = 15.68\%$$

Solution 21

The appropriate discount rate should reflect the risk of the project, or target firm in this case. Since both Succotash and the target firm are in the same line of business, the business risk of both firms is the same. Succotash could use the unlevered cost of equity calculated in Problem 20 with the APV method and add the present value of the interest tax shield and any other financing side effects. Succotash could also discount the target's cash flow at a WACC that reflects Succotash's capital structure. In this approach, the equity beta reflecting Succotash's financial risk is:

$$\beta_U = [S/(S + (1 - T_c)B)]\ \beta_{equity}$$

$$.9036 = [\$7/(\$7 + (.66)\$3)]\beta_{equity}$$

$$\beta_{equity} = 1.16$$

The cost of equity is

$$r_s = 8\% + 1.16(8.5\%) = 17.86\%$$

The weighted average cost of capital is

$$WACC = .3(8\%)(.66) + .7(17.86\%) = 14.09\%$$

Succotash could use this rate to discount the after-tax earnings.

Solution 22

The most that Succotash should pay is the price that makes NPV = 0. Discounting the target firm's cash flow at the WACC from Problem 21, we find

$$V \text{ (to Succotash)} = \$3,943,900(1 - .34)/.1409$$

$$= \$18.474 \text{ million.}$$

Note that with Succotash's capital structure the value of the target to Succotash is less than the current market value ($20 million) of the target firm.

Solution 23

Because Sawtooth's maintains a constant debt ratio, the project's NPV can be found most easily using the WACC:

$$WACC = .40 \times 6\% \times (1 - .35) + .60 \times 20\% = 13.56\%.$$

Depreciation is $760,000/4 = $190,000 per year, and the depreciation tax shield is $66,500 per year. After tax cash flow is

$$CF = \$380,000(1 - .35) + \$66,500 = \$313,500.$$

The present value of this cash flow at the WACC is $921,750, and NPV = $161,750.

Solution 24

The FTE approach to finding net present value is shown in the following table.

Year	0	1	2	3	4
Investment	−760,000				
EBITDA		380,000	380,000	380,000	380,000
Depreciation		190,000	190,000	190,000	190,000
Earnings before tax		190,000	190,000	190,000	190,000
Tax (35%)		66,500	66,500	66,500	66,500
Earnings after tax		123,500	123,500	123,500	123,500
Cash flow		313,500	313,500	313,500	313,500
Value (using wacc)	921,750	733,239	519,167	276,066	0
Debt (.4×Value)	368,700	293,296	207,667	110,426	0
Interest (6%)		22,122	17,598	12,460	6,626
Interest tax shield		7,743	6,159	4,361	2,319
Repayment of principal		75,404	85,629	97,240	110,426
Cash flow to equity	−553,050	223,716	216,432	208,161	198,767

The value of the project at any time is the present value of the future cash flows discounted at WACC=13.56%. For example, the value at time 2 is

$$V_2 = \frac{\$313,500}{(1.1356)} + \frac{\$313,500}{(1.1356)^2}$$
$$= \$519,167$$

The cash flow to equity for years 1 to 4 equals

fte = cash flow − interest + interest tax shield − repayment of principal.

For year zero, the flow to equity equals value minus debt ($553,050 = $921,750 − $368,700). This is what a new investor would have to pay to acquire all the equity. The internal rate of return of these cash flows equals 20%, the cost of levered equity. Note: although not needed for this problem, the correct cost of unlevered equity is 14.4671%.

CHAPTER 18

DIVIDEND POLICY:
WHY DOES IT MATTER?

CHAPTER MISSION STATEMENT

The purpose of Chapter 18 is to review the mechanics of paying dividends and to discuss the issues surrounding the affect dividend policy has on firm value. Dividend policy is irrelevant, as shown by Miller and Modigliani, with perfect capital markets. With personal taxes and transaction costs, dividend policy may be important. Conflicting empirical evidence leaves the issue unresolved. Dividends, as opposed to dividend policy, are important. An appendix discusses stock dividends and stock splits.

The key concepts discussed in this chapter are outlined below.

- ♦ Types of dividends
  - • regular cash dividends
  - • stock dividends
  - • stock splits
- ♦ Cash Dividends
  - • declaration date
  - • date of record
  - • ex-dividend date
  - • date of payment
- ♦ Irrelevance of dividend policy
  - • MM's proposition
  - • perfect capital markets
  - • homogeneous expectations
  - • fixed investment policy
  - • homemade dividends
- ♦ Relevance of dividend policy
  - • taxes, personal and corporate
  - • issue costs
  - • opportunity costs
- ♦ Expected returns and dividends
- ♦ Real-world factors
  - • taxes
  - • information effects
  - • tax clienteles

CONCEPT TEST

1. Strictly speaking, a cash payment to shareholders which is not paid out of current earnings is called a _____.

2. Most public companies pay _____ dividends _____ times a year.

3.   A dividend paid in the form of additional shares of stock is called a _____.

4.   If a distribution of shares of stock increases the number of outstanding shares by less than _____ it is called a _____.

5.   Instead of paying cash dividends, a corporation can distribute money to its shareholders by means of a stock _____.

6.   A cash dividend expressed as dollars per share is called _____.

7.   A cash dividend expressed as a percentage of market price is called the _____.

8.   A cash dividend expressed as a percentage of earnings per share is called the _____.

9.   The mechanics of dividend payment involve the following number of dates: _____.

10. Chronologically, the first significant date in the process of paying a dividend is the _____ date.

11. The second significant date in the process of paying a dividend is the _____ date.

12. The third significant date in the process of paying a dividend is the _____ date.

13. The last significant date in the process of paying a dividend is the _____ date.

14. A dividend becomes a liability of the firm on the _____ date.

15. Suppose you own a share of stock. If you sell it on the ex-dividend date, will you receive the dividend payment?

16. If you buy a share of stock two days before the date of record, will you receive the dividend payment?

17. Typically, a stock goes _____ two days before the record date.

18. If you buy a share of stock before the record date and you receive the dividend, the stock must have been selling _____.

19. A stock is selling for $100 at the close of trading on the last with-dividend date. The dividend is $2. If there are no taxes, then the opening price the next day will be about _____.

20. In the previous question, suppose that there are no capital gains taxes and that dividends are taxed at a 30% rate. The opening price would be about $_____.

21. A stockholder who is dissatisfied with the dividend policy of the firm can, by buying or selling shares of stock, substitute _____ dividends for the firm's dividends.

22. True or false: Dividends may be irrelevant?

23. True or false: Dividend policy may be irrelevant

24. A firm should consider immediately paying out extra cash to stockholders if the corporate tax rate is _____ than stockholder tax rates.

25. _____ are an example of a tax-paying group that may have a preference for high dividends.

26. The _____ associated with new equity sales result in a preference for a low dividend payout.

27. Two factors which are often cited as arguments favoring a high dividend payout are the desire that shareholders may have for _____ and the _____.

28. Stock prices often react to announcements of changes in dividends. This reaction may stem from the _____ of dividends.

29. The _____ argument states that different groups of investors have, different preferences regarding the level of dividends. One natural basis for the existence of such groups is differing _____.

ANSWERS TO CONCEPT TEST

1. distribution
2. regular cash; four
3. stock dividend
4. 25; stock dividend
5. repurchase
6. dividends per share
7. dividend yield
8. dividend payout
9. four
10. declaration
11. ex-dividend
12. record
13. payment
14 declaration
15. yes
16. no
17. ex-dividend
18. cum dividend
19. $98
20. $98.60
21. homemade
22. false
23. true
24. higher
25. corporations
26. flotation costs
27. current income; resolution of uncertainty
28. information content
29. clientele effect; tax rates

PROBLEMS

Problem 1

On February 20, 1998 the Kellogg Corporation declared a regular quarterly cash dividend of $ .225 per share payable on March 13, 1998 to shareholders of record on Monday March 2, 1998. What is the last day you could by Kellogg's stock and still receive this dividend?

Use the following information to solve Problems 2-6.

The market value balance sheet for Springbok Corporation is shown below. There are 250 shares outstanding.

Assets		Liabilities and owners' equity	
Cash	$500		
Fixed assets	2,000	Equity	$2,500

Problem 2

Springbok has declared a dividend of $.80 per share. The stock goes ex-dividend tomorrow. What is the price of the stock today? What will its price be tomorrow? (Assume no taxes)

Problem 3

Springbok, instead, has declared a 12% stock dividend. The stock goes ex-dividend tomorrow. What will the ex-dividend price be?

Problem 4

Instead of paying a cash dividend, Springbok has announced that it is going to repurchase $200 of stock. What is the effect of this repurchase? Ignoring taxes, show how this repurchase is effectively the same as a $.80 dividend per share.

Problem 5

Suppose that capital gains are not taxed, but dividends are taxed at a 40% rate, and that taxes are withheld at the time the dividend is paid. If Springbok is going to pay an $.80 dividend per share, what is the ex-dividend price?

Problem 6

Suppose that, in Problem 5, capital gains are taxed at a 20% rate. What is the ex-dividend price?

Problem 7

Spume Company is in the same risk class as Froth & Company. Spume has an expected dividend yield over the next year of 10%, while Froth pays no dividends. The required return on Froth & Company is 20%. Capital gains are not taxed, but dividends are taxed at 40%. What is the required pre-tax return on Spume?

Problem 8

Now suppose that Spume's dividend next year will be $10, and after paying the dividend the stock will sell for $100. Froth's current stock price is $50 per share, and shareholders expect next year's price will be $60. Assume that dividends are taxed at 40%, as in Problem 7, and capital gains are taxed at 20%. What is Spume's current stock price?

Problem 9

You own 20 shares of stock in Gann Aircraft. You are certain that you will receive a $.50 per share dividend at date 1. At date 2, Gann will pay a liquidating dividend of $13.80 per share. The required return is 20%. Assuming no taxes, what is the price per share of the common stock? Suppose that you would rather have equal dividends in each of the next two years; how can you accomplish this by using homemade dividends?

Problem 10

Try this one on your own. Suppose that, in Problem 9, you wanted only $5 at date 1. What is your homemade dividend at date 2?

Problem 11

The Spruce Company's stock is selling for $100 per share. Next year the firm expects to pay a $5.00 dividend, which will increase by 10% per year thereafter. The required return on Spruce stock is 15%. Calculate the cum-dividend and ex-dividend stock prices over the next three years.

Problem 12

Using the information in Problem 11, and assuming that dividends are taxed at 20%, recalculate the cum-dividend and ex-dividend prices. Assume that capital gains escape taxes.

Problem 13

The Spruce Company has some extra cash on hand and decides to invest it in some utility company preferred stock. Consolidated Edison has $5.00 preferred currently selling at $67.50 per share. If Spruce buys some of this stock, what will be the after tax return? Spruce's tax rate is 34%.

SOLUTIONS

Solution 1

Given the regular three-day settlement plan effective since June 7, 1995, the stock will go ex-dividend two business days prior to the record date. Thus, the ex-day is the record date March 2 less two business days. Since March 2, 1998 is a Monday, the ex-day is Thursday February 26, 1998. To be on the record books and receive the dividend on March 13th you must buy the stock no later than Wednesday February 25, 1998, three business days before the record date.

Solution 2

Since the balance sheet shows market values, the stock is worth $10 per share today (cum dividend). The ex-dividend price will be $9.20. Notice that once the dividend is paid, Springbok has $200 less cash, so the total equity is worth $2,300, or $9.20 per share.

Solution 3

After the stock dividend is paid, 280 shares will be outstanding. The total value of the shares is still $2,500; that is, the total market value of the equity is unchanged. Therefore, the per share value is ($2,500/280) = $8.93. Notice that this is not 12% less than the old price; rather the old price is 112% of the new price: [$8.93(1.12)] = $10.

Solution 4

Springbok will purchase 20 shares, leaving 230 outstanding. The total equity value will be $2,300, so that the market price is still $10 per share.

Consider an investor who owns 20 shares. With the cash dividend, this investor receives $16 in cash and has 20 shares (each worth $9.20), for a total value of $200. Using the $16, the investor could purchase 1.739 more shares and have 21.739 shares worth $9.20 each. With the repurchase, the investor has 20 shares worth $10 each, if she does not sell any shares. Alternatively, if she wanted cash, she could just sell 1.6 shares for $10 each. As a result, she would have 18.4 shares (each worth $10), and $16 in cash, for a total of $200 again.

Solution 5

The price will decrease by the after-tax amount of the dividend, or [$.80(1 − .40)] = $.48. The ex-dividend price will be $9.52.

Solution 6

This problem is somewhat more difficult. Consider the following scenario: suppose you buy a share just before the stock goes ex-dividend, and then sell immediately thereafter. You will have an after-tax dividend of $.48 and a capital loss of D, the decline in the stock price. Since this loss is tax deductible, your after-tax loss is [D × (1 − .20)]. You will be indifferent with regard to buying the share with the dividend only if $.48 = D × (.80)]. In this scenario, the price decrease will be ($.48/.80) = $.60.

In reality, capital gains are not taxed until the gain (or loss) is realized, so the size of the price decline would be much more difficult to determine; however, it would probably be less than the amount of the dividend but more than the after-tax value of the dividend.

Solution 7

The 10% dividend yield is equivalent to a 6% after-tax return. Since the total expected after-tax return is 20%, the expected capital gain is 14%. The after-tax return is thus 'grossed up' to a pre-tax return of (10% + 14%) = 24%.

Solution 8

Since Spume and Froth are in the same risk class, they must provide the same after-tax return. The after tax return on Froth is [$60 − $50](1 − .20) = $8.00 or 16%. Spume must provide the same after tax return. Thus,

$$.16 = (\text{After-tax div} + \text{after-tax gain})/P_0$$

$$= [\$10(1 − .4) + (\$100 − P_0)(1 − .20)]/P_0$$

Solving for the current price,

$$P_0 = \$89.58$$

Solution 9

The value of your stock is the present value of the dividends, discounted at 20%, or $10 per share. Therefore, the total value of your position is $200. An annuity of $130.91 per year for two years has the same present value. At date 1, your stock will be worth the present value of the liquidating dividend, or $11.50 per share. You will receive $10 in total dividends at date 1. You will have to sell $130.91 − $10.00 = $120.91 worth of stock, or ($120.91/11.5) = 10.514 shares, leaving you with 9.486 shares. At the end of the second year, you will receive [9.486($13.80)] in dividends, for a total of $130.91, thereby accomplishing your goal.

Solution 10

Your liquidating dividend will be $282, which is $6 greater than it would have been.

Solution 11

The return on Spruce stock is 15% per year of which 5% represents dividend yield and 10% is capital gains. The value of the stock will grow 15% in a given year, i.e., the cum-dividend price in a given year will be 15% higher than the ex-dividend price the prior year. Over time, the ex-dividend price will grow 10% per year. The following table shows the prices:

Year	Cum-price	Div	Ex-price
0			$100.00
1	$115.00	$5.00	110.00
2	126.50	5.50	121.00
3	139.15	6.05	133.10

Notice that the dividend yield is always 5%, e.g., consider buying the stock at year 2 for $121.00 and receiving a dividend of $6.05 the following year. The dividend yield is $6.05/$121.00 = .05 or 5%. Note also that the ex-prices grow at 10% per year, while the cum-prices grow at neither 10% nor 15%.

Solution 12

With personal taxes on dividends, and other factors held constant, the stock price decline on the ex-day will be the after-tax dividend rather than the pre-tax dividend. For example, at year 1, the after tax dividend is $5.00(1 − .20) = $4.00. Thus, the ex-dividend price will be $111.00. The prices are shown in the following table.

Year	Cum-price	Dividend Pre-tax	Post-tax	Ex-price
0				$100.00
1	$115.00	$5.00	$4.00	111.00
2	127.65	5.55	4.44	123.21
3	141.69	6.16	4.93	136.76

Note that we forced the after tax return to be 15%. This return now consists of 4% dividend return after-tax plus 11% capital gains. The pre-tax return is 16%.

Solution 13

The pretax yield is $5.00/$67.50 = .074 or 7.4%. Since 70% of intercorporate dividends are excluded from taxes, Spruce's after-tax dollar return is $5.00[1 − (.3)(.34)] = $4.49; the percentage return is $4.49/$67.50 = .0665 or 6.65%.

APPENDIX 18A

STOCK DIVIDENDS AND STOCK SPLITS

The appendix provides examples of stock dividends and stock splits and discusses the benefits and costs of these strategies. In principle, stock dividends or splits should not affect firm value. Conventional wisdom, however, suggests that stock dividends or splits are beneficial because they keep stock prices within a popular trading range. But evidence suggests that trading costs increase after stock splits.

The key concepts discussed in the appendix are presented below.

♦Stock dividend
♦Stock split
♦Popular trading range
♦Post-split trading costs
♦Reverse split

CONCEPT TEST

1.   Keeping stock prices within a proper trading range allows small investors to buy stock in _____.

2.   The argument in favor of a proper trading range is weakened by the presence of _____ investors such as _____.

3.   A counter argument to the notion of a proper trading range is that a stock split reduces _____ by increasing _____.

4.   Stock splits are likely to increase two types of transaction costs: _____ and _____.

ANSWERS TO CONCEPT TEST

1.   round lots   3.   liquidity; transaction costs
2.   institutional; mutual funds   4.   brokerage fees; bid-ask spreads

CHAPTER 19

ISSUING EQUITY SECURITIES TO THE PUBLIC

CHAPTER MISSION STATEMENT

The purpose of Chapter 19 is to provide a brief overview of how firms issue securities to the public. The chapter addresses the institutional details of a cash offering, a rights offering, and an initial public offering. The costs of the issuance process are discussed. The mechanics of a rights offering are detailed. The new issue puzzle is discussed. Finally, the chapter describes the shelf registration process and venture capital.

The key concepts presented in Chapter 19 are outlined below.

- ◆The public issue
  - ●initial public offering
  - ●seasoned new issue
- ◆Alternative issue methods
  - ●cash offer
  - ●rights offer
- ◆Investment banker arrangements
  - ●firm commitment
  - ●best efforts
  - ●competitive offer
  - ●negotiated offer
- ◆Costs of new issues
  - ●underwriting discount
  - ●direct expenses
  - ●indirect expenses
  - ●abnormal returns
  - ●underpricing
  - ●green-shoe-option
- ◆New-issues puzzle
- ◆Shelf registration
- ◆Private equity market

CONCEPT TEST

1. The _____ administers federal laws and regulations concerning the public sale of securities.

2. With two exceptions, a _____ is required for all public issues.

3. The first exception applies to loans that mature within _____.

4. The second exception to the requirement described in Question 2 involves issues of _____ in size. This is called the _____ exemption, and it is governed by _____.

5. The two kinds of public issues are _____ and _____.

6. A public issue sold to existing shareholders is a _____.

7. The first public equity issue by a corporation is called an _____ or _____.

8. A _____ is a new issue by a corporation that has previously issued securities.

9. In order to spread the risk of a new issue, underwriters frequently form underwriting _____.

10. The basic compensation in an underwritten cash offer is called the underwriting _____.

11. A _____ is an advertisement listing the names of the underwriters of a new issue.

12. If an underwriter purchases the entire issue from the firm at a fixed price, then this is called _____ underwriting.

13. If the underwriter promises only to attempt to sell the issue, then this is called _____ underwriting.

14. A _____ allows the underwriter to purchase additional shares at the initial price for a period of time subsequent to the offering date.

15. In an auction, it is sometimes remarked that the highest bidder is the one who made the biggest mistake. This is an example of a _____.

16. Following an announcement of a new issue, the value of existing shares is observed to _____ on average.

17. On average, new issue prices appear to be too _____. This tendency is called _____.

18. If a firm's articles of incorporation contain a _____ then a new issue of common stock must first be offered for sale to existing stockholders.

19. In a rights offer, the cost of a new share is called the _____ price.

20. In a rights offer, the ex-rights date is _____ trading days before the _____ date.

21. Prior to the ex-rights date, the shares are said to be selling _____ or _____.

22. After the ex-rights date, the shares are said to be selling _____.

23. If a rights issue is underwritten, the arrangement is usually _____ underwriting, for which the underwriter is paid a _____.

24. The value of one right is the difference between the _____ price and the _____ price.

25. In a rights offering, shareholders are usually given an _____ which enables them to buy additional shares if any are available.

26. The least expensive way to sell securities to the public is a _____.

27. The most common way in which securities are sold to the public is through an _____.

28. SEC _____ allows corporations to register securities that it reasonably expects to sell over the next _____ years. This is called _____.

29. Start up firms and firms in financial distress can raise capital in the _____.

30. Four sources of venture capital are _____, _____, _____, and _____.

ANSWERS TO CONCEPT TEST

1. Securities and Exchange Commission (SEC)
2. registration statement
3. nine months
4. less than $5.0 million; small-issues; Regulation A
5. general cash offer; rights offer
6. rights offer
7. initial public offer (IPO); unseasoned new issue
8. seasoned new issue
9. syndicates
10. spread
11. tombstone
12. fixed commitment
13. best efforts
14. green shoe option
15. winner's curse

16. decline
17. low; underpricing
18. preemptive right
19. subscription
20. two; holder-of-record
21. rights-on; cum rights
22. ex rights
23. standby; standby fee
24. rights-on; ex-rights
25. oversubscription privilege
26. pure rights offer
27. underwritten cash offer
28. Rule 415; two; shelf registration
29. private equity market
30. wealthy families; private partnerships and corporations; industrial or financial corporations; informal venture-capital market

PROBLEMS

Problem 1

Quahog Company has just floated an IPO. Under a fixed commitment agreement, Quahog received $10 for each of the 1 million shares sold. The initial offering price was $11 per share, and the stock rose to $14 per share in the first few minutes of trading. Quahog paid $60,000 in direct legal and other costs. Indirect costs were $40,000. What was the flotation cost as a percentage of funds raised?

Problem 2

Firms Atech and Btech have announced IPO's; each firm's stock will be sold for $10 per share. One of these issues is undervalued by $2, the other is overvalued by $1, but you do not know which is which (better informed investors, however, may know which is which). You plan to buy 100 shares of each firm's stock. If an issue is rationed, you will only get half your order. If you get 100 shares of each firm's stock, what is your profit? What profit do you get if the underpriced issue is rationed?

Problem 3

Circle Media Enterprises has announced a rights offer to raise $45 million for a new publishing project. The stock currently sells for $40 per share and there are 5.4 million shares outstanding. What is the maximum possible subscription price? What is the minimum possible subscription price?

Problem 4

Using the information from the previous question, suppose that Circle Media sets the subscription price at $10 per share. How many shares must be sold? How many rights are required in order to buy one share?

Problem 5

In the previous question, what is the ex-rights price? What is the value of a right?

Problem 6

In the previous question, demonstrate the fact that a shareholder with 100 shares, and no desire (or money) to buy additional shares, is not harmed by the rights offer.

Problem 7

Take another look at Problem 3. Suppose that Circle Media Enterprises had set the subscription price at $30. How many shares must be sold? How many rights are required in order to buy one new share?

Problem 8

Based on your answer to Problem 7, what is the ex-rights price? What is the value of one right?

Problem 9

Suppose that the Giant Sequoia Corporation wants to issue 1.0 million new shares in a seasoned equity offering. The firm contracts with Budget Investment Bank to handle the issue. The bank advises that to insure a successful offer, the offering price should be set 10% below the current market price of $100 per share. The firm has 10 million shares outstanding. If the offering price is set at $90, what will be the stock price after the issue of 1.0 million new shares?

Problem 10

Giant Sequoia Corporation decides to forego the underwritten seasoned equity offering and instead do a rights offering. Sequoia will set the subscription price at $80 per share and issue 1.0 million shares. How many rights will be require to buy one share?

Problem 11

What is the ex-rights price of Giant Sequoia's stock?

Problem 12

What is the value of a Giant Sequoia right?

Problem 13

Suppose that the Little Sequoia Company, an offshoot (spinoff) of the Giant Sequoia Corporation, decides to go public in an initial public offering (IPO). Gross proceeds of the issue will be $20 million = 1 million shares × $20 subscription price. Little Sequoia's investment banker, Bulge Bracket Investment Bankers, Ltd., advises that the underwriting spread will be 8% and other direct costs will be 4%. At the end of the first day's trading the stock closes at $22 per share. How much did the IPO cost Little Sequoia's owners? How much did the firm net?

SOLUTIONS

Solution 1

Quahog received $10 million. The underwriter spread was $1 million total. The direct and indirect costs were $100,000. The stock was underpriced by $3 per share, or $3 million total. Total costs were $4.1 million, so the flotation cost was 41% of the financing obtained.

Solution 2

If you are able to purchase all the shares for which you bid, you earn a profit of $100 (=$2×100−$1×100). However, if the undervalued issue is rationed while the overvalued issue is not rationed, you should expect to get 50 shares of the former issue. Your profit would be $0 (=$2×50−$1×100). This is the outcome you should expect if both informed and uninformed investors bid for the shares. Notice that, on average, these new issues are underpriced by 5% ($.50 per $10). The fact that you expect to make a zero profit illustrates the winner's curse.

Solution 3

In principle, the minimum subscription price could be arbitrarily small as long as it is not zero, so there is no minimum. This illustrates the fact that a rights offer cannot be underpriced. The maximum is $40, because the issue would not sell at a price higher than the current market value. In practice, a price of $40 would be too high because the market price could fall below this value during the offer and the issue would not sell.

Solution 4

At $10 per share, 4.5 million shares must be sold in order to raise $45 million. There are 5.4 million shares outstanding, so it will take (5.4/4.5) = 1.2 rights to buy one new share.

Solution 5

Someone who owned no Circle Media stock could buy 120 shares for $4,800 and then exercise the 120 rights to acquire 100 shares for $1,000. Thus, 220 shares can be purchased for $5,800, or $26.36 per share. The ex-rights price is $26.36, and the value of one right is ($40 – $26.36) = $13.64.

Solution 6

Before the rights offer, the 100 shares were worth $4,000. After the offer, they are worth $2,636. However, the 100 rights could be sold for $1,364, so the stockholder would have $2,636 worth of stock and $1,364 in cash from the sale of the rights, for a total of $4,000.

Solution 7

Circle Media must sell 1.5 million shares. Then 3.6 rights are required in order to buy one new share.

Solution 8

The ex-rights price is $37.83, so the value of one right is $2.17.

Solution 9

The post issue stock price will be the total value of the firm divided by the total number of shares outstanding. Total value of the firm is the initial value, 10 million shares times $100 per share = $1,000 million, plus the amount of funds raised, 1 million shares times $90 per share = $90 million, or $1,090 million. Total number of shares is the original 10 million plus the new 1 million shares or 11 million. Thus, the new value per share is $1,090/11 = $99.09 per share. Note that the initial shares are now worth $990.9 million, a loss of $9.1 million. What the existing shareholders lost, the new shareholders gained. New shareholders paid $90 million for shares worth $99.09 million.

Solution 10

Initially there are 10 million shares outstanding, so Giant Sequoia issues 10 million rights. To sell 1 million shares with 10 million rights, each right must be "worth" 1/10 share. Thus, 10 rights are needed to buy one share.

Solution 11

The ex-rights price, assuming all rights are exercised, is just the new total value of the firm divided by the new number of shares outstanding (similar to Problem 9). If all rights are exercised, there will be 1 million new shares and the firm will raise $80 million. The new, ex-rights, price is $1,080 million divided by 11 million shares or $98.18 per share. Note that unlike Problem 9, existing shareholder are not worse off even though the stock price fell from $100 to $98.18.

Solution 12

Since 10 rights allow you to buy $98.18 worth of stock for $80, the 10 rights must be worth $18.18. Thus, each right must be worth $1.82. Alternately, the difference between the old stock price of $100 and the new price of $98.18 must reflect the value of one right.

Solution 13

The cost of the IPO to Sequoia's owners consists of the underwriting fee (spread), other direct costs, and the underpricing. Underwriting fees are $20 million × .08 = $1.6 million. Other direct costs are $20 million × .04 = $.8 million. Underpricing results from selling stock worth $22 for $20, the cost is 1 million shares × $2 per share = $2 million. Thus, total costs are $1.6 + $.8 + $2.0 = $4.4 million. Net proceeds are $20 million – $1.6 million – $.8 million = $17.6 million.

CHAPTER 20

LONG TERM DEBT

CHAPTER MISSION STATEMENT

The purpose of Chapter 20 is to review the basic features of long-term debt and discuss the issue of bond refunding. The chapter describes the standard features of bonds which affect their value, such as security, sinking funds, protective covenants, and call provisions. Bond ratings are discussed, along with the emerging importance of high-yield, non-investment grade, debt. Finally, the chapter describes several unusual varieties of bonds.

The key concepts discussed in Chapter 20 are outlined below.

- ◆Bond basics
  - ●public issues
  - ●indenture
  - ●bond terminology
  - ●security
  - ●covenants
  - ●sinking fund
  - ●call provision
- ◆Bond refunding
  - ●zero sum game
  - ●refunding paradox
- ◆Bond ratings
  - ●investment grade
  - ●junk bonds
- ◆Bond types
  - ●floating rate
  - ●deep discount
  - ●income
- ◆Private placement

CONCEPT TEST

1. The _____ is the written agreement between the corporation and the trustee.

2. Bonds usually have a _____ value of _____.

3. Bond prices are quoted net of _____.

4. If the coupon interest payment is mailed directly to the owner, the bond must be in _____ form.

5. With a _____ bond, a coupon must be presented before an interest payment is made.

6.   If the pledged assets for a secured bond are securities, then these securities are called the _____.

7.   If the collateral for a secured bond is real property, then the bond is a _____ security.

8.   An unsecured bond is called a _____.

9.   A bond indenture contains _____ that limit the firm's activities.

10.   An indenture might prohibit the firm from merging with another firm. This is an example of a _____.

11.   An indenture might require that the firm supply audited financial statements every quarter. This is an example of a _____.

12.   A _____ is an account managed by the bond trustee for the purpose of repaying the bonds prior to maturity.

13.   An _____ mortgage permits the company to issue additional mortgage bonds on the specified property, while a _____ mortgage restricts the company's ability to do so.

14.   A _____ gives the corporation the option of repurchasing or _____ an entire bond issue at a stated price.

15.   If the option described in Question 14 is inactive for the first ten years, then this is a _____ and the bonds are _____ during this period.

16.   Replacing all or part of an outstanding bond issue prior to maturity is called bond _____.

17.   The two largest bond rating agencies are _____ and _____.

18.   The highest bond rating is _____.

19.   The lowest bond rating is _____.

20.   Bonds rated below BBB are called _____ bonds.

21.   Bonds with _____ ratings have higher interest rates.

22.   Bonds with adjustable coupons payments are called _____ bonds.

23.   Bonds that have no coupon payments are called _____ bonds.

24.   Bonds that pay coupon interest payments only when corporate income is above a certain level are called _____ bonds.

25. The primary advantage of bonds with adjustable coupon interest payments is that they reduce the risk associated with _____.

ANSWERS TO CONCEPT TEST

1. indenture
2. face; $1,000
3. accrued interest
4. registered
5. bearer
6. collateral
7. mortgage
8. debenture
9. private covenants
10. negative covenant
11. positive covenant
12. sinking fund
13. open-end; closed-end

14. call provision; calling
15. deferred call; call protected
16. refunding
17. Moody's and Standard and Poor's
18. AAA or Aaa
19. D
20. junk
21. lower
22. floating-rate
23. original-issue deep-discount or zero-coupon or pure-discount
24. income
25. uncertain future inflation

PROBLEMS

Problem 1

How much will you have to pay today, August 15th, for an 8% coupon bond quoted at 95? The bond pays interest semiannually, on June 1 and December 1.

Problem 2

Timberlake Industries has decided to float a perpetual bond issue. The coupon interest payment will be 7.5% (the current interest rate). There is an equal chance that, in one year, the market rate of interest will be either 5% or 15%. What will the market value of the bonds be one year from now if they are noncallable? If they are callable at par plus $75?

Problem 3

Timberlake has a perpetual bond with coupon payment C outstanding that is selling at par value. The bond is callable at $1,075. As in problem 2, there is an equal chance that next year interest rates will be either 5% or 15%. What is the coupon interest payment (C)?

Problem 4

In Problem 3, what is the cost to Timberlake of the call provision?

Problem 5

Hanna Company has issued a 5-year, pure-discount, 12% bond. Assuming that the IRS allows straight-line calculation of the interest, calculate the annual interest deduction available to Hanna. Compare this with the true implicit interest. What is the benefit of the straight-line method?

Problem 6

The Topeka Corporation wants to call its $100 million of 10.5% coupon perpetual bonds and replace them with $100 million of perpetual bonds at the current market rate of 8%. If called, each existing bond receives a call premium of one year's interest. In addition, the underwriting fees would amount to 12% of the $100 million. What is the net present value of this refunding operation?

Problem 7

Refer back to Problem 6. What is the NPV of the refunding if the interest savings are for only 15 years?

Problem 8

The Tarpon Spring Corporation intends to issue a callable bond and wants to know what coupon rate will allow the bond to be sold at par. If called next year, the call premium will be $100. The current one year interest rate is 8%. Consensus opinion believes that there is a 30% probability that rates will fall to 5%, a 20% probability that the rate will increase to 10%, and a 50% chance that rates will stay at 8%. What coupon rate must Tarpon set on its perpetual bonds to sell them at par?

Problem 9

The Tarpon Spring Company in Problem 8 announces that it will set the coupon at 8%, the current interest rate. If the same beliefs about the future course of interest rates apply, what will be the price of Tarpon Spring's bonds?

Problem 10

What if, in Problem 9, the bond were not callable. What will be the current price of a bond?

SOLUTIONS

Solution 1

Bonds are sold at the quoted price plus accrued interest (unless they're quoted "flat"). If you had purchased the bond on June 1, the accrued interest would have been zero. By purchasing the bond on August 15, you must pay the seller 75 days accrued interest plus the quoted price of $950. Accrued interest is (8%/365 days)(75 days) = $16.44. Total price is $950 + $16.44 = $964.44.

Solution 2

If the bond is not callable, then, in one year, the bond will be worth either ($75/.05) = $1,500 or ($75/.15) = $500. The expected value of the future price is $1,000. The present value of the $1,000 plus the first $75 coupon interest payment is ($1,075/1.075) = $1,000. so the bond will sell for par.

If the bond is callable, then either it will be called at $1,075 (if rates fall to 5%) or it will sell for $500. The expected value of the future price is [($1,075 + $500)/2] = $787.50. The present value is [($787.50 + $75)/1.075] = $802.33.

Solution 3

In one year, the bond will be worth either (C/.15) or it will be called for $1,075. If the bond sells for par, then:

$$\$1,000 = [C + .5(C/.15) + .5(1,075)]/(1.075)$$

$$\$537.50 = [C + .5(C/.15)] = 4\ 1/3\ C$$

$$C = \$537.50/4.333 = \$124.04.$$

Solution 4

If the bond had a coupon interest payment of $124.04 and was not callable, then in one year it would be worth either $2,480.80 or $826.93. The expected value is $1,653.86. The bond would sell for [($1,653.86 + $124.04)/1.075 = $1,653.86. The cost of the call provision is thus $653.86. The size of this cost stems from the volatility of interest rates in this example.

Solution 5

The bond will sell for $1,000/(1.12)^5 = [$1,000(.56743)] = $567.43. The total interest paid is ($1,000 − $567.43) = $432.57. Under the straight-line method, the annual interest deduction is ($432.57/5) = $86.51. The implicit interest in the first year is [$567.43(.12)] = $68.09. With four years remaining to maturity, the bond will sell for [$1,000(.63552)] = $635.52. The implicit interest in the second year is thus [$635.52(.12)] = $76.26. The necessary computations can be summarized as:

Year	Bond value	Interest deduction	Implicit interest
0	$567.43	$86.51	$68.09
1	635.52	86.51	76.26
2	711.78	86.51	85.41
3	797.19	86.51	95.66
4	892.86	86.51	107.14
Totals		$432.57	$432.57

Notice that, except for some round-off error, the total interest deducted is the same under either method. The straight-line method allows the corporation to receive the tax benefit early, however, thereby increasing the present value of the tax shield.

Solution 6

The net present value of the refunding is the present value of the interest savings less the cost of the refunding. The 2.5% spread in rates means that Topeka will save $100 million $\times$ .025 = $2.5 million per year forever. The present value is $2.5 million/.08 = $31.25 million. The cost of the refunding is the $100 million $\times$ .12 = $12 million underwriting fee plus the call premium of $105 per bond $\times$ ($100 million/$1,000) = $10.5 million. Thus, total costs are $22.5 million, and the NPV = $31.25 - $22.5 = $8.75 million.

Solution 7

The NPV of the refunding is the present value of the interest savings less the cost of the refunding. The costs are the same as in Problem 6, $22.5 million. The present value of the interest savings is now $2.5 million per year $\times$ 8.5595 = $21.399 million, where 8.5595 is the present value of an annuity factor for 8% and 15 periods. The NPV becomes $21.399 - $22.5 = -$1.101.

Solution 8

If interest rates fall to 5% it is likely that the bond price will rise above the call price $1,000 + $100 = $1,100, and the bonds will be called. If, on the other hand, interest rates rise or stay the same, the bonds will not be called. The coupon rate will be such that the present value of the expected pay-off next year will be $1,000. That is, if C is the coupon payment, then:

$$\$1,000 = [.3(C + \$1,100) + .2(C + C/.10) + .5(C + C/.08)]/1.08$$

Solving for C:

$$C = \$81.081$$

or, the coupon rate should be 8.108%.

Solution 9

The current bond price will be the present value of next year's expected pay-offs. That is,

$$P_o = [.3(\$80 + \$1,100) + .2(\$80 + \$80/.10) + .5(\$80 + \$80/.08)]/1.08$$

$$P_o = \$1,070/1.08 = \$990.74$$

Solution 10

If the bond is not callable, then the current price is:

$$P_o = [.3(\$80 + \$80/.05) + .2(\$80 + \$80/.10) + .5(\$80 + \$80/.08)]/1.08$$

$$P_o = \$1,220/1.08 = \$1,129.63$$

CHAPTER 21

OPTIONS AND CORPORATE FINANCE: BASIC CONCEPTS

CHAPTER MISSION STATEMENT

The purpose of Chapter 21 is to show how stocks and bonds, and some corporate decisions, may be thought of as options. The chapter describes call and put options, and discusses what factors affect their value. The chapter presents two methods of determining option values at any point in the life of an option. First, the two-state model is described whereby the price of an option can be determined by creating a portfolio of borrowing and buying stock that duplicates the payoffs to owning a call option. The two-state method is used, primarily, to motivate the intuition behind the famous Black-Scholes option pricing model. The chapter explains how stocks and bonds may be viewed as options on the firm's assets. Finally, the chapter discusses how capital structure policy and investments in real assets should be viewed in an option framework.

The key concepts presented in this chapter are outlined below.

♦Options
- Call options
- Put options
- Put-Call parity

♦Valuing options
- boundary values
- exercise price
- expiration date
- stock price
- stock variability
- interest rate

♦Option pricing formula
- two-state model
- Black-Scholes model

♦Stocks and bonds as options
- loan guarantees
- capital structure policy
- real projects

CONCEPT TEST

1. If you pay money to acquire the right to buy a specified asset at a fixed price anytime during the next 90 days, you have _____ a _____ option.

2. If you receive money in exchange for the potential obligation to buy a specified asset at a fixed price anytime during the next 90 days, you have _____ a _____ option.

3.   If you receive money in exchange for the potential obligation to sell a specified asset at a fixed price anytime during the next 90 days, you have _____ a _____ option.

4.   If you pay money to acquire the right to sell a specified asset at a fixed price anytime during the next 90 days, you have _____ a _____ option.

5.   The fixed price in an option contract is called the _____ or_____ price.

6.   The act of buying or selling an asset under the terms of an option contract is called _____ the option.

7.   The maturity date on an option is called the _____ date.

8.   An option that can only be exercised on the day it matures is a _____ option.

9.   An option that can be exercised anytime up to the day it matures is an _____ option.

10. If the exercise price on a call option is less than the stock price, then the option is said to be _____.

11. If the exercise price on a call option is greater than the stock price, then the option is said to be_____.

12. Another term for selling an option is _____ an option.

13. What is the value of a call option with an exercise price of zero.

14. Five factors affecting an option's value are: _____, _____, _____, _____, and _____.

15. Of the five factors which determine a call option's value, only one has an inverse relationship with the option's value. Which one?

16. Of the five factors affecting a put option's value, two have an inverse relationship with the option's value. Which two?

17. The equity in a levered firm can be viewed as a _____ option on the underlying assets of the firm.

18. The formula for valuing call options is called the _____ call option pricing equation.

19. Suppose you purchase the assets of a firm and sell a call option back to the original owner as a part of the deal. What corporate security have you effectively created for yourself?

20. Suppose you are a sole proprietor and thus have unlimited liability for business debts. To protect yourself. you purchase insurance. What corporate security have you effectively created for yourself?

21. If we view the equity in a levered firm as a call option, who owns the assets?

22. The value of risky debt can be viewed as the value of risk-free debt _____ the value of a _____ option.

ANSWERS TO CONCEPT TEST

1.   purchased; call
2.   sold; put
3.   sold; call
4.   purchased; put
5.   exercise; striking
6.   exercising
7.   expiration
8.   European
9.   American
10. in the money
11. out of the money
12. writing
13. the same as the asset value

14. stock price; exercise price; time to expiration; risk-free rate; volatility of the underlying asset
15. exercise price
16. stock price; interest rate
17. call
18. Black-Scholes
19. a risky bond
20. levered equity
21. the bondholders
22. less; put

PROBLEMS

Problem 1

Next year, only two outcomes are possible when a call option on Wautoma Inc. common stock expires. With equal probability, the stock price will be either $50 or $30 per share. The current stock price is $35. The option's exercise price is $40. The borrowing rate is 10%. What are the expected payoffs next year if you buy an option contract today?

Problem 2

Say, instead, you decide to buy N shares of Wautoma stock partially with borrowed money. How many shares must you buy such that the payoff next year exactly matches the payoff in Problem 1?

Problem 3

Using the payoffs from Problems 1 and 2, calculate the price of a call option.

Use the following information about the Wabash Corporation to solve Problems 4-8.

The price of Wabash Corporation common stock will be either $25 or $40 at the end of the year. A standard call option contract for the purchase of 100 shares of Wabash stock has an expiration date in one year. Investors can borrow and lend at 12%.

Problem 4

Suppose the current price of Wabash stock is $30 and that the exercise price of the call is $35. What are the possible values of the call contract on the expiration date?

Problem 5

For the data in Problem 4, what is the current value of the call contract?

Problem 6

Suppose that the option described in Problem 4 has an exercise price of $20. What is the value of the call contract?

Problem 7

Suppose a call contract for 100 shares of Wabash common stock, with an exercise price of $30, sells for $1,000. What is the current value of the stock?

Problem 8

Calculate the value of the call if the current stock price is $30 and the exercise price is $35.

Problem 9

Twain Corporation, the publisher of "Roughing It" magazine, is currently selling at $50 per share. Next year, the stock price will be either $40 or $65. Call options and put options on Twain stock with an exercise price of $48 and are selling for $12 and $2, respectively. What is the appropriate interest rate?

Problem 10

Calls on Wasatch Corporation common stock are currently selling for $10; puts are selling for $8. The exercise price of both options is $80 and the expiration date is in one year. The risk-free rate is 12%. What is the value of Wasatch common stock?

Problem 11

For the data in Problem 10, what is the maximum you can make if you buy the put? If you buy the call?

Options and Corporate Finance

Problem 12

Suppose that a stock is 'at the money,' meaning that the current price of the stock is equal to the exercise price of the option. What is the relationship between the value of the call and the value of the put?

Problem 13

In February 1993, a call on Cool Breeze, Inc., common stock, with a September 1993 expiration date sells for $5.45. The exercise price of the call is $60. Treasury bills coming due in September 1993 are priced to pay a yield of 12.6% and Cool Breeze common stock is selling for $55 per share. What is the value of a September 1993 put on Cool Breeze common stock with an exercise price of $60?

Problem 14

Use the Black-Scholes model to determine the price of a six-month call option, given the following information:

$$S = \$80, E = \$70, r = .10, \ d_1 = .82, \ d_2 = .74$$

Problem 15

Calculate the Black-Scholes price for a 9-month call option given the following:

$$S = \$80, E = \$70, \sigma = .30, r = .10$$

Problem 16

Here are some additional problems to be solved using the Black-Scholes model. Try them on your own. The interest rate given is annual. Your answers may differ slightly from those in the solution because of rounding in the standard normal distribution table, Table 21.3 in the text.

Stock price	Exercise price	Risk free rate	Maturity (months)	Variance	Call price
$50	$60	8%	6	20%	
25	15	6%	9	30%	
50	60	8%	6	40%	
0	10	9%	12	65%	
90	30	7%	forever	22%	
50	0	8%	6	44%	

The following information about the Winnipesaukee Company applies to Problems 17-18.

Winnipesaukee Company has a discount bank loan that matures in one year and requires the firm to pay $1,000. The current market value of the firm's assets is $1,200. The annual variance of the value of the firm's assets is .30 and the annual risk-free interest rate is 6%. Winnipesaukee is considering two mutually exclusive investments. Project A has an NPV of $100, and Project B has an NPV of $150. If Project A is accepted, the firm's variance will increase to .40. If Project B is accepted, the variance will decrease to .25.

Problem 17

What is the market value of the firm's debt and equity before undertaking any investment?

Problem 18

What is the value of the firm's assets, debt, and equity after accepting Project A? What is the value of the firm's assets, debt and equity after accepting Project B? Which project would the stockholders choose? Why?

Problem 19

Quotes for Wasatch call options are flashing on your computer screen. You notice that the calls with two-months until maturity are priced at $13 7/8 while the calls which expire in three-months are priced at $16 1/8. The stock has a variance of .20 and a current price is $110. The options have an exercise price of $100. The risk free rate is 5%. Should you buy either or both calls? You believe that the Black-Scholes formula correctly prices calls.

Problem 20

Using the information from Problem 19, calculate the value of two more Wasatch call options with the same expiration dates but with $110 striking prices.

SOLUTIONS

Solution 1

Next year, if the stock price is $50 you will exercise the option and buy 100 shares of Wautoma stock for $40 per share - representing a profit of $1,000. If, on the other hand, the stock price is $30, you will let the option expire, and your payoff is zero. The expected payoff is .5($1,000) + .5(0) = $500.

Solution 2

The easiest way to determine how many shares you need to buy is to consider the case where the stock price next year is $30 and the payoff is zero. Your N shares will be worth $30N; thus, for a zero payoff, the principal and interest on your loan must also equal \$30N. Now, if the stock price is \$50, your stock is worth \$50N and your loan balance is still \$30N. Thus, when the stock price equals \$50 your net pay off is (\$50N - \$30N) = \$20N. Compare this with the payoff on the call option in Problem 1. Thus, \$20N = \$1,000, or N = 50 shares. The following table shows these outcomes.

	Payoffs	
	Stock price = \$50	Stock price = \$30
Stock position	\$50×N	\$30×N
Borrowing	-\$30×N	-\$30×N
Net Payoff	\$20×N	\$ 0

Solution 3

Since the payoffs next year are the same whether you buy a call option contract or borrow and buy 50 shares, the net cost of each strategy today must be the same. Buying 50 shares costs \$35×50 = \$1,750. Next year, you must pay back \$30N or \$1,500; the present value of this is \$1,500/1.10 = \$1,363.64. Your net cost under the borrow and buy stock strategy is \$1,750 - \$1,363.64 = \$386.36. Thus, the cost of purchasing a call option contract (100 shares) must also be \$386.36, or \$386.36/100 = \$3.86 per call.

Solution 4

On the expiration date, Wabash stock will be worth either \$25 per share or \$40 per share. If the stock is worth \$25 per share, the option to buy at \$35 is worthless. If the stock is worth \$40 per share, then the call option is worth [(\$40 - \$35)(100)] = \$500.

Solution 5

If you buy the call, then, at the end of the year, you will have either \$0 or \$500, as indicated in Problem 4. Now determine a strategy consisting of borrowing and buying stock that produces the same payoffs as the call. It can be shown that the number of shares per option that must be purchased is equal to the difference between the call payoffs divided by the difference between the stock payoffs. In this case, you must purchase:

$$(\$500 - 0)/(\$4,000 - \$2,500) = 1/3 \text{ share per option.}$$

or a total of 33 1/3 shares.

If you buy 33 1/3 shares, you will have either \$833.33 or \$1,333.33 at the end of the year. If you arrange a loan that requires you to repay \$833.33, the net payoff from borrowing and buying 33 1/3 shares of stock is either \$500 or \$0 the same as the call option payoffs. At an interest rate of 12%, you can borrow (\$833.33/1.12) = \$744.04. At \$30 per share, 33 1/3 shares of stock cost \$1,000. Therefore, the net investment required to duplicate the call option is (\$1,000 - \$744.04) = \$255.96, which is equal to the value of the call option contract.

Solution 6

If you buy the contract with an exercise price of $20, then your payoff at the end of the year will be either $500 or $2,000. The number of shares of stock required to replicate the call is:

$$(\$2,000 - \$500)/(\$4,000 - \$2,500) = 1 \text{ per option.}$$

The cost of buying 100 shares is $3,000. Your payoff from owning 100 shares will be either $2,500 or $4,000. If you borrow enough to repay $2,000 on a loan, then you have replicated the payoffs from the option. Thus, you will borrow ($2,000/1.12) = $1,785.71. The net cost of replicating the option is ($3,000 − $1,785.71) = $1,214.29, which is equal to the value of the call option contract.

Solution 7

The number of shares required in order to replicate the call is ($1,000/$1,500) = 2/3 per call, or a total of 66 2/3 shares. Your payoff on 66 2/3 shares will either be $1,666.67 or $2,666.67. To duplicate the call payoffs, borrow the present value of $1,666.67, or ($1,666.67/1.12) = $1,488.10. The total value of the 66 2/3 shares is thus ($1,488.10 + $1,000) = $2,488.10 and the current value of the stock is ($2,488.10/66.67) = $37.32 per share.

Solution 8

From Solution 5, you need 1/3 share per option, or 33 1/3 shares. This will cost $700 (=1/3×100×$21). To replicate the call, you borrow the present value of $833.33 (=33 1/3×$25), or $744.05. The value of the call contract appears to be ($700 − $744.05) = −$44.05; however, since the value of the call cannot be negative, the call is actually worth zero.

How can the option to buy a share of stock that may be worth $40 for only $35 be worth nothing? The inconsistency here arises from the fact that the current stock price cannot be $21. You can borrow $21 at a 12% interest rate, and buy one share of stock. Under the worst case scenario, the share will be worth $25, but you will have to repay only [($21)(1.12)] = $23.52 on the loan. As a result, you would earn, at a minimum, a costless, riskless $1.48. There is an arbitrage opportunity here because the return on the stock (19% or 90%) is always greater than the riskless 12% interest rate. Therefore, the stock must sell for more than $21.

Solution 9

A strategy of buying the stock, buying puts, and selling calls will produce a risk free return. The table below shows that the payoff next year will be $48 whether the stock goes up to $65 or falls to $40.

	Stock falls to $40	Stock rises to $65
Buy stock	$40	$65
Buy put	8	0
Sell call	0	-17
Net payoff	$48	$48

The net investment on this strategy is $40 (=$50+$2−$12). Thus, given a certain payoff next year of $48, and a net investment today of $40, the risk free interest rate is 20% (48/40 = 1+r).

Solution 10

We can use the put-call parity theorem to solve this problem. The present value of the exercise price is ($80/1.12) = $71.43. The put-call parity theorem states that the put premium minus the call premium plus the current stock price equals the present value of the exercise price. Therefore, the value of the common stock is the value of X in the following equation:

$$\$8 - \$10 + X = \$71.43.$$

so that the value of the common stock is $73.43.

Solution 11

If you buy the put, the most profitable outcome would result if the stock price decreases to zero. In this case, you earn $80 if you exercise the put on the expiration date. The present value of this $80 is $71.43. In principle, there is no upper limit to what you can make on the call. For either option, the profit is reduced by the premium paid for the option.

Solution 12

From the put-call parity theorem, the call premium minus the put premium is equal to the current stock price minus the present value of the exercise price. If the current stock price is equal to the exercise price, then the current stock price must be greater than the present value of the exercise price; the difference is the exercise price times the risk-free rate, which is equal to the difference between the call premium and the put premium.

Solution 13

Using the put call parity theorem, and seven months to the expiration date, the value of the put is equal to the call premium plus the present value of the exercise price minus the price of the stock. The present value of the exercise price is [$60/1.126^{(7/12)}$] = $55.99, so that the value of the put is ($5.45 + $55.99 − $55) = $6.44.

Solution 14

We must evaluate the following:

$$C = SN(d_1) - Ee^{-rt} N(d_2)$$

$$= (\$80)\ N(.82) - (\$70)\ e^{-.10 \times .5}\ N(.74)$$

The values of $N(.82)$ and $N(.74)$ can be determined from Table 21.3 in the text (or any table of areas under the standard normal distribution). The table indicates that .2929 is the probability that d_1 is greater than zero and less than .82. Therefore, the probability that d_1 is less than .82 is equal to .2939 plus the probability that d_1 is less than zero; this latter value is .50, so that $N(.82)$ is $(.2939 + .50) = .7939$. Similarly, for d_2, $N(.74)$ is .7704. The value of the option is \$12.21.

Solution 15

The call option value is determined from the following substitutions:

$$C = SN(d_1) - E\ e^{-rt}\ N(d_2)$$

$$= (\$80)\ N(d_1) - (\$70)\ e^{(-.10 \times .75)}\ N(d_2)$$

where

$$d_1 = [\ln(S/E) + (r + .5\sigma^2)t]/(\sigma\ \sqrt{t})$$

$$= [\ln(80/70) + (.10 + (.5)(.3)^2)(.75)]/[(.3)\ \sqrt{(.75)} = .9325$$

$$d_2 = d_1 - \sigma\ \sqrt{t}$$

$$= .9325 - (.3)\ \sqrt{(.75)} = .6727$$

$N(d_1)$ is approximately .8245, and $N(d_2)$ is approximately .7494, and the value of the option is \$17.29.

Solution 16

Stock price	Exercise price	Risk free rate	Maturity (months)	Variance	Call price
$50	$60	8%	6	20%	$ 3.61
25	15	6%	9	30%	11.18
50	60	8%	6	40%	6.18
0	10	9%	12	65%	0.00
90	30	7%	forever	22%	90.00
50	0	8%	6	44%	50.00

Solution 17

To value the equity of the firm before a project is accepted, we use the Black-Scholes model with a value of S = $1,200, an exercise price of E = $1,000, a variance of 30%, a maturity of one year, and a riskfree rate of 6%. The value of equity is $381.70, which means that the value of debt must equal ($1,200 − $381.70) = $818.30.

Solution 18

With Project A, the value of the assets increases to ($1,200 + $1,00) = $1,300. With the new variance of .40, the value of the equity increases to $491.03, and the value of the debt decreases to $808.97.

With Project B, the value of the assets increases to ($1,200 + $150) = $1,350. With the new variance of .25, the value of the equity increases to $484.61, and the value of the debt increases to $865.39.

The stockholders would choose Project A, even though it has a lower NPV, because it has the greater effect on the value of the equity. The increased variance that results from accepting Project A benefits stockholders at the expense of bondholders. The reduction in variance that occurs with the acceptance of Project B makes the bonds safer and therefore benefits the bondholders.

Solution 19

The Black-Scholes formula is used to price each call. The results are presented below.

Two-months to expiration:

$d_1 = .65897$ $\qquad\qquad$ $N(d_1) = .74507$

$d_2 = .47640$ $\qquad\qquad$ $N(d_2) = .68310$

$C = \$14.21$

Three-months to expiration:

$$d_1 = .59394 \qquad N(d_1) = .72370$$

$$d_2 = .37034 \qquad N(d_2) = .64443$$

$$C = \$15.96$$

Given the quoted prices of $13 7/8 and $16 1/8 for the two and three month expiration dates, respectively, you should buy the two-month call and sell the three-month call.

Solution 20

The prices of these options are shown below. The solution to Problem 19 illustrates how the option price increases as the time to expiration increases. The prices shown below indicate that increasing the striking price reduces the value of the call, with the two-month call being more sensitive to the change in striking price.

Two-months to expiration:

$$d_1 = .13693 \qquad N(d_1) = .55447$$

$$d_2 = -.04564 \qquad N(d_2) = .48180$$

$$C = \$8.43$$

Three-months to expiration:

$$d_1 = .16770 \qquad N(d_1) = .56660$$

$$d_2 = -.05591 \qquad N(d_2) = .47774$$

$$C = \$10.43$$

CHAPTER 22

OPTIONS AND CORPORATE FINANCE: EXTENSIONS AND APPLICATIONS

CHAPTER MISSION STATEMENT

The purpose of Chapter 22 is to extend the discussion of options in Chapter 21 to practical financial decisions that include option-like properties. The chapter examines executive stock options and compensation, the option to change a firm's production plan, the option to postpone an investment, and the option to shutdown or reopen a project. The chapter emphasizes that optionality is present in many corporate decisions. The chapter elaborates on the two-state binomial option pricing model.

The key concepts presented in Chapter 22 are outlined below.

♦Why options?
♦Valuing executive compensation
♦Flexible production
♦Waiting to invest
♦Binomial option pricing model
  ●risk neutral valuation
  ●binomial tree
  ●simulation
♦Shutdown and reopen decisions
  ●valuing a gold mine

CONCEPT TEST

1. The biggest part of total compensation for many executives is _____.

2. One reason for using options as part of executive compensation is to _____ the interests of managers with shareholders.

3. Including options as part of an executive's compensation puts at _____ his compensation and ties his pay with the firm's _____.

4. Flexible production is _____ valuable than fixed production, but it also costs _____.

5. A drawback to a flexible production facility is that it is _____ efficient than a dedicated production facility.

6. One option-like feature common to most projects is the option to _____.

7. The ability to wait for lower interest rates is like a _____ option on a_____.

8. A general and powerful method for valuing options when the Black-Scholes formula does not apply is the _____ or _____ approach.

9.   In the risk neutral approach to valuing options, the probability q is the _____ probability of good news.

10. A binomial tree where the nodes come together after each move is known as a _____ tree.

11. If q is not risk adjusted, but merely the probability of an up move, then the appropriate discount rate must be a _____ rate.

12. A gold mine can be thought of as a package of _____ on the price of gold.

13. In an option framework, the extraction cost of gold is the option's _____.

14. The price at which you open or close the gold mine will deviate further from the extraction cost the more _____ the price of gold.

ANSWERS TO CONCEPT TEST

1.   options
2.   align
3.   risk; performance
4.   more; more
5.   less
6.   wait to invest
7.   call; bond

8.   binomial; two-state
9.   risk adjusted
10. recombining
11. risk adjusted
12. call options
13. exercise price
14. volatile

PROBLEMS

Problem 1

During 1997, Gordon F. Teter President and CEO of Wendy's International was granted options on 181,061 shares. These at-the-money options have an exercise price of $27.125 and have an expected life of four years. What is the value of these options if the volatility of Wendy's stock is 28.1% and the risk free rate is 5.83%?

Problem 2

What will be the value of Mr. Teter's options in one year if Wendy's stock price increases by 20%? What will be the value if the price falls by 20%?

Problem 3

The Springbok Company is building a new plant to manufacture athletic shoes. Springbok has the choice of building a plant dedicated to manufacturing basketball shoes or building a flexible production plant that could easily switch between manufacturing basketball shoes and tennis shoes. The option offered by the flexible plant could be valuable because, although the demand for basketball shoes is high right now, in two years the demand might be half of what it is now. The demand for tennis shoes is relatively constant. At today's demand, Springbok could sell one million pairs of basketball shoes with a profit margin of $50 per pair for the dedicated plant and $40 for the less efficient flexible plant. There is a 50% chance that demand will stay high. In two years, if demand falls by half, then the profit margin for basketball shoes will fall to $30. On the other hand, in two years the demand for tennis shoes will be one million pairs with a profit margin of $30 per pair. Whatever course the firm follows, the plant will cost $150 million and will last for 10 years. The appropriate discount rate is 12%. Should Springbok build the flexible plant?

Problem 4

In Problem 3, would your decision change if there was a 60% chance that demand for basketball shoes would fall by half in two years?

Problem 5

Terra Firma Development is deciding whether to exercise its right to put up a luxury apartment complex, to forego the project altogether, or to sell its rights to another developer who has offered to buy the right for $50,000. The apartment complex would cost $10 million and could be sold in two years when the project is complete for $12 million. The current discount rate is 10%, but there is a 50-50 chance that rates could soon change to 12% or 8%. What decision would you recommend?

Problem 6

Ultra Alloy Products is evaluating a $3.0 million project that will manufacture high tensile strength flanges which will be used in high pressure steam applications. Initial projections call for the firm to sell 5,000 units with a net cash flow of $250 per unit each year for the next five years. The appropriate discount rate is 15%. These new flanges, although much more durable than existing flanges, are very expensive and may not be widely accepted. If demand is less than expected, Ultra Alloy can abandon the plant after one year and net $1.5 million. If sales fall below 5,000 units after the first year, how low can demand go before Ultra Alloy abandons the project?

Problem 7

Ultra Alloy is revising its initial projections. The firm now believes that after the first year there is a 50-50 chance that demand will increase to 10,000 units if the new flange is accepted, or else fall to zero. If demand falls to zero, the project can be abandoned to net $1.5 million. Reevaluate the project's NPV.

Problem 8

Nevada Nuggets is deciding whether to buy the right to open an abandoned gold mine in central Nevada.

The price of gold is currently $350 per ounce and in the next year the price could increase by 20% or decline by 10%. The mine could extract and refine gold for $360 per ounce. If the mine is opened, 1 million ounces of gold could be extracted. If the rights are purchased and the mine is not opened, then Nevada Nuggets would have to spend $1 million on environmental cleanup. The risk free rate is 8%. What is the value of the right to open the mine?

SOLUTIONS

Solution 1

The value of Mr. Teeter's options can be found using the Black-Scholes model. The stock price and the exercise price equal $27.125, the time to expiration is four years, and the risk free rate is 5.83%. This yields values of $d_1 = .6959$ and $d_2 = .1339$, $N(.6959) = .7568$ and $N(.1339) = .5533$. From the Black-Scholes model

$$C = SN(d_1) - Ee^{-rt} N(d_2)$$

$$= (\$27.125) N(.6959) - (\$27.125) e^{-.0583 \times 4} N(.1339)$$

$$= \$8.64$$

The value of the options equals $8.64 × 181,061 = $1,564,367. Note that this overstates the value because we ignored the impact of dividends. If we include the effect of a 1.11% dividend yield, the value of each call is $7.77, and the total value would be $1,406,844.

Solution 2

Following the method of Solution 1, but substituting time to expiration of three years and a stock price of $32.55 if the price rises 20% and a price of $21.70 if the price falls by 20%, provides the option prices and values are shown in the following table.

Stock Price	$21.70	$27.125	$32.55
d_1	.1442	.6959	.9773
d_2	−.3425	.1339	.4906
$N(d_1)$	.5574	.7568	.8358
$N(d_2)$	.3660	.5533	.6881
Option price	$3.76	$8.64	$11.53
Options value	$680,789	$1,564,367	$2,087,633

The table shows that if the stock price increases 20% over the next year, the value of the options increase by 33%. But if the stock price declines 20%, the value of the options decline by 56%. Thus, total compensation is linked to shareholder wealth.

Solution 3

The choice of which plant to build is not clear, even though each would cost $150 million and last for 10 years. At first glance the flexible plant seems attractive, but it is less efficient than the dedicated plant. Thus, the decision must be based on the present value of each plant. Each plant will have a present value that equals the expected value of the present values under the high demand and high-low demand for basketball shoes environment. With low demand, the flexible plant switches to tennis shoes. For the dedicated plant,

$$PV(High) = \frac{\$50}{(1.12)} + \frac{\$50}{(1.12)^2} + ... + \frac{\$50}{(1.12)^{10}} = \$282.51$$

$$PV(High-Low) = \frac{\$50}{(1.12)} + \frac{\$50}{(1.12)^2} + \frac{\$15}{(1.12)^3} + ... + \frac{\$15}{(1.12)^{10}} = \$143.90$$

The expected present value of the dedicated plant is

$$\$213.21 = \tfrac{1}{2}(\$282.51) + \tfrac{1}{2}(\$143.90)$$

For the flexible plant,

$$PV(High) = \frac{\$40}{(1.12)} + \frac{\$40}{(1.12)^2} + ... + \frac{\$40}{(1.12)^{10}} = \$226.01$$

$$PV(High-Low) = \frac{\$40}{(1.12)} + \frac{\$40}{(1.12)^2} + \frac{\$30}{(1.12)^3} + ... + \frac{\$30}{(1.12)^{10}} = \$186.41$$

The expected present value of the dedicated plant is

$$\$206.21 = \tfrac{1}{2}(\$226.01) + \tfrac{1}{2}(\$186.41)$$

Thus, because of its lower profit margins, the flexible plant is slightly inferior to the dedicated plant. Although, one could argue that the present values are close enough so that it may be worthwhile to go with the flexible plant just to have available the option to switch production processes.

Solution 4

In this problem, since only the probability changes, we can use the present values for each demand scenario from problem 3. Thus, for the dedicated plant, the expected present value is

$$\$199.34 = .40 \times \$282.51 + .60 \times \$143.90$$

and for the flexible plant, the expected present value becomes

$$\$202.25 = .40 \times \$226.01 + .60 \times \$186.41$$

Thus, with the revised probability, the flexible plant looks more attractive.

Solution 5

Terra Firma is facing a negative net present value project with the current 10% discount rate

$$NPV = -\$10 + \$12/(1.10)^2 = -\$0.083 \text{ million,}$$

so the offer of $50,000 for the right to build seems attractive. But it may be more worthwhile to wait and see what happens to interest rates. If rate rise to 12% the project remains negative net present value and should be foregone. But if rates fall to 8%, the project's NPV becomes

$$NPV = -\$10 + \$12/(1.08)^2 = \$0.288 \text{ million.}$$

The expected NPV of waiting is $144,000 = ½ ($0) + ½ ($288,000). Thus, Terra Firma should wait to see if rates fall to 8%.

Solution 6

If Ultra Alloy Products' project goes as expected it will generate $1.25 million (= $250 × 5,000) net cash flow per year, and will have a net present value of

$$NPV = -\$3.0 + \sum_{t=1}^{5} \frac{\$1.25}{(1.15)^t} = \$1.19 \text{ million.}$$

If demand falls after the first year, then Ultra Alloy will abandon the project if the present value at year 1 of net cash flow from years 2 through 5 is less than $1.5 million. The minimum level of sales, S, satisfies the following equation.

$$\$1.5 \text{ million} = \sum_{t=1}^{4} \frac{\$250 \times S}{(1.15)^t}$$

Thus, the project will be abandoned if sales fall below 2,102 units per year, assuming unit sales remain constant over the four years.

Solution 7

Under the revised plan, if at the end of one year demand increases to 10,000 units for each of the next four years, the project will have a present value of

$$\$7.14 \text{ million} = \sum_{t=1}^{4} \frac{\$2.50}{(1.15)^t}.$$

If demand falls to zero, the project will be abandoned for $1.5 million. The expected value of the project at year one is

$$\$4.32 \text{ million} = \tfrac{1}{2}\,(\$1.5) + \tfrac{1}{2}\,(\$7.14).$$

The revised NPV of the project becomes

$$NPV = -\$3.0 + \frac{\$1.25}{(1.15)} + \frac{\$4.32}{(1.15)} = \$1.84 \text{ million}.$$

Solution 8

The value of the right to open the gold mine can be found using the risk-neutral approach for evaluating a one-period binomial option pricing model. With gold as the underlying asset, the current price of gold must be the present value of the expected future price of gold using risk adjusted probabilities (q). Thus,

$$\$350 = [q \times \$350\,(1.20) + (1 - q) \times \$350\,(0.90)]/(1.08).$$

Solving for q, the risk-adjusted probability of an increase in the price of gold, shows q = .60. The current value of the right to open the mine must be the present value of the expected payoff:

$$PV(\text{right}) = [q \times \text{profit from 1 million ounces of gold} + (1- q) \times \text{cleanup cost}]/(1 + r)$$

$$PV(\text{right}) = [.60 \times (\$420 - \$360) \times 1 \text{ mill. oz.} + .40 \times (-\$1 \text{ mill.})]/(1.08)$$

$$PV\,(\text{right}) = \$32.963 \text{ million}.$$

Thus, the most Nevada Nuggets should pay for the right to open the mine is $32.963 million. This value does not depend on the actual probability that the price of gold will increase.

CHAPTER 23

WARRANTS AND CONVERTIBLES

CHAPTER MISSION STATEMENT

The purpose of Chapter 23 is to describe two securities, warrants and convertible bonds, issued by firms which have option-like characteristics. The chapter compares warrants with call options and discusses the dilutive nature of warrants. Convertible bonds are described. The chapter discusses how convertibles are valued as part straight debt, part stock, and part option. The chapter emphasizes that neither warrants nor convertibles represent cheap financing. The chapter concludes by discussing several economic reasons why convertibles may be issued.

The key concepts presented in Chapter 23 are outlined below.

- ◆Warrants
  - ●comparison with calls
- ◆Warrant pricing
  - ●Black-Scholes model
- ◆Convertible bonds
- ◆Convertible bond value
  - ●straight bond
  - ●conversion value
  - ●option value
- ◆Issuing warrants and convertibles
  - ●spurious reasons
  - ●valid reasons
- ◆Conversion policy

CONCEPT TEST

1. The holder of a _____ has the right to buy common stock from an investor at a fixed price for a specified time period.

2. The holder of a _____ has the right to buy common stock from the corporation at a fixed price for a specified time period.

3. A corporate security (e.g., a bond or preferred stock) that can be exchanged for a fixed number of shares of common stock is said to be _____.

4. Warrants are normally issued in combination with _____.

5. A convertible bond might allow the owner to exchange a $1000 face value bond for shares of common stock at $40. The $40 is the _____.

6.   The bond described in the previous question can be exchanged for _____ shares of stock. This figure is called the _____.

7.   For the bond described in Question 5, suppose the stock were selling for $60 at the time the bond was issued. The $20 differential is called the _____.

8.   The price at which a convertible bond would sell if it did not have the conversion privilege is called the _____.

9.   The amount that a convertible bond would be worth if it were immediately exchanged for common stock is its _____.

10.   The minimum value of a convertible bond is equal to the maximum of its _____ or its _____.

11.   The value of a convertible bond generally exceeds the minimum value indicated in Question 10 by the _____.

12.   Is it true that a convertible bond will have a lower coupon rate than an otherwise identical nonconvertible bond?

13.   Is it true that issuing convertible bonds is always preferable to issuing otherwise identical nonconvertible bonds?

14.   In terms of security, most convertible bonds are _____.

15.   Since investors prefer not to convert convertible bonds before maturity, most convertible bonds are _____.

16.   If the conversion value is greater than the call price on a convertible bond, the effect of a call is to _____.

17.   From the corporation's point of view, the optimal time to call a convertible bond is when the call price _____ the conversion value.

18.   In retrospect, a firm would have been better off selling _____ rather than convertible bonds if the stock price has increased significantly.

19.   In retrospect, a firm would have been better off selling _____ rather than convertible bonds if the stock price has decreased significantly.

20.   In practice, firms tend to call convertible bonds when the conversion value _____ the call price.

21. Would a firm with a high growth rate be more or less likely to issue convertibles than a firm with a low growth rate?

22. Would a firm with highly uncertain future prospects be more or less likely to issue a bond/warrant package than a firm with relatively certain prospects?

23. Would a convertible bond tend to have more or fewer restrictive covenants than an otherwise identical nonconvertible bond?

ANSWERS TO CONCEPT TEST

1.	call option	13.	no
2.	warrant	14.	subordinated debentures
3.	convertible	15.	callable
4.	privately placed debt	16.	force conversion
5.	conversion price	17.	equals
6.	25; conversion ratio	18.	straight debt
7.	conversion premium	19.	common stock
8.	straight bond value	20.	exceeds
9.	conversion value	21.	more
10.	straight bond value; conversion value	22.	more
11.	option value	23.	fewer
12.	yes		

PROBLEMS

Use the following information to answer Problems 1-4.

The Sweet Crude Company's only asset is 20,000 barrels of oil. The oil was purchased a few years ago for about $18 per barrel and is now worth $25 per barrel. The firm has 1,000 shares outstanding and intends to issue 500 warrants. Each warrant will cost $180 and give the holder the option to buy one share of Sweet Crude for $550.

Problem 1

What is the stock price per share immediately before the warrants are issued?

Problem 2

What is the stock price per share just after the warrants are sold if (a) the proceeds from the issue are immediately paid out to existing shareholders as a dividend? or (b) the proceeds are retained and used to purchase more oil?

Problem 3

Now assume that the warrants are about to expire. What is the minimum oil price per barrel that would cause the warrants to be exercised? Assume part (a) in Problem 2 applies, i.e., the firm uses the proceeds from the warrant sale to pay a dividend.

Problem 4

Assume that the price of oil jumps to $30 per barrel, and the firm has its original 20,000 barrel inventory. If the warrants are now converted, what is the new stock price?

Problem 5

Years later, Sweet Crude Company is capitalized with equity and convertible bonds. The convertible debt has a face value of $1,000, a coupon rate of 10%, 10 years to maturity, and a conversion price of $550 per share. The yield on similar nonconvertible bonds is 11%. What is the minimum price at which Sweet Crude's convertible debt should sell if the market price of Sweet's stock is $590 per share? What is the price if the stock price is $500 per share?

Problem 6

You have been hired to value a new 30-year callable, convertible bond. The bond has a 6% coupon rate, with interest payable annually. The conversion price is $100 and the stock currently sells for $50.12. The stock price is expected to grow at 10% per year. The bond is callable at $1,100, but based on prior experience, it would not be called unless the conversion value was $1300. The required return on this bond is 8%. What value would you assign?

Problem 7

Suppose that the bond described in Problem 6 were not callable. What would its value be? (Assume that the dividend yield on the stock is negligible.)

Problem 8

For the bond described in Problem 6, what is the minimum price at which the bond could sell when it is issued? (Assume that comparable nonconvertible bonds are priced to yield 7%.)

Problem 9

Suppose that the bond described in Problem 6 sells for $900. What is the option value of the bond?

Problem 10

Consider the convertible bond described in Problem 6; suppose that, ten years after the bond is issued, the price of the firm's common stock increases to $120 per share and that yields for comparable nonconvertible bonds decline to 6%. What is the straight debt value of the bond? What is the conversion value of the bond? Why is the conversion value now the minimum value of the bond?

Problem 11

A bond with ten detachable warrants has been offered for sale at a price of $1,000. The bond matures in 30 years and has an annual coupon payment of $100. Each warrant gives the owner the right to purchase five shares of stock at $15 per share. Ordinary bonds (i.e., bonds without warrants) of similar quality are priced to yield 14%. What is the value of a warrant?

Problem 12

Using the data from Problem 11, determine the maximum current price of the firm's stock.

Use the following information to solve Problems 13-20.

Sweetwater Company has 6,500 shares of stock outstanding. The market value of Sweetwater's assets is $950,000. The market value of outstanding debt is $200,000. Some time ago, Sweetwater issued 100 warrants that are now about to expire. Each warrant gives the owner the right to purchase ten shares of stock at a price of $75 per share.

Problem 13

What is the price per share of Sweetwater stock?

Problem 14

What is the value of one warrant?

Problem 15

What is the effective exercise price of the warrants?

Problem 16

What is the profit from exercising one warrant?

Problem 17

Suppose that a call option to buy ten shares of stock in a company comparable to Sweetwater has an exercise price of $75. The comparable company, Sour Pete, is identical to Sweetwater, except that it has no warrants outstanding. What is the price of this firm's stock? What is the profit from exercising this call option?

Problem 18

Let q be the ratio of total shares that can be purchased using warrants to shares currently outstanding for Sweetwater. Show numerically that the value of a warrant to buy one share is $[1/(1 + q)]$ of the value of a call option with an exercise price of $75 on an identical firm such as Sour Pete without warrants outstanding.

Problem 19

Suppose that Sweetwater declares a 3-for-1 stock split. If the warrants are protected, what adjustments would be made?

Problem 20

Suppose that Sweetwater declares a 20% stock dividend. If the warrants are protected, what adjustments would be made?

SOLUTIONS

Solution 1

The assets of Sweet Crude are worth $25 per bbl $\times$ 20,000 bbls = $500,000. Per share, the assets are worth $500,000/1,000 = $500.

Solution 2

Under part (a), after the sale and before the dividend is paid, the firm's assets are $500,000 worth of oil and 500 $\times$ $180 = $90,000 cash from the warrants. The firm pays a $90,000/1,000 = $90 dividend to each shareholder. The $500,000 worth of oil remaining is the value of the shares (ex-dividend) plus warrants. Since the warrants are worth $90,000, the shares must be worth $500,000 - $90,000 - $410,000 or $410 per share.

Under question (b), the firm uses the $90,000 proceeds to buy more oil at $25 per barrel. The firm buys $90,000/$25 = 3,600 barrels of oil. The firm is worth $25 per bbl $\times$ 23,600 bbls = $590,000. Of this, $90,000 represents the warrants and the remaining $500,000 represents the 1,000 shares. Thus, the share price is $500 per share. Note that the stated price of $180 per warrant cannot represent a fair price for both (a) and (b). If $180 is a fair warrant price for scenario (a) where the stock price is $410, then clearly $180 is too low for scenario (b) where the stock price is $500 - much closer to the exercise price.

Solution 3

For the warrants to be exercised, the price per share must be at least $550. If the warrants are exercised, the firm gets $500 \times \$550 = \$275,000$ and issues 500 shares. The 1,500 shares outstanding must be worth $1,500 \times \$550 = \$825,000$. The value of the firm's assets consists of 20,000 bbls $\times P_{bbl} + \$275,000$. We want to find the price of oil, P_{bbl}, that makes the assets worth $825,000. Thus,

$$\$825,000 = 20,000 \times P_{bbl} + \$275,000$$

$$P_{bbl} = \$27.50$$

Solution 4

The assets of the firm are 20,000 bbls $\times$ $30 per bbl = $600,000 plus $550 $\times$ 500 = $275,000 cash from the warrant conversion, or $875,000. After the conversion, there are 1,500 shares outstanding. The stock price is $875,000/1,500 = $583.33.

Solution 5

The minimum at which a convertible bond will sell is the maximum of its value as a straight bond or the value of the stock in which it could be converted, the conversion value. As straight debt, the bond is worth

$$\text{straight debt} = \sum_{t=1}^{10} \frac{\$100}{(1.11)^t} + \frac{\$1,000}{(1.11)^{10}}$$
$$= \$941.11$$

If converted into stock, each bond is equivalent to $1,000/$550 = 1.818 shares. At the current stock price of $590, this is worth

$$\text{conversion value} = \$590 \times 1.818 = \$1,072.62$$

Thus, the minimum price is $1,072.62, but it will sell for more since there is still ten years before maturity assuming that the bond is not callable. If the stock price is $500, then the conversion value is $500 $\times$ 1.818 = $909.00. The bond will sell for at least $941.11.

Solution 6

We must first determine when the bond is likely to be called. The conversion ratio is ($1,000/$100) = 10, so the bond will be called when the stock price reaches $130 per share. The time required for the stock price to grow from $50.12 to $130 can be determined by solving for n in the following equation:

$$\$130 = \$50.12 \times (1.10)^n$$

The value of n can be most easily determined using a trial-and-error approach or by locating, in the future value tables, the value of n such that $[(1.10)^n] = (\$130/\$50.12) = 2.5938$; thus, we determine that n is approximately 10 years.

If we buy the bond, we expect to receive an annuity of $60 per year, for 10 years, and then to convert to stock worth $1,300. The present value of the annuity, discounted at 8%, is $402.60. The present value of the $1,300, to be received in ten years, is $602.15. Therefore, the bond is worth $1,004.75.

Solution 7

If the bond is not callable, it will not be converted until maturity. At a growth rate of 10% per year, the stock price is expected to be $874.564 per share in 30 years. Therefore, the conversion value is expected to be $8745.64 at that time. At a discount rate of 8%, the present value of the conversion value is $869.12. The present value of the annuity of $60 per year for 30 years is $675.47. The value of the bond is ($869.12 + $675.47) = $1,544.59.

Solution 8

The minimum value is the greater of either the straight debt value or the conversion value. The conversion value is [10($50.12)] = $501.20. The straight debt value, using a discount rate of 7%, is $875.91. Therefore, the minimum price is the straight debt value of $875.91.

Solution 9

The option value is the difference between the selling price of the bond and the minimum price of $875.91, as determined in Problem 8; therefore, the option value is $24.09.

Solution 10

The straight debt value of the bond is now $1,000, and the conversion value is [($120)(10)] = $1,200. The bond can not sell for less than its conversion value because such a price would provide an arbitrage opportunity for an investor who bought the bond, converted to common stock, and then sold the common stock for $1,200.

Solution 11

If there were no warrants, the bond would be worth $719.89. The total value of the warrants is ($1,000 − $719.89) = $280.11. Since there are ten warrants, each is worth $28.01.

Solution 12

The straight bond value is $719.89. Each bond enables the owner to buy a total of 50 shares of stock for $15 per share. The minimum value of the warrants is [50(S − $15)]; the solution to Problem 11 indicates that the total value of the warrants is $280.11. Therefore, the current stock price is at most the value of S in the following equation:

$$50(S - \$15) = \$280.11$$

Solving for S, we find that the current stock price is at most S = [$15 + ($280.11/50)] = $20.60.

Solution 13

The total value of the warrants and stock is ($950,000 – $200,000) = $750,000. If all of the warrants are exercised, then the number of shares increases by 1,000, to a total of 7,500 shares outstanding. The total equity value would be [$750,000 + ($75)(1,000)] = $825,000, and the per share price is ($825,000/7,500) = $110.00.

Solution 14

The total value of the stock, just before exercise of the warrants, is [($110.00)(6,500)] = $715,000. Since the total value of the warrants and stock is $750,000, the value of the warrants is ($750,000 – $715,000) = $35,000, and the value of one warrant is $350.00 or $35 for each of the 10 shares.

Solution 15

The warrantholders will pay a total of $75,000 if they exercise the warrants. They will own 1,000 of 7,500 shares outstanding, or 2/15 or 13.33% of the equity. Effectively, they pay [(13/15)($75,000)] = $65,000 to acquire the shares. The effective exercise price per share is $65.00. Ignoring the proceeds from the warrant exercise, the value of 2/15 of the equity is $100,000. Therefore, the value of the warrants is ($100,000 – $65,000) = $35,000, as calculated above.

Solution 16

The holder of one warrant can purchase ten shares of stock for $75 per share. Each share has a value of $110.00, so the warrantholder has a profit of $35.00 per share, or a total profit of [($35)(10)] = $350, as indicated in Problem 14. Note that this is an alternative approach to determining the value of a warrant.

Solution 17

For this identical firm, Sour Pete, the stock is worth [($950,000 – $200,000)/6,500] = $115.3846 per share. The exercise of a call option does not affect either the number of shares outstanding or the value of the firm, so exercise of the call option results in a profit of [($115.3846 – $75)(10)] = $403.8462.

Solution 18

In the identical firm, the stock is worth $115.3846 per share. At a $75 exercise price, the payoff on a call option is $40.3846. From Problem 14, the payoff per share on the warrants is $350. The ratio q is (1,000/6,5000) = .1538, and [1/(1 + q)] = .8667. Using this ratio, the payoff per share for each warrant is ($40.3846/1.1538 = $35.00 (or $350 for the 10-share warrant) which is the solution to Problem 14. Since this ratio is constant, the value of the call option is always (1 + q) times the value of the warrant.

Solution 19

Each warrant would give the owner the right to buy 30 shares at a price of $25 per share.

Solution 20

Each warrant would give the owner the right to buy 20% more shares at a price that is 20% less. The number of shares would thus be 12 and the exercise price would be ($75/1.20) = $62.50.

CHAPTER 24

LEASING

CHAPTER MISSION STATEMENT

The purpose of Chapter 24 is to discuss the institutional details of leasing and describe the proper way to evaluate financial leases. The chapter reviews operating leases and distinguishes them from financial, or capitalized, leases. The chapter shows how to determine cash flows from leases, and evaluate the lease versus purchase decision. The chapter shows that risk-free after-tax cash flows should be discounted at the after-tax risk-free rate. Likewise, nearly risk-free lease cash flows should be discounted at the firm's after-tax interest rate on secured debt. The debt displacement aspect of leasing is explained. Finally, the chapter discusses when leasing is beneficial to both lessee and lessor. An appendix illustrates the APV approach of evaluating leases.

The key concepts presented in this chapter are outlined below.

- ♦Leases
  - ●operating leases
  - ●financial leases
- ♦Accounting and leasing
- ♦Tax rules and leasing
- ♦Cash flow from leasing
- ♦Discount rate
- ♦Debt displacement
- ♦Does leasing ever pay
- ♦Reasons for leasing

CONCEPT TEST

1. In a lease arrangement, the owner of the asset is the _____.

2. In a lease arrangement, the user of the asset is the _____.

3. In a lease arrangement, the _____ gets the tax benefit from depreciating the asset.

4. An _____ lease is short-term (usually 3 to 5 years) and is sometimes called a _____ or _____ lease.

5. A _____ lease is long-term and is sometimes called a _____ lease.

6. If a lease can be canceled at the lessee's option, it is probably an _____ lease.

7. If the payments under a lease are sufficient to recover the cost of the asset, then the lease is said to be _____ and is probably a _____ lease.

8. A financial lease originates as either a _____ or a _____.

9.   If a firm previously owned a leased asset, then the lease is probably a _____ arrangement.

10. If the lessor borrows a substantial fraction of the purchase price of the asset, then the financial lease is called a _____.

11. The cash flow benefit to the lessee is that the lessee does not pay the _____.

12. For the lessee, the costs associated with leasing are the _____ and the _____.

13. A financial lease is a source of financing much like _____.

14. If the firm has an optimal capital structure, then an indirect cost of leasing is the resulting _____.

15. The appropriate discount rate for valuing a lease is the _____.

16. In a perfect market, there is no particular reason for financial leasing to exist since the lease would be a _____ transaction.

17. If markets are perfect, and the lessor concludes that a lease has an NPV of $100, then the NPV for the lessee is _____.

18. The primary advantage of leasing in an imperfect market is _____.

19. A major reason for short-term leasing is _____.

20. Prior to FAS 13, all leases were _____ financing.

21. A financial lease is likely to be beneficial to all parties when the lessor's tax bracket is _____ than the lessee's.

In Questions 22-24 indicate whether, from an accounting perspective, the lease is a capital lease or an operating lease, and also indicate whether the IRS might view the lease as a loan.

22. You lease a Porsche 911 for six years. At the end of the sixth year, you have the option to purchase the car for $1.

23. You lease a computer with a five-year economic life. The lease term is three years and the present value of the lease payments is 80% of the cost of the computer. You can purchase the computer for its fair market value at the end of the lease.

24. You lease a Boeing 747 for two years at $1 million per year. You can buy it at its fair market value of $200 million when the lease expires. During the lease, you cannot issue additional debt for other purposes.

ANSWERS TO CONCEPT TEST

1. lessor	13. secured borrowing
2. lessee	14. debt displacement
3. lessor	15. after-tax cost of secured borrowing
4. operating; service; maintenance	16. zero NPV
5. financial; capital	17. -$100
6. operating	18. tax avoidance
7. fully-amortized; financial	19. transactions costs
8. direct lease; sale and lease-back	20. off-balance-sheet
9. sale and lease-back	21. higher
10. leveraged lease	22. financial; might be a loan
11. purchase price	23. operating; probably a lease
12. after-tax lease payments; lost depreciation benefit	24. operating; might be a loan

PROBLEMS

Use the following information to solve Problems 1-5.

Aileron Airlines Inc., is in desperate need of a new airplane. The purchase price is $150 million. It can be leased for 10 years at $20 million per year. Aileron is in the 34% tax bracket and can borrow on a secured basis at 12%. Aircraft are depreciated on a straight-line basis to a zero residual value over 10 years. Since regulations require that planes be permanently grounded after 10 years, the actual residual value is negligible.

Problem 1

What is Aileron's after-tax cash outflow from leasing instead of buying?

Problem 2

What is the net present value of the lease? Should Aileron lease or buy? What is the value of the lease from the lessor's point of view.

Problem 3

What amount of debt is displaced by the lease?

Problem 4

Suppose that Aileron has sufficient tax-loss carryforward to avoid paying taxes for ten years, and that the lease payment is $26.1 million. Should the firm lease or buy?

Problem 5

What is the value of the lease described in Problem 4, from the lessor's point of view? (Assume that the lessor is in the 34% tax bracket and can borrow on a secured basis at 12%.)

Problem 6

An asset costs $50,000, has a useful life of five years and no salvage value. Assume that the asset will be depreciated on a straight-line basis. The corporate tax rate on ordinary income is 34%. The relevant interest rate for secured debt is 10%. The annual lease payments are $12,500 paid at the end of each of the next five years. What are the annual cash outflows for the lessee?

Problem 7

For the lease described in Problem 6, what is the net present value of the lease for the lessee?

Problem 8

Suppose that the lease payments described in Problem 6 are paid at the beginning of each year; what is the net present value of the lease for the lessee?

Problem 9

For the lease described in Problem 6, what lease payment will make the lessee indifferent between leasing and purchasing the asset?

Problem 10

Suppose that the lessee in Problem 6 is a smaller, less profitable company than the lessor; as a result, the lessee is in a 20% tax bracket and pays 15% interest on unsecured debt. The lease payment is $14,000 per year, paid at the end of each of the next five years. Calculate the net present value of the lease for the lessee.

Problem 11

For the lease described in Problems 6 and 10, what is the net present value of the lease for the lessor?

Problem 12

Referring to the data in Problem 10, what lease payment would make the lessee indifferent regarding whether to accept the lease?

Use the following information to solve Problems 13-18.

CHCL, Inc. is a railroad car leasing firm. They only lease out covered hopper cars that are used to ship grain, and the railroad cars are the firm's primary assets. Business has been growing and the firm is harvesting bountiful profits. This keeps the firm in the 40% tax bracket. CHCL, Inc. can borrow at 8% and has an overall weighted-average cost of capital (WACC) of 12%.

The standard lease arrangement calls for the lessee to make six $24,000 payments. The first payment is due at lease inception, and the remaining five are paid at twelve month intervals. There is no purchase option; CHLC sells the cars for scrap at the end of the lease. Experience suggests that the cars can be scrapped for about 20% of their initial value.

A new covered hopper car costs $60,000 and is depreciated to zero over a five-year period. The percentage of the original price of the asset which can be depreciated each year is fixed at 20%, 30%, 20%, 20%, and 10%, respectively over each of the five years.

Problem 13

What are the cash flows to CHLC, Inc. from leasing one covered hopper car?

Problem 14

What is the net present value to CHCL, Inc. from leasing one car?

Problem 15

What must CHLC, Inc. charge to break even on the lease?

Problem 16

Golden Grain Bakery will lease one covered hopper car from CHCL, Inc. using the standard lease contract. Golden Grain is in the 20% tax bracket, can borrow at 8%, and has the same 12% cost of capital as CHCL, Inc. What are the lease cash flows from the lessee's point of view?

Problem 17

What is the NPV of the lease from the lessee's, Golden Grain's, point of view?

Problem 18

What is the most Golden Grain Bakery should be willing to pay for the lease?

Problem 19

The Cumulo & Nimbus Railroad is evaluating whether to lease or purchase a new locomotive. The locomotive, if purchased, will cost $1,200 thousand and could be depreciated on a straight line basis over four years. If purchased, a local bank will provide a $1,200 thousand loan at 10% to be paid back in four $300 thousand principal payments plus interest on the outstanding balance. Principal and interest payments are paid at the end of each year. If leased, annual lease payments are $360 thousand paid at the end of the year. Cumulo & Nimbus is in the 30% tax bracket. Assume that the locomotive will be worthless at the end of four years. Should C & N buy or lease the locomotive?

Problem 20

What is the break-even lease payment for Cumulo & Nimbus?

Problem 21

Calculate the debt capacity created by leasing the locomotive. Show that the principal and after-tax interest payments of a loan equal to the debt capacity exactly duplicates the after-tax lease cash flows.

Problem 22

Calculate the NPV of the lease using the adjusted present value (APV) approach described in the appendix to Chapter 24.

Problem 23

Cumulo & Nimbus will lease the locomotive from a lessor in the 40% tax bracket. What is the NPV of the lease from the lessor's point of view?

SOLUTIONS

Solution 1

The after tax cash outflow is:

$$L(1 - T_c) + T_c(Dep) =$$

$$(\$20,000,000)(1 - .34) + .34(15,000,000) = \$18,300,000$$

Solution 2

Aileron saves the $150 million purchase price by paying $18.3 million per year for ten years. The appropriate discount rate is the after-tax cost of borrowing, which is $[.12(1 - .34)] = .0792$. The NPV of the lease is thus:

$$\$150,000,000 - \$18,300,000(6.7344) = +\$26,761,185$$

Aileron should lease instead of buy. The lessor loses $26.761 million on the deal.

Solution 3

The after-tax cash flows from the lease are $18.3 million. At an interest rate of 7.92%, we can borrow $[(\$18.3 \text{ million})(6.7344)] = \$123.239$ million by agreeing to make these same after-tax payments on a loan. Therefore, the debt displaced is $123.239 million. Notice that this $123.239 million plus the NPV of the lease is equal to the $150 million raised by the lease.

Solution 4

The cost of leasing instead of buying is the $26.1 million lease payment. The discount rate is 12%. The NPV of the lease is thus:

$$\$150,000,000 - \$26,100,000(5.6502) = \$2,529,780$$

Therefore, the firm should lease.

Solution 5

For the lessor, the cash flows are:

$$\$26,100,000(.66) + (.34)(\$15,000,000) = \$22,326,000$$

At 7.92%, the lessor's NPV is:

$$-\$150,000,000 + \$22,326,000(6.7344) = \$352,214$$

Solution 6

The annual after-tax cash outflow is:

$$L(1 - T_c) + T_c(\text{Dep}) =$$

$$(\$12,500)(1 - .34) + .34(10,000) = \$11,650$$

Solution 7

The appropriate discount rate is $[.10(1 - .34)] = .066$. The NPV of the lease is:

$$\$50,000 - \$11,650(4.1445) = \$1,717$$

Solution 8

The present value of the after-tax cash flows is now equal to:

$$\$11,650(4.1445)(1.066) = \$51,470$$

The NPV of the lease is ($50,000 - $51,470) = -$1,470. Thus, the lease becomes unacceptable to the lessee because the increase in the present value of the outflows resulting from the earlier payment.

Solution 9

The lessee will be indifferent if the net present value of the lease is zero. Therefore, the lease payment is the value of L which is the solution to the following equation:

$$\$50,000 - (.66L)(4.1445) - (\$3400)(4.1445) = 0$$

The value of L is $13,128. Note that the lessor will also have a net present value of zero for a lease payment of $13,128. If the lease payment is greater than this amount, the lessor will have a positive NPV, while the lessee will have a negative NPV, and the sum of the two will be zero. Similarly, for lease payments below $13,128, the lease has a positive NPV for the lessee and a negative NPV for the lessor. Both the lessor and the lessee can have positive NPV for a given lease only if the two parties have different tax rates and/or different interest rates for secured debt.

Solution 10

The after tax cash outflow is:

$$L(1 - T_c) + T_c(Dep) =$$

$$(\$14,000)(1 - .20) + .20(10,000) = \$13,200$$

The appropriate discount rate is $[.15(1 - .20)] = .12$. The NPV of the lease is:

$$\$50,000 - \$13,200(3.6048) = \$2,417$$

Since the NPV is positive, this lease is acceptable to the lessee. Even though the lease payment here is greater than the lease payment calculated in Problem 9, the lease has a positive NPV here primarily because the relevant discount rate is much greater than in the previous problem. The higher discount rate makes the present value of the lease payments smaller and consequently makes the NPV greater. The lower tax rate also affects the above calculations because it makes the after-tax cost of the lease payments greater but also decreases the after-tax value of the depreciation deduction.

Solution 11

The after tax cash inflow for the lessor is:

$$L(1 - T_c) + T_c(Dep) =$$

$$(\$14,000)(1 - .34) + .34(10,000) = \$12,640$$

The appropriate discount rate for the lessor is 6.6%. For the lessor, the NPV of the lease is:

$$-\$50,000 + \$12,640(4.1445) = \$2,386$$

Solution 12

The lease payment is the value of L which makes the net present value of the lease zero, as indicated in the following equation:

$$\$50,000 - (.80L)(3.6048) - (\$2,000)(3.6048) = 0$$

The value of L is $14,838.

Note that in this case, the NPV of the lease for the lessor plus the NPV of the lease for the lessee is not equal to zero. The reason is that the tax rates and the relevant interest rates differ for the two parties to the lease. In fact, the lease payment which makes the lessor indifferent is $13,128, as indicated in the solution to Problem 9. Furthermore, we see in Problem 11 that a lease payment of $14,000 provides a positive NPV to the lessor, so that a payment of $14,838 would be more profitable to the lessor.

The lease payment of $14,838 is called the reservation payment of the lessee; this is the maximum lease payment the lessee would pay. The reservation payment of the lessor is $13,128, which is the minimum payment the lessor would accept. A negotiated lease payment would have to be between these two figures.

Solution 13

The cash flows (in thousands) associated with the CHCL, Inc. lease are:

	0	1	2	3	4	5
Purchase price	-$60.0					
After-tax lease payment	14.40	14.40	14.40	14.40	14.40	14.40
Depreciation tax shield		4.80	7.20	4.80	4.80	2.40
After-tax residual value						7.20
Total	-$45.60	19.20	21.60	19.20	19.20	24.00

Solution notes: The depreciation tax shield in year 2, for example, is [.30($60,000)(.40)] = $7,200. The after-tax residual value is [.20(60,000)(1 - .40)] = $7,200. The cars are depreciated to zero over their life, so the 'excess' depreciation must be 'recaptured'.

Solution 14

The after-tax residual value is riskier than the other cash flows. Because the hopper cars are CHLC, Inc's primary assets, the WACC is a reasonably appropriate discount rate for the residual value. All other cash flows are discounted at the after-tax cost of borrowing, 4.8%. The present value of the residual is [$7.2(.5674)] = $4.09. The present value of the other cash flows equals $83.87 thousand. The total present value is $87.96 thousand, so the net present value is (-$45.6 + $87.96) = $42.36 as shown below.

$$NPV = -\$45.60 + \frac{\$19.20}{(1.048)} + \frac{\$21.60}{(1.048)^2} + \frac{\$19.20}{(1.048)^3}$$

$$+ \frac{\$19.20}{(1.048)^4} + \frac{\$16.80}{(1.048)^5} + \frac{\$7.20}{(1.12)^5} = \$42.36$$

Solution 15

In order to just break even, NPV = 0, CHLC, Inc. needs to charge $10,812 to break even. To find this value, set the present value of the after tax lease payment equal to the initial cost ($60.00) net of the present value of the depreciation tax shield ($21.18) and the present value of the salvage value ($4.09), and solve for the before tax lease payment.

$$A^6_{4.8\%} (1.048)(1-.4)PMT = \$60.00 - \$21.18 - \$4.09$$

$$PMT = \$10,812.$$

Note that the annuity factor is multiplied by (1.048) because the lease payments are a six-period annuity due and the annuity factor is for an six-period ordinary annuity.

Solution 16

The following table shows the cash flows to Golden Grain Bakery. The company saves the cost of the hopper car, but foregoes the depreciation tax shield and the car's salvage value, and must make the tax deductible lease payments.

	0	1	2	3	4	5
Purchase price	$60.0					
After-tax lease payment	-19.20	-19.20	-19.20	-19.20	-19.20	-19.20
Lost depreciation tax shield		-2.40	-3.60	-2.40	-2.40	-1.20
After-tax residual value						-9.60
Total	$40.80	-21.60	-22.80	-21.60	21.60	-30.00

The table shows that the lease is like a loan, the firm gets effectively a cash infusion at time zero and then makes a series of payments. The lease is better than borrowing if the present value of the payments is less than the initial financing.

Solution 17

The NPV of the lease is shown below.

$$NPV = \$40.80 - \frac{\$21.60}{(1.064)} - \frac{\$22.80}{(1.064)^2} - \frac{\$21.60}{(1.064)^3}$$

$$- \frac{\$21.60}{(1.064)^4} - \frac{\$20.40}{(1.064)^5} - \frac{\$9.60}{(1.12)^5} = -\$54.83$$

This is not a good lease for Golden Grain Bakery. The large NPV for CHLC, Inc. comes at the expense of Golden Grain. The absolute values of the NPVs are not equal because of the different tax rates.

Solution 18

The most Golden Grain should pay is the payment that makes the lease NPV = 0. The calculations parallel Solution 15 above. In order to just break even, set the present value of the after tax lease payment equal to the initial cost ($60.00) net of the present value of the depreciation tax shield ($10.18) and the present value of the salvage value ($5.45), and solve for the before tax lease payment.

$$A^6_{6.4\%} (1.064)(1-.2) \, PMT = \$60.00 - \$10.18 - \$5.45$$

$$PMT = \$10,734.$$

Note that the annuity factor is multiplied by (1.064) because the lease payments are an annuity due and the annuity factor is for an ordinary annuity. From Problem 15, the lowest lease payment that CHLC, Inc. is willing to charge is $10,812. Thus, since Golden Grain would pay at most $10,734, there is no lease payment that would make the lease positive NPV for both parties.

Solution 19

The lease versus purchase cash flows are presented in the following table.

	0	1	2	3	4
Purchase price	$1,200				
After-tax lease payment		-252	-252	-252	-252
Lost depreciation tax shield		-90	-90	-90	-90
Total	$1,200	-342	-342	-342	-342

The value of the lease relative to the purchase option is the $1,200 equivalent financing provided by the lease less the after-tax net lease payments discounted at the after-tax borrowing rate:

$$NPV = \$1,200 - \Sigma[\$342/(1.07)^t]$$

$$= \$1,200 - \$1,158.43 = \$41.57$$

Since the NPV is positive, leasing is better than purchasing the locomotive. Note that the loan repayment schedule is not important to the solution of the problem. If 10% is the market rate of interest, then the present value of the loan, whatever the repayment schedule, is $1,200 thousand. If in doubt, calculate the present value of the principal and interest payments on a pretax and after-tax basis.

Solution 20

The break-even, or reservation, lease payment is the payment that makes the NPV equal zero. That is, the lease payment L that solves the following equation:

$$NPV = 0 = \$1,200 - \Sigma[(\$L(.7) + 90)/(1.07)^t]$$

$$\$1,200 = (.7L + 90)(3.3872)$$

$$L = \$377.54,$$

where 3.3872 is the present value annuity factor for 4 years at 7%. Cumulo & Nimbus would be indifferent between leasing and purchasing if the lease payment was $377.54.

Solution 21

The debt capacity created by the lease is the present value of the after-tax lease payments. That is,

$$\text{debt capacity} = \Sigma[\$342.0/(1.07)^t]$$

$$= \$1,158.43 \text{ thousand}$$

If you borrowed this amount, your repayment schedule would be:

	0	1	2	3	4
Principal	$1,158.43	897.52	618.34	319.63	0
Interest					
(pre-tax)		115.84	89.75	61.83	31.96
(after-tax)		81.09	62.83	43.28	22.37
Principal payment		260.91	279.17	298.72	319.63
Total		342.00	342.00	342.00	342.00

Solution 22

The APV approach calculates the value of leasing by finding the NPV as if the purchase was all equity financed and subtracting the lost interest tax shield. Finding the all equity NPV is easy, it's just the difference between the $1,200 not spent and the after-tax cash flow determined in Problem 19, $342 per year, discounted at the pre-tax rate of 10%. That is,

$$\text{all equity NPV} = \$1200 - \Sigma[\$342.0/(1.10)^i]$$

$$= \$1200 - 1,084.09 = \$115.91$$

Calculating the lost interest tax-shield is tricky. By leasing the asset, you lose the tax shield associated with not borrowing an amount equal to the debt capacity created by the lease. Note that the interest tax shield is not based on the purchase price of the asset, $1,200 thousand in our case, but on the $1,158.43 you could have borrowed with equivalent after-tax payments. The present value of the lost tax-shield is then (interest payments from Problem 21):

$$\text{PV(tax shield)} = .30 \times [\$115.84/(1.10) + \$89.75/(1.10)^2$$

$$+ \$61.83/(1.10)^3 + \$31.96/(1.10)^4]$$

$$= .30 \times \$247.77 = \$74.33$$

The NPV of the lease is $115.91 - $74.33 = $41.58, the same value (within rounding error) as determined in Solution 19.

Solution 23

Since the lessor and Cumulo & Nimbus have different tax rate, each will face a different NPV from the lease. The lessor's cash flows are shown in the following table.

	0	1	2	3	4
Purchase price	-$1,200				
After-tax lease payment		216	216	216	216
Depreciation tax shield		120	120	120	120
Total	-$1,200	336	336	336	336

The NPV of the lease is:

$$NPV = -\$1,200 + \Sigma[\$336.0/(1.06)^t]$$

$$= -\$1,200 + \$1,164.28 = -\$35.72$$

Since the NPV is negative, the lessor will lose money on the lease. To break-even, the lessor must charge $377.18 per year. Compare this value with Cumulo & Nimbus' break-even payment in Problem 20. Within rounding error they are the same. Thus, $377 would be a fair lease payment to both parties.

CHAPTER 25

DERIVATIVES AND HEDGING RISK

CHAPTER MISSION STATEMENT

The purpose of Chapter 25 is to introduce the concept of hedging, or reducing risk through financial contracts. The chapter discusses forward contracts, futures contracts, the differences between them, and how they are used to reduce risk. The pricing of forward contracts is discussed. The concept of duration is introduced. Duration hedging is described and illustrated. The chapter concludes with a discussion of swaps contracts.

The key concepts presented in Chapter 25 are outlined below.

- ◆Forward contracts
- ◆Futures contracts
    - ●delivery option
    - ●marked-to-market
    - ●exchange traded
- ◆Hedging
    - ●short hedge
    - ●long hedge
- ◆Pricing forward contracts
    - ●pricing futures contracts
- ◆Duration hedging
    - ●duration
    - ●matching liabilities with assets
- ◆Swaps contracts
    - ●interest rate swaps
    - ●currency swaps
    - ●exotics

CONCEPT TEST

1. Procedures for reducing risk are referred to as _____.

2. The financial instruments used for hedging are _____ and _____.

3. A _____ is an agreement to make an exchange of assets at a future date.

4. The seller of a forward contract is referred to as the _____ of the contract.

5. A cash transaction differs from a forward contract in that the exchange of assets occurs _____ for the cash transaction.

6. The difference between a forward contract and an option is that, in the case of the forward contract, the participants are _____ the terms of the contract.

7.   When a trader buys or sells a futures contract, he contracts with the exchange _____, rather than with an individual trader.

8.   Forward contracts traded on an organized exchange are referred to as _____.

9.   The _____ provisions of futures contracts are designed to reduce the likelihood of a default by either the buyer or the seller of the contract.

10. A producer of a commodity can use a _____ to reduce the risk of a decline in the price of the commodity.

11. A processor of a commodity can use a _____ to reduce the risk of an increase in the price of the commodity which the processor must purchase.

12. Long-term bonds are subject to _____ price volatility for a given change in interest rates than are short-term bonds.

13. The greater price volatility for a long-term bond arises from the _____ over a longer period of time.

14. Price volatility is _____ related to maturity and _____ to coupon rate.

15. Financial institutions frequently use the concept of duration in order to _____ against interest rate risk.

16. Firms use swaps to change their _____ exposures.

17. A firm would use an interest rate swap to exchange a _____ rate obligation for an agreement to pay a _____ rate.

18. A multinational firm can use currency swaps to hedge _____ risk.

ANSWERS TO CONCEPT TEST

1.   hedging
2.   forward contracts; futures contracts
3.   forward contract
4.   writer
5.   immediately
6.   obligated to perform
7.   clearinghouse
8.   futures contracts
9.   mark-to-the-market

10. short hedge
11. long hedge
12. greater
13. compounding of interest
14. positively; inversely
15. immunize
16. risk
17. fixed; floating
18. exchange rate

PROBLEMS

Problem 1

Closing prices for coffee futures are shown in the following table. Suppose that you establish a one contract long hedge on March 25 at the closing price. On April 7 the short position notifies the clearinghouse of the intent to deliver. Each contract is for 37,500 pounds of coffee. On what day does delivery take place?

Date	Closing Price (cents/pound)
Mar 25	143.55
Mar 26	146.25
Mar 27	146.45
Mar 30	146.00
Mar 31	146.25
Apr 1	143.75
Apr 2	144.30
Apr 3	140.55
Apr 6	141.65
Apr 7	142.00
Apr 8	144.55
Apr 9	146.30

Problem 2

What price is paid for the coffee upon delivery?

Problem 3

What are the cash flows associated with your long position? What price do you pay for the coffee?

Use the following table of semiannual spot rates to answer Problems 4-10.

Time from today	Semiannual rate
6 months	0.050
12 months	0.055
18 months	0.058
24 months	0.060
30 months	0.060
36 months	0.060
42 months	0.062
48 months	0.063
54 months	0.065
60 months	0.065
66 months	0.065

Problem 4

Find the price of a Treasury bond with a 10%-coupon rate, a $1,000 maturity value and five years to maturity, using the semiannual spot rates shown above.

Problem 5

Suppose you sign a contract today specifying that a five-year Treasury bond, as described in Problem 4, will be delivered to you in six months. If you pay for the bond today, what is the price you would pay? (Note that this is not a forward contract because you pay for the bond today, rather than on the delivery date. Also note that the bond to be delivered has a five-year maturity on the delivery date.)

Problem 6

Suppose that the contract in Problem 5 is a forward contract, so that payment for the Treasury bond will be made six months from today, when the bond is delivered, rather than today. What is the price of the forward contract, to be paid in six months?

Problem 7

Suppose that all semiannual spot rates shown in the table increase by 10 basis points. (A basis point is one one-hundredth of a percentage point, or .01% = .0001.) What is the value of the five-year, 10% coupon bond described in Problem 4?

Problem 8

Suppose that, as in Problem 5, you sign a contract today specifying that a five-year Treasury bond will be delivered to you in six months. If you pay for the bond today, and interest rates have increased by 10 basis points, what is the price you would pay?

Problem 9

Suppose that the contract in Problem 8 is a forward contract, with delivery of a five-year Treasury bond six months from today. What is the price of the forward contract, to be paid in six months?

Problem 10

Suppose that the spot rates indicated in the spot-rate table decrease by 10 basis points. What is the present value of a five-year Treasury bond, with a 10% coupon rate, to be delivered six months from today, if the bond is paid for today? What is the price of a forward contract to purchase the Treasury bond six months from today?

Problem 11

Melissa's Mortgage Banking Company has made a commitment to lend $500,000 in mortgage loans. The terms of the loans specify a thirty-year loan with a 10% interest rate and annual payments of principal and interest. The market rate for thirty-year mortgages is also 10%. Melissa will make the loans six months from today. What are the annual mortgage payments on the loans? If the loans are paid monthly, what are the monthly payments?

Problem 12

Suppose that, when Melissa makes the loans described in Problem 11, she immediately sells the loans to an insurance company. If the interest rate for 30-year mortgages has increased to 11% at that time, at what price will Melissa be able to sell the mortgages? If the interest rate has declined to 9%, at what price will Melissa sell the mortgages? (Assume that the mortgages specify annual payments of principal and interest.)

Problem 13

In order to hedge against the interest-rate risk indicated in Problem 12, Melissa decides to sell five $100,000 Treasury bond futures contracts which specify delivery of Treasury bonds with an 8%-coupon rate and a twenty-year maturity. The delivery date of the contracts is in six months, at the same time that Melissa will extend the mortgage loans. If the interest rate for long-term Treasury bonds is currently 9%, what is the price of the futures contract? [Assume that all relevant semiannual spot rates are equal to (.090/2) = .045.]

Problem 14

Suppose that Melissa sells the five futures contracts today and that, six months from today, interest rates for twenty-year Treasury bonds have increased to 10%. What is the price of the futures contract on that date.

Problem 15

Suppose that Melissa makes the commitment on the mortgage loans described in Problem 11 and sells the five Treasury-bond futures contracts described in Problem 13; furthermore, in the next six months, interest rates on thirty-year mortgages increase from 10% to 11% and yields on twenty-year Treasury bonds increase from 9% to 10%. What is the effect on Melissa's position?

Problem 16

Three zero-coupon bonds each have a maturity value of $1,000 and are priced to yield 8%. The maturities of the three bonds are 2 years, 5 years and 15 years, respectively. Calculate the current price of each bond.

Problem 17

Suppose that the yields for the three bonds described in Problem 16 increase to 9%. Which of the three bonds has the greatest percentage change in price?

Problem 18

Calculate the duration for a ten-year bond, with a $1,000 face value and an 8%-coupon rate. The bond is selling at par. Assume that the bond pays annual interest.

Problem 19

Calculate the duration of the bond described in the previous problem, but now assuming that the yield to maturity is 12%. Calculate the duration if the yield to maturity is 4%.

Problem 20

The Avarice Savings & Loan has the following market value balance sheet. Calculate the duration of Avarice's assets?

Assets	Market value	Duration
Federal funds	$ 100	0 months
Accounts receivable backed loans	400	2 months
Short term debt	350	9 months
Long term debt	200	3 years
Mortgages	250	15 years
Total	$1,300	

Liabilities and Equity	Market value	Duration
Checking and savings deposits	$ 400	0 months
Certificates of deposit	450	14 months
Long term funding	250	10 years
Equity	200	
Total	$1,300	

Problem 21

Calculate the duration of Avarice's liabilities.

Problem 22

Avarice S & L wants to change the duration of its liabilities in a way to make it immune from interest rate risk. What must be the new duration?

Problem 23

Avarice S & L wants to change the duration of its assets in a way to make it immune from interest rate risk. What must be the new duration?

Problem 24

You have just leased out a small commercial office building that you own. Terms of the lease call for annual payments of $14,400 for the next five years. You want to hedge against increases in interest rates by using futures contracts on three year, 6.57% coupon Treasury bonds. The prevailing market rate applicable for both the lease and the T-bond is 10.0%. Calculate the present value and duration of the lease.

Problem 25

Calculate the present value and duration of the T-bond.

Problem 26

If interest rates rise to 12%, calculate the value change to the lease, T-bonds, and hedged position.

Problem 27

Five years ago, a firm agreed to borrow $100 million for 5 years with annual interest paid a year end based on LIBOR at the beginning of the year. The firm preferred to borrow at a fixed rate. Thus, the firm entered into a swap agreement that required it to pay 8% and receive LIBOR. When the swap was set up, LIBOR was 7.5%, and over the following four years LIBOR was 8%, 9%, 9.5%, 7.5%. What payments did the firm make on its loan?

SOLUTIONS

Solution 1

The long hedge involves entering into one futures contract to take delivery of 37,500 pounds of coffee during the delivery month. The writer of the contract may choose to deliver on any day in the month, and here chooses to initiate the delivery sequence on April 7. Delivery takes place two days later on April 9.

Solution 2

The delivery price is set to the closing price on the day the short notifies the clearinghouse of his intent to deliver. Thus, the coffee will be sold at 142.00 cents per pound. One futures contract is for 37,500 pounds, therefore the long must pay $53,250.00.

Solution 3

The cash flow associated with marking-to-market are shown in the following table. As the long position, you must pay the clearinghouse when the price drops and you will receive payment when the price rises. Your cash flows from March 25 to April 7 are:

$$2.70 + 0.20 - 0.45 + 0.25 - 2.50 + 0.55 - 3.75 + 1.10 + 0.35 = -1.55$$

Date	Closing Price (cents/pound)	Cash Flow (cents/pound)
Mar 25	143.55	
Mar 26	146.25	2.70
Mar 27	146.45	0.20
Mar 30	146.00	−0.45
Mar 31	146.25	0.25
Apr 1	143.75	−2.50
Apr 2	144.30	0.55
Apr 3	140.55	−3.75
Apr 6	141.65	1.10
Apr 7	142.00	0.35
Apr 8	144.55	
Apr 9	146.30	

Your effective price is the agreed upon March 25 price of 143.55 cents per pound. You pay 142.00 cents per pound on April 9 plus you lost 1.55 cents per pound on the futures position. Your effective price is $142.00 + 1.55 = 143.55$ cents per pound., or $\$1.4355 \times 37,500$ lbs $= \$53,831.25$. Payments must be made to the clearinghouse within one day. For example, within one day of March 26 the short must pay you $\$.0270 \times 37,500 = \$1,012.50$ per contract. Note that establishing a long position in a futures contract hedges against price rises, in this problem, however, the price moved against you, so you lost money on the hedge.

Solution 4

The bond described here pays semiannual coupon interest payments of $[(.10)(\$1,000)/2] = \$50$. The present value of the bond is found by discounting each of the future payments at the appropriate spot rate. For example, the present value of the first interest payment is $(\$50/1.050) = \$47.619$; the present value of the second payment is $[\$50/(1.055)^2] = \$44.923$. Complete calculations are shown below:

Time from today	Semiannual rate	Payment	Present value
6 months	0.050	$ 50	$47.619
12 months	0.055	50	44.923
18 months	0.058	50	42.219
24 months	0.060	50	39.605
30 months	0.060	50	37.363
36 months	0.060	50	35.248
42 months	0.062	50	32.817
48 months	0.063	50	30.669
54 months	0.065	50	28.368
60 months	0.065	1,050	559.362
Present value			$ 898.193

Solution 5

The first interest payment for the five-year bond will be paid one year from today. The present value of this payment, discounted at the 12-month spot rate from Problem 4, is $[\$50/(1.055)^2] = \$44.923$. The complete calculation is indicated in the table below:

Time from today	Semiannual rate	Payment	Present value
12 months	0.055	$ 50	44.923
18 months	0.058	50	42.219
24 months	0.060	50	39.605
30 months	0.060	50	37.363
36 months	0.060	50	35.248
42 months	0.062	50	32.817
48 months	0.063	50	30.669
54 months	0.065	50	28.368
60 months	0.065	1,050	26.636
66 months	0.065	1,050	525.223
Present value			$ 843.071

Therefore, you would pay $843.07 today for a Treasury bond to be delivered to you six months from today. At that time, the bond will have five years to maturity.

Solution 6

The price to be paid (P_{FC}) is equal to the present value calculated in Problem 5, times one plus the six-month spot rate: [($843.07)(1.05)] = $885.22. This calculation reflects the fact that, rather than paying for the bond today, the forward contract specifies payment in six months; therefore, the size of the payment must include interest over the next six months.

Solution 7

Each of the semiannual interest rates increases by .10% = .0010. Therefore, the present value of the first interest payment is [$50/(1.051)] = $47.574; the present value of the second payment is [$50/(1.056)^2] = $44.838. The present value of the bond is $891.51. As we expect, the present value of the bond decreases with the increase in interest rates.

Solution 8

The present value of the first interest payment, to be received in 12 months, is [$50/(1.056)^2] = $44.838. The present value of the bond is $836.02. As a result of the increase in interest rates, the present value of the bond has decreased from the value calculated in Problem 5.

Solution 9

P_{FC} is equal to the present value calculated in Problem 8 times one plus the six-month spot rate: [($836.02)(1.051)] = $878.66. Note that, as a result of the increase in the spot rates specified in Problem 7, the price of the forward contract has decreased from $885.22, as calculated in Problem 6, to $878.66

Solution 10

If the Treasury bond is paid for today, the price is $850.20. The price of the forward contract, to be paid six months from today, is $891.86. The decrease in spot rates results in an increase in the price of the forward contract, compared to the value indicated in Problem 6.

Solution 11

Using the present value annuity factor for a thirty-year annuity, at 10% interest, the annual payments are ($500,000/9.426914) = $53,039.63. Monthly payments are $4,387.86.

Solution 12

When the insurance company buys the mortgages from Melissa, the insurance company is buying a thirty-year annuity, with annual payments of $53,039.63. At a discount rate of 11%, the present value of these payments is [($53,039.63)(8.693793)] = $461,115.56. Therefore, if the interest rate increases from 10% to 11% during the six-month period, Melissa will lose $38,884.44. On the other hand, if the interest rate for thirty-year mortgages declines to 9%, then the present value of the mortgages will increase to $544,910.75, and Melissa will gain $44,910.75.

Solution 13

The first coupon interest payment for the Treasury bond is $40, to be paid one year from today, and the maturity value plus the last interest payment, or $1,040, will be paid 20.5 years from today. We can discount all of these payments, at the 4.5% semiannual rate, to today, and then multiply the present value by 1.045 to find the price of the futures contract six months from today. However, since all the semiannual spot rates are identical, we need only determine the present value of the Treasury bond, as of date 1, with payments beginning as of date 2. The present value of the Treasury bond is $907.99. (Although this calculation is based on the valuation of a forward contract, it is a reasonable approximation for the value of a futures contract.) The futures contract calls for delivery of $100,000 face-value of Treasury bonds, so the price of the futures contract is [(100)($907.99)] = $90,799. Since Melissa will sell five contracts, the price is [(5)($90,799)] = $453,995.

Solution 14

The present value of a $1,000 Treasury bond with an 8%-coupon rate and twenty years to maturity is $828.41. The price of the futures contract is [(5)(100)($828.41)] = $414,205.

Solution 15

The increase in mortgage rates results in a loss in the value of the mortgage commitments of $38,884.44. Since Melissa has sold the futures contracts, the decrease in the price of the futures contract represents a gain of $39,790. Therefore, the net gain is $905.56. Note that by hedging, Melissa has avoided a loss in the value of the loan commitments equal to $38,884.44, and has also gained $905.56.

Solution 16

The present value of the two-year bond is $[1,000/(1.08)^2] = \$857.33$. The present value of the five-year bond is $[\$1,000/(1.08)^5] = \$680.58$, and the present value of the fifteen-year bond is $[\$1,000/(1.08)^{15}] = \$315.24$.

Solution 17

The present values are now: $841.68, $649.93 and $274.54, for the two-year, five-year and fifteen-year bonds, respectively. The percentage decreases in price are: 1.825%, 4.504%, and 12.911%. As expected, the bond with the longest maturity also has the greatest percentage decrease in price.

Solution 18

Since the bond is selling at face value, its yield to maturity is equal to its coupon rate. To find the duration, we first calculate the present value of each interest payment, then express these present values as a percentage of the price of the bond. The resulting weights are multiplied by the 'maturity' of each payment to find the duration. The following table demonstrates these calculations:

Year	Payment	Present value	Relative value	Relative value × year
1	$80	$74.074	.074074	.074074
2	80	68.587	.068587	.137174
3	80	63.507	.063507	.190520
4	80	58.802	.058802	.235210
5	80	54.447	.054447	.272233
6	80	50.414	.050414	.302481
7	80	46.679	.046679	.326755
8	80	43.222	.043222	.345772
9	80	40.020	.040020	.360179
10	1,080	500.249	.500249	5.002490
		$1,000.000	1.000000	7.246888

The last column shows that the duration is 7.25 years. This implies that the 10-year bond has the same sensitivity to small changes in interest rates as a 7.25 year zero coupon bond.

Solution 19

The duration of the 10-year bond will change as interest rates change. With a yield to maturity of 12%, the 8% coupon bond will have a value of $773.991 and a duration of 6.837 years. With a 4% yield to maturity, the value will be $1,324.436 and the duration will equal 7.637 years. As these values show, for a given bond there is an inverse relation between yield to maturity and duration.

Solution 20

The duration of the assets is:

$$\text{Duration} = (\$100/\$1,300)(0 \text{ yrs}) + (\$400/\$1,300)(2/12 \text{ yrs})$$

$$+ (\$350/\$1,300)(.75 \text{ yrs}) + (\$200/\$1,300)(3 \text{ yrs})$$

$$+ (\$250/\$1,300)(15 \text{ yrs}) = 3.60 \text{ yrs}$$

Solution 21

The duration of the liabilities is:

$$\text{Duration} = (\$400/\$1,100)(0 \text{ yrs}) + (\$450/\$1,100)(14/12 \text{ yrs})$$

$$+ (\$250/\$1,100)(10 \text{ yrs}) = 2.75 \text{ yrs}$$

Solution 22

For Avarice to be immune from interest rate risk the following must hold:

$$\text{Duration assets} \times \text{value of assets} = \text{Duration liabilities} \times \text{value of liabilities.}$$

Then, solving for duration of liabilities,

$$\text{Duration liabilities} = 3.60 \text{ yrs} \times \$1,300/\$1,100 = 4.25 \text{ yrs}$$

Solution 23

For Avarice to be immune from interest rate risk the following must hold:

$$\text{Duration assets} \times \text{value of assets} = \text{Duration liabilities} \times \text{value of liabilities.}$$

Then, solving for duration of assets,

$$\text{Duration assets} = 2.75 \text{ yrs} \times \$1,100/\$1,300 = 2.33 \text{ yrs}$$

Solution 24

The present value of the lease is:

$$\text{PV(lease)} = \Sigma\$14,400/(1.10)^t = \$54,587.33$$

The duration of the lease is:

$$\text{Duration(lease)} = [\Sigma(\$14,400 \times t)/(1.10)^t]/\$54,587.33$$

$$= 2.810 \text{ years}$$

Solution 25

The present value of the T-bond is:

$$PV(\text{T-bond}) = \Sigma \$65.7/(1.10)^t + \$1,000/(1.10)^3 = \$914.70$$

The duration of the T-bond is:

$$\text{Duration(T-bond)} = [(\$65.7 \times 1)/(1.10) + (\$65.7 \times 2)/(1.10)^2$$

$$+ (\$1,065.7 \times 3)/(1.10)^3]/\$914.70$$

$$= \$2,570.35/\$914.70$$

$$= 2.810 \text{ years}$$

Solution 26

If interest rates rise to 12%, the value of the lease falls to $51,908.78, a decline of $2,678.55. The hedge position is 54.58733 T-bonds to match the original value of the lease (note: in practice only an integer number of bonds are available). When rates rise to 12%, the value of the futures position falls to $869.58 per bond or a change of ($914.70 − $869.58) × 54.58733 = ($45.120) × 54.58733 = $2,462.98. This is a gain to you. Thus, the net change in value is −$2,678.55 + $2,462.98 = −$215.57. Since the hedge is not perfect, the net change is not zero. But, by hedging you lost only $215.57 rather than $2,678.55.

Solution 27

The cash flows (millions $) from the 5-year $100 million floating rate loan and the floating for fixed swap are shown in the following table. The swap turned the firm's floating rate loan into an 8% fixed-rate loan.

	0	1	2	3	4	5
LIBOR (%)	7.5	8.0	9.0	9.5	7.5	
Loan						
Pay LIBOR	+100	−7.5	−8.0	−9.0	−9.5	−107.5
Swap						
Pay fixed		−8.0	−8.0	−8.0	−8.0	−8.0
Receive LIBOR		+7.5	+8.0	+9.0	+9.5	+7.5
Net Payments	+100	−8.0	−8.0	−8.0	−8.0	−108.0

CHAPTER 26

CORPORATE FINANCIAL MODELS AND LONG-TERM PLANNING

CHAPTER MISSION STATEMENT

The purpose of Chapter 26 is to describe the long-term financial planning process. Financial planning models are simple devices that allow managers to formulate how to achieve the firm's goals and how investment and financing decisions consistent with these goals interact. The chapter discusses and illustrates how to construct pro forma financial statements from the sales forecast. The chapter concludes by discussing corporate growth as an objective, and how financial planning models assist in understanding the relationship between growth and the firm's financing and investment needs.

The key concepts presented in Chapter 26 are outlined below.

- ♦Corporate financial planning
  - ●time frame
  - ●level of aggregation
- ♦Financial-planning model
  - ●sales forecast
  - ●pro forma statements
  - ●asset requirements
  - ●financial requirements
  - ●plug
  - ●economic assumptions
- ♦External funds needed
- ♦Sustainable growth

CONCEPT TEST

1. The two dimensions of financial planning are the _____ and the _____.

2. The process of combining smaller investment proposals into a single larger asset requirement is called _____.

3. All financial plans require a _____.

4. Projected future accounting statements are called _____ statements.

5. A financial plan usually addresses projected capital spending or _____.

6. A financial plan usually addresses dividend and debt policy, or, more generally, _____.

7. In order to reconcile the various financial statements in a financial plan, a _____ variable must be designated.

8. A financial plan must include a set of _____ such as projected interest rates.

9. Financial planning models frequently assume that most variables are proportional to _____.

10. In contrast to the goal of maximization of shareholder wealth, many corporations use an explicit _____ as a goal.

11. Assume a firm's assets and net income are proportional to sales, its debt and dividend policy are fixed, and it will not issue new equity. In this case, the plug variable is _____.

12. The plug variable in question 11 is called the firm's _____.

13. The time horizon considered by most short-term financial plans is _____.

14. The time horizon considered by most long-term financial plans is _____.

15. Amber Corporation has a return on equity of 16% and pays out 30% of net income in the form of dividends. Its approximate growth rate is _____.

ANSWERS TO CONCEPT TEST

1. time dimension; level of aggregation
2. aggregation
3. sales forecast
4. pro forma
5. asset requirements
6. financing requirements
7. plug
8. economic assumptions

9. sales
10. growth rate
11. growth
12. sustainable growth rate
13. 12 months
14. 2 to 5 years
15. $(.16)(1 - .3) = 11.2\%$

PROBLEMS

Use the following information for the Sansar Company to solve Problems 1-5. All the financial statements are from the most recent reporting period.

Income statement	
Sales	$5,000
Cost of sales	3,500
Depreciation	800
Interest	200
Tax (35%)	175
Net income	$ 325
Dividends	130

Balance sheet

Current assets	$ 850	Current liabilities	$ 320
Net fixed assets	3,275	Long term debt	1,330
		Equity	2,475
Total	$4,125		$4,125

Problem 1

Sansar forecasts that sales next year will be $5,600. Calculate the external funds needed (EFN).

Problem 2

Assume that Sansar has sufficient excess capacity to support a sales level of $5,300 with no new fixed assets. Calculate EFN for projected sales of $5,600.

Problem 3

Sansar believes that an industry slowdown is possible over the next year. In this case, sales growth will be 4%. Calculate EFN, assume no new fixed assets, and interpret your answer.

Problem 4

Assuming that Sansar is operating at full capacity, what is the maximum sales increase possible before external financing is required?

Problem 5

Assume that no new equity will be sold, the dividend payout is fixed, and the debt/equity ratio is fixed; what is Sansar's maximum sustainable growth rate? In answering, assume that the debt/equity ratio is based on total debt.

Use the most recent financial statements for Nortada, Inc. shown below to solve Problems 6-8.

Income statement

Sales	$6,130
Cost of sales	5,330
Tax (34%)	272
Net income	$ 528
Dividends	0

	Balance sheet		
Net working capital	$2,590	Long term debt	$3,530
Fixed assets	8,000	Equity	7,060
Total	$10,590		$10,590

Problem 6

Prepare a pro forma income statement, balance sheet, and sources and uses statement for Nortada, assuming that sales grow by 20%. New long-term debt is the plug variable. Depreciation (included in costs on the income statement) is 10% of beginning fixed assets.

Problem 7

Rework Problem 6 assuming that Nortada is operating its plant and equipment at only 70% of capacity, and that long-term debt does not change. Use new equity as the plug variable. How do you interpret your answer?

Problem 8

Try this one on your own. Assume that Nortada is operating at full capacity, no dividends will be paid, no new equity will be sold, and the debt/equity ratio remains constant; what is its maximum sustainable growth rate?

Problem 9

Experience has shown that the Quahog Company's sales are sensitive to the state of the economy. The company's financial officer believes that sales will increase by 6% plus 1.5 times the expected change in GDP. Furthermore, the company's financial planning staff have determined that current assets (CA), fixed assets (FA), current liabilities (CL), and net profit (NP) are related to sales by the following relationships.

$$CA = \$25,000 + .15 \text{ Sales}$$
$$FA = \$50,000 + .40 \text{ Sales}$$
$$CL = \$5,000 + .05 \text{ Sales}$$
$$NP = .05 \text{ Sales}$$

Last year's balance sheet is shown below. Sales were $500,000. The firm's dividend payout ratio is 20%. Economic predictions suggest that next year GDP will increase by 4%. Calculate a pro forma balance sheet for Quahog.

Quahog balance sheet

Net working capital	$100,000	Current liabilities	$ 30,000
Fixed assets	150,000	Long term debt	70,000
		Common stock	100,000
		Retained earnings	50,000
Total	$250,000		$250,000

Problem 10

Revised expectations suggest that next year the economy will be in recession, and GDP growth will be minus two percent (-2%). Quahog Company's response to the coming recession is to cut costs and increase the profit margin to 6%. Recalculate a pro forma balance sheet for Quahog using these new assumptions.

Use the following information about Arcadia Enterprises to answer Problems 11-14.

Arcadia Enterprises would like to grow 10% per year for the foreseeable future. The firm's financial statements are provided below ($ in thousands).

Income statement

Sales	$1,400
Cost of sales	700
Depreciation	200
Interest	150
Tax (34%)	119
Net income	$ 231
Dividends	169

Balance sheet

Current assets	$1,891	Current liabilities	$1,173
Net fixed assets	1,689	Long term debt	945
		Common stock	959
		Retained earnings	503
Total	$3,580		$3,580

Problem 11

If the firm grows 10% next year, what is Arcadia's need for external financing.

Problem 12

Calculate the sustainable growth rate for Arcadia.

Problem 13

What dividend pay-out ratio should Arcadia adopt to achieve its 10% growth objective?

Problem 14

Construct a pro forma balance sheet for Arcadia Enterprises.

Problem 15

Yodel Corporation forecasts that sales will grow 20% next year. The firm's current financial statements are provided below ($ in thousands). If assets grow proportionally with sales, what will be Yodel's external funds needed (EFN)? Assume that Yodel maintains the same net profit margin and dividend payout ratio.

Income statement

Sales	$230,000
Costs	207,000
Gross Profit	23,000
Tax (35%)	8,050
Net income	$ 14,950
Dividends	5,980
Retained Earnings	8,970

Balance sheet

Current assets	$200,000	Current debt	$100,000
Net fixed assets	300,000	Long term debt	122,222
		Common stock	150,000
		Retained earnings	127,778
Total	$500,000		$500,000

Problem 16

Construct a pro forma income statement and balance sheet for Yodel Corporation. Assume that Yodel maintains the same current debt-to-long term debt and debt-to-equity ratios when it raises the external funds needed calculated in Problem 15.

SOLUTIONS

Solution 1

The asset/sales ratio is ($4,125/$5,000) = .825. Profit margin is 6.5%, and the payout ratio is 0.40. Current liabilities will vary spontaneously with sales; however, the amount of long-term debt is under management control and generally does not vary spontaneously. Thus, holding long term debt constant, we can use current liabilities/sales ($320/$5,000 = .064) as the debt/sales ratio. EFN is calculated as follows:

$$EFN = (Assets/Sales) \times \Delta S - (Debt/Sales) \times \Delta S - [p(Projected\ Sales)(1-d)]$$

$$= (.825)(\$600) - (.064)(\$600) - (.065)(\$5,600)(1-.40) = \$238.20$$

The pro forma balance sheet is shown below. Next year's net income will be $364 and the firm will pay dividends of $145.60.

Pro forma balance sheet

Current assets	$ 952.00	Current liabilities	$ 358.40
Net fixed assets	3,668.00	Long term debt	1,330.00
		Equity	2,693.40
		EFN	238.20
Total	$4,620.00		$4,620.00

Solution 2

At the full capacity sales level of $5,300, current assets would be [($850/$5,000)($5,300)] = $901, and fixed assets would be $3,275. That is, at full capacity no new fixed assets are required, but $51 additional current assets are required. Total assets would thus be $4,176. The asset/sales ratio at full capacity is ($4,176/$5,300) = .7879, so total assets would increase proportionally with sales for the $300 additional sales above full capacity. Thus, EFN would be:

$$EFN = [51 + (.7879)\$300] - (.064)(\$600) - (.065)(\$5,600)(1-.40) = \$30.57$$

The pro forma balance sheet, given that sales of $5,300 represents full capacity, is shown below.

Pro forma balance sheet

Current assets	$ 952.00	Current liabilities	$ 358.40
Net fixed assets	3,460.37	Long term debt	1,330.00
		Equity	2,693.40
		EFN	30.57
Total	$4,412.37		$4,412.37

Solution 3

In this case, sales will increase by $200 to $5,200, just below full capacity. Current assets will increase by $34 (= $850/$5,000 × $200) while fixed assets remain fixed. EFN is:

$$EFN = \$34 - (.064)(\$200) - (.065)(\$5,200)(1 - .40) = -\$181.60$$

A negative value for EFN indicates that Sansar will have a surplus for the year; no external financing will be required.

Pro forma balance sheet

Current assets	$ 884.00	Current liabilities	$ 332.80
Net fixed assets	3,275.00	Long term debt	1,330.00
		Equity	2,677.80
		EFN	-181.60
Total	$4,159.00		$4,159.00

Solution 4

Denote the maximum sales level as ($5,000 + x). We can solve for x by setting EFN equal to zero:

$$EFN = (.825)(x) - (.064)(x) - (.065)(\$5,000 + x)(1 - .40) = 0$$

Solving for x, we get x = $270.08, and a sales level of $5,270.08. This implies that sales could grow by 5.40% before any new financing is required. This is not the maximum sustainable growth rate, however, because the debt/equity ratio will decline in this case. This happens because retained earnings increases while borrowing remains unchanged. (See Problem 5.)

Solution 5

The debt/equity ratio (L) is 2/3 (=$1,650/$2,475), the asset/sales ratio (T) is .825, the dividend payout ratio (d) is 0.40 (=$130/$325), and the profit margin (p) is 6.5% . The maximum sustainable growth rate is:

$$\Delta S/S_o = p(1 - d)(1 + L)/[T - p(1 - d)(1 + L)]$$

$$= [.065(0.60)(5/3)]/[.825 - (.065)(0.60)(5/3)] = 8.55\%$$

Solution 6

Assuming all items are proportional to sales, the pro forma income statement and balance sheet are:

Income statement	
Sales	$7,356
Cost of sales	6,396
Tax (34%)	326
Net income	$ 634
Dividends	0

Balance sheet			
Net working capital	$3,108	Long term debt	$5,014
Fixed assets	9,600	Equity	7,694
Total	$12,708		$12,708

Depreciation is $[.10(\$8,000)] = \$800$. The sources and uses statement is:

Sources and uses

Sources

Net income	$ 634
Depreciation	800
Operating cash flow	$1,434
Borrowing	$1,484
New stock issued	0
Financing cash flow	$1,484
Total sources	$2,918

<u>Uses</u>

Increases in NWC	$ 518
Capital spending	2,400
Dividends	$ 0
Total uses	$2,918

Solution note: Net capital spending rose by $1,600. There was $800 in depreciation during the year, so gross capital spending was $2,400.

Solution 7

At 70% of capacity, sales were $6,130, so $6,130 = (.7)(Full capacity sales). Full capacity sales are thus $8,757. If sales increase by 20%, no new fixed assets will be needed. The pro forma income statement is unchanged from Problem 6. The balance sheet would look like:

Balance sheet

Net working capital	$3,108	Long term debt	$3,530
Fixed assets	7,200	Equity	6,778
Total	$10,308		$10,308

Depreciation is again $800. The sources and uses would be:

Sources and uses

<u>Sources</u>

Net income	$ 634
Depreciation	800
Operating cash flow	$1,434
Borrowing	$ 0
New stock issued	−916
Financing cash flow	$−916
Total sources	$ 518

<u>Uses</u>

Increases in NWC	$ 518
Capital spending	0
Dividends	$ 0
Total uses	$ 518

Solution note: No new assets were purchased and depreciation was $800, so fixed assets declined by $800. Beginning equity was $7,060, and retained earnings were $634, for a total of $7,694. Ending equity (the plug variable) is $6,778, so $7,694 – $6,778 = $916 in common stock was repurchased.

Solution 8

The maximum growth rate that can be sustained is 8.09%.

Solution 9

Next year's sales are forecast to be 6% + 1.5(4%) = 12% higher than last year, or $500,000(1.12) = $560,000. Using the established relationships,

$$CA = \$25,000 + .15\ (\$560,000) = \$109,000$$

$$FA = \$50,000 + .40\ (\$560,000) = \$274,000$$

$$CL = \$5,000 + .05\ (\$560,000) = \$\ 33,000$$

$$NP = .05\ (\$560,000) = \$28,000$$

Dividends are .20($28,000) = $5,600, and retained earnings are $22,400. The two remaining entries we need to determine are long term debt and equity. Assume that the firm's debt/assets ratio remains constant. Then, from last year's balance sheet debt/assets = ($30 + $70)/$250 = 0.40. Thus, next year's total debt must be .40 × ($109,000 + $274,000) = $153,200. Long term debt is $153,200 – CL = $153,200 – $33,000 = $120,200. For the balance sheet to balance, equity must be $157,400. The pro forma balance sheet is shown below.

Balance sheet (pro forma)			
Current assets	$109,000	Current liabilities	$ 33,000
Fixed assets	274,000	Long term debt	120,200
		Equity	157,400
		Retained earnings	72,400
Total	$383,000		$383,000

Solution 10

Quahog's sales are expected to increase only 6% + 1.5(-2%) = 3%, to $515,000. With these sales, net profit will be NP = .06($515,000) = $30,900. Other balance sheet entries are calculated as in Problem 9. The new pro forma balance sheet is shown below.

Balance sheet (pro forma)

Current assets	$102,250	Current liabilities	$ 30,750
Fixed assets	256,000	Long term debt	112,550
		Equity	140,230
		Retained earnings	74,720
Total	$358,250		$358,250

Solution 11

If sales grow 10% next year, assume that net income also increases by 10%. This is not an unreasonable assumption for a one-year forecast. Net income will become $231(1.10) = $254.10. Arcadia will need to finance increased net working capital, increased fixed assets including depreciation, and pay a dividend assuming a constant pay-out ratio. All are assumed to increase with sales. The increase in net working capital is .10($1,891 − $1,173) = $71.80; the increase in fixed assets plus depreciation is .10($1,689) + deprec. = $168.90 + deprec.; the dividend is pay-out ratio × net income = ($169/$231) × $254.10 = $185.90. Total required funds are $71.80 + $168.90 + deprec. + $185.90 = $426.60 + deprec. Total funds provided by operations are net income + deprec. = $254.10 + deprec. Net requirements are $426.60 + deprec. − $254.10 − deprec. = $172.50. If the debt/equity ratio (1.4487) remains constant, then the firm will need to issue $102.0545 long term debt and $70.4455 new equity. Note: D/E = 1.4487 implies D/V = 1.4487/2.4487, or D = .5916V.

Solution 12

Sustainable growth is determined by the following formula.

$$\Delta S/S_o = p(1 - d)(1 + L)/[T - p(1 - d)(1 + L)]$$

$$= [.1650(62/231)(1.4487)]/[2.5571 - (.1650)(62/231)(1.4487)] = .0257$$

Arcadia's high dividend pay-out ratio and high asset-to-sales ratio limits the firm's long-run growth rate.

Solution 13

To find the dividend pay-out ratio consistent with 10% growth, set the sustainable growth formula equal to .10 and solve for d.

$$\Delta S/S_o = p(1 - d)(1 + L)/[T - p(1 - d)(1 + L)]$$

$$.10 = [.1650(1 - d)(1.4487)]/[2.5571 - (.1650)(1 - d)(1.4487)]$$

$$d = .0273$$

Solution 14

Balance sheet (pro forma)

Current assets	$2,080	Current liabilities	$ 1,290
Net fixed assets	1,858	Long term debt	1,047
		Common stock	1,030
		Retained earnings	571
Total	$3,938		$3,938

Solution 15

Assets are proportional to sales, therefore current assets, fixed assets, and total assets increase 20% to $240, $360, and $600 million. Net income increases by 20% to $17.94 million, and additions to retained earnings (ΔRE) are 60% of net income or $10.764 million. Since the balance sheet must balance, using EFN as the plug:

$$TA_1 = TD_0 + CS_0 + RE_1 + EFN$$

$$\$600,000 = \$222,222 + \$150,000 + \$138,542 + EFN$$

$$EFN = \$89,236$$

where TA_1 is the new value of total assets, TD_0 equals the original total debt, CS_0 equals the initial value of common stock, and RE_1 is the new value of retained earnings. Management must decide whether to raise EFN by issuing current debt, long term debt, common stock, or some combination of all three securities.

Solution 16

Yodel's debt-to-equity ratio equals .80 = $222,222/$277,778. The change in total debt (TD) plus new stock issued (SI) must equal external funds needed: $\Delta TD + SI = EFN$. The change in total debt equals the debt-to-equity ratio times the change in equity ($\Delta E = SI + \Delta RE$). Using these relations to find the amount of new stock issued, we find:

$$\Delta TD = .8 \times \Delta E = .8 \times (SI + \$10,764)$$

$$\Delta TD + SI = .8 \times (SI + \$10,764) + SI = EFN = \$89,236$$

$$SI = \$44,792 \text{ and } \Delta TD = \$44,444$$

To maintain the relative proportion of current to long term debt, Yodel must issue current debt (CD) equal to $36,363 = $44,444 × ($100,000/$122,222) and long term debt (LTD) equal to $8,081 = ($44,444 − $36,363). The pro forma balance sheet is constructed using these values for ΔCD, ΔLTD, and SI. Note that the debt-to-equity ratio remains at 80%.

Income statement

	Current	Pro forma
Sales	$230,000	$276,000
Costs	207,000	248,400
Gross Profit	23,000	27,600
Tax (35%)	8,050	9,660
Net income	$14,950	$17,940
Dividends	5,980	7,176
Retained Earnings	8,970	10,764

Pro forma balance sheet

Current assets	$240,000	Current debt	$136,363
Fixed assets	360,000	Long term debt	130,303
		Common stock	194,792
		Retained earnings	138,542
Total	$600,000		$600,000

CHAPTER 27

SHORT-TERM FINANCE AND PLANNING

CHAPTER MISSION STATEMENT

The purpose of Chapter 27 is to discuss the management of short-term assets and short-term liabilities, or the management of net working capital. The chapter discusses how unsynchronized cash inflows and cash outflows create the need for short-term financing. The chapter traces the sources and disbursement of cash, and discusses various policies for managing current assets. The chapter describes cash budgeting, which is the primary tool for short-term financial planning.

The key concepts presented in this chapter are outlined below.

- ♦Tracing cash and net working capital
- ♦Sources and uses of cash
- ♦Operating cycle and cash cycle
- ♦Short-term financial policy
  - ●investment in current assets
  - ●financing policy for current assets
- ♦Cash budgeting
  - ●sources of cash
  - ●disbursement of cash
  - ●cash balance
- ♦Short-term financial plan
  - ●unsecured loans
  - ●secured loans

CONCEPT TEST

1. Current assets are expected to _____ within _____.

2. Current assets appear on the balance sheet in order of their _____.

3. Of the current assets, _____ is typically the least liquid.

4. Other than cash, the most liquid current asset is typically _____.

5. Money owed to a firm by its customers is a current asset called _____.

6. Money owed by the firm to its suppliers is a current liability called _____.

7. Short-term bank borrowing is a current liability often called _____.

8. Short-term finance is concerned with the firm's _____ activities.

In Questions 9-13, indicate whether the action will increase cash (a source) or decrease cash (a use), all other things equal.

9.   Fixed assets rise.

10.   New equity is sold.

11.   New long-term debt is sold.

12.   Accounts payable increase.

13.   Accounts receivable increase.

14.   The cash flow time line consists of an _____ cycle and a _____ cycle.

15.   The length of the operating cycle is equal to the sum of the _____ turnover period and the _____ turnover period.

16.   The time required to order, produce, and sell a product is the _____ turnover period.

17.   The time required to collect the cash receipt from a sale is the _____ turnover period.

18.   The length of time the firm is able to delay payment on its purchases is the _____ turnover period.

19.   The cash cycle is the difference between the _____ cycle and the _____ period.

20.   A firm keeps large amounts of cash and inventory on hand. Its current asset policy is considered _____.

21.   A firm finances short-term assets exclusively with short-term debt. Its short-term financial policy is considered _____.

22.   Costs that rise with the level of investment in current assets are called _____ costs.

23.   Costs that decline with the level of investment in current assets are called _____ costs.

24.   The costs identified in Question 23 can be classified as either _____ costs or costs related to _____.

25.   The primary tool of short-term planning is the _____.

26.   A _____ loan is the most common means of covering a temporary cash deficit.

27.   The loan identified in Question 26 is often arranged through a _____.

28.   A banking arrangement often requires the firm to keep money on deposit in a low-interest or non-interest paying account. This requirement is called a _____.

29.   The security on a secured short-term loan is usually either _____ or _____.

30.   Short-term notes issued by large, highly-rated corporations are called _____.

ANSWERS TO CONCEPT TEST

1.	convert to cash; 12 months	16.	inventory
2.	accounting liquidity	17.	accounts receivable
3.	inventory	18.	accounts payable
4.	marketable securities	19.	operating; accounts payable
5.	accounts receivable	20.	flexible
6.	accounts payable	21.	restrictive
7.	notes payable	22.	carrying
8.	short-run operating	23.	shortage
9.	decrease	24.	trading (or order); safety reserves
10.	increase	25.	cash budget
11.	increase	26.	short-term unsecured
12.	increase	27.	line of credit
13.	decrease	28.	compensating balance
14.	operating; cash	29.	accounts receivable; inventory
15.	inventory; accounts receivable	30.	commercial paper

PROBLEMS

Problem 1

Over the course of the year, the Prism Company had the following events occur:

1. Net income was $100
2. Depreciation was $30
3. Accounts payable rose by $20
4. A $10 dividend was paid
5. Inventories were increased by $120
6. Short-term bank borrowing rose by $80
7. Accounts receivable rose by $30

Prepare a statement showing the sources and uses of cash.

Use the following selected information from Oberon Corporation's financial statements to solve Problems 2-6.

	Beginning	Ending
Inventory	$1,000	$1,400
Accounts receivable	1,800	2,100
Accounts payable	900	1,100
Sales (all credit)	$30,000	
Cost of goods sold	16,000	

Problem 2

Calculate the inventory turnover period.

Problem 3

Calculate the accounts receivable turnover period.

Problem 4

Calculate the accounts payable deferral period.

Problem 5

Calculate the operating cycle.

Problem 6

Calculate the cash cycle.

Use the following information on Osiris Company to solve Problems 7-9.

Osiris has estimated sales for the next four quarters as:

	Q1	Q2	Q3	Q4
Sales	$510	$870	$450	$600

Accounts receivable at the beginning of the year were $210. Osiris has a 60-day collection period. Osiris' purchases from suppliers in a quarter are equal to 50% of the next quarter's forecast sales. Projected sales for the year following the current one are uniformly 10% higher than the current year's forecast sales. The payables deferral period is 45 days. Wages, taxes, and other expenses are one-third of sales, and interest and dividends are $10 per quarter. No capital expenditures are planned. Osiris is required to maintain a $20 minimum compensating balance.

Problem 7

Calculate Osiris' projected cash collections.

Problem 8

Calculate Osiris's projected cash outflows.

Problem 9

Calculate the net cash balance and cumulative financing surplus (or deficit) for Osiris. What do you observe?

Some selected items from Isis Company's beginning and ending balance sheets and income statement are shown below. Use this information to solve Problems 10-15.

	Beginning	Ending
Accounts receivable	$1,300	$1,540
Inventory	1,130	1,210
Accounts payable	560	610
Sales (all credit)	$15,000	
Cost of goods sold	10,675	

Problem 10

Calculate the inventory turnover period, the accounts receivable turnover period and the operating cycle for Isis.

Problem 11

Calculate the accounts payable deferral period and the cash cycle for Isis.

Problem 12

Suppose that Isis is able to reduce its inventory turnover period by 10 days. How will this affect the firm's short-term financing requirements?

Problem 13

Suppose that Isis is able to reduce its accounts receivable turnover period by 5 days. How will this affect its short-term financing requirements?

Problem 14

Suppose that Isis is able to extend its accounts payable deferral period by 5 days. How will this affect the firm's short-term financing requirements?

Problem 15

Given the changes presented in Problems 12-14, what is the new operating cycle? What is the new cash cycle?

Use the following balance sheet and income statements for the Fresnel Corporation to answer Problems 16-17.

Balance Sheet

	1993	1992
Cash	$200	$200
Marketable securities	100	150
Accounts receivable	400	300
Inventory	600	700
Total current assets	$1,300	$1,350
Fixed assets	$10,000	$12,000
Total assets	$11,300	$13,350
Accounts payable	$200	$250
Notes payable	500	600
Accrued expenses payable	100	80
Taxes payables	200	220
Total current liabilities	$1,000	$1,150
Long-term debt	$2,300	$3,600
Equity	8,000	8,600
Total liabilities and equity	$11,300	$13,350

Income Statement
(December 31,1992)

Net sales	$5,750
Cost of goods sold	2,085
General and Admin. expenses	1,550
Depreciation	600
Profit before tax	1,515
Tax	515
Net profit	1,000
Dividends	$400
Retained earnings	600

Problem 16

Construct Fresnel's sources and uses of cash statement.

Problem 17

Calculate Fresnel's operating cycle and cash cycle. Assume all sales are credit sales.

Use the following information to answer Problems 18-20.

Suppose that sales over the next four quarters for the Fraunhofer Company are estimated as follows:

	Q1	Q2	Q3	Q4
Sales	$200	$300	$250	$400

Accounts receivable at the beginning of the year are $120. Fraunhofer has a 45-day collection period. That is, half (45/90) of the sales in a given quarter will be collected during the current quarter and half during the following quarter. Purchases from suppliers during a quarter are equal to 60% of next quarter's forecast sales. Fraunhofer's payments to suppliers are equal to the previous period's purchases. Wages, taxes, and other expenses are 20% of sales; interest and dividends are $20 per quarter. A capital expenditure of $100 is planned in the second quarter.

Problem 18

Construct a table showing Fraunhofer's projected beginning receivables, cash collections, and ending receivables over the next four quarters.

Problem 19

Construct a table showing Fraunhofer's cash disbursements over the next four quarters.

Problem 20

Construct a table showings Fraunhofer's cash balance in each of the next four quarters. Fraunhofer maintains a $10 minimum cash balance to guard against unforeseen contingencies and forecasting errors.

SOLUTIONS

Solution 1

The Prism Company's sources and uses statements are shown below:

<u>Sources of cash</u>

Cash flow from operations	
Net income	$100
Depreciation	30
Decrease in net working capital	
Increase in accounts payable	20
Increase in notes payable	80
	$230

<u>Uses of cash</u>

Dividends	10
Increase in net working capital	
Increase in inventory	120
Increase in accounts receivable	30
	$160
Change in cash balance	$70

Solution 2

The inventory turnover period is the average length of time required to order, produce and sell a product. For Oberon, cost of goods sold was $16,000. Average inventory during the year was [($1,000 + 1,400)/2] = $1,200, so Oberon 'turned over' its inventory ($16,000/$1,200) = 13.33 times during the year. There are 365 days in a year, so inventory turned over every (365/13.33) = 27.38 days, on average.

Solution 3

Average receivables were $1,950. Credit sales were $30,000, so receivables turned over ($30,000/$1,950) = 15.38 times during the year, or every (365/15.38) = 23.73 days, on average.

Solution 4

Average payables were $1,000. Cost of goods sold was $16,000, so payables turned over 16 times during the year, or every (365/16) = 22.81 days, on average.

Solution 5

The operating cycle is the sum of the inventory period and the accounts receivables period. Using the results from Problems 2 and 3, the operating cycle is (27.38 + 23.73) = 51.11 days.

Solution 6

The cash cycle is the operating cycle less the accounts payable deferral period. Using the results from Problems 4 and 5, the cash cycle is (51.11 – 22.81) = 28.30 days.

Solution 7

With a 60-day collection period, Osiris collects 1/3 (30/90) of sales in the quarter in which they occur; 2/3 are collected the following quarter. Cash collections are thus:

	Q1	Q2	Q3	Q4
Beginning receivables	$210	$340	$580	$300
Sales	510	870	450	600
Cash collections	380	630	730	500
Ending receivables	340	580	300	400

Solution 8

With a 45-day deferral period, half of purchases from suppliers are paid in the quarter in which they are ordered and half are deferred one quarter. Projected sales in the first quarter of the next year are [$510(1.10)] = $561. The projected cash outflows are:

	Q1	Q2	Q3	Q4
Payment of accounts	$345	$330	$263	$290
Wages, taxes, other expenses	170	290	150	200
Long-term financing expenses (interest and dividends)	10	10	10	10
Total	$525	$630	$423	$500

Solution 9

The net cash balance is:

	Q1	Q2	Q3	Q4
Total cash receipts	$380	$630	$730	$500
Total cash disbursements	525	630	423	500
Net cash flow	-145	0	307	0
Cumulative excess cash balance	-145	-145	162	162
Minimum cash balance	20	20	20	20
Cumulative finance surplus	-$165	-$165	$142	$142

Osiris has a highly seasonal sales pattern. Because purchases are made in advance and collections are deferred, Osiris will have an ongoing pattern of short-term deficits (Q1, Q2) followed by surpluses.

Solution 10

The inventory turnover period and accounts receivable turnover period are shown below.

$$\text{Inventory turnover period} = 365 \times \frac{\text{average inventory}}{\text{cost of goods sold}} = 365 \times \frac{\$1,170}{\$10,675} = 40.0 \text{ days}$$

$$\text{Accounts receivable turnover period} = 365 \times \frac{\text{avg acct receiv}}{\text{credit sales}} = 365 \times \frac{\$1,420}{\$15,250} = 34.0 \text{ days}$$

The operating cycle is 74.0 days (= 40.0 + 34.0).

Solution 11

The accounts payable deferral period is shown below.

$$\text{Accounts payable deferral period} = 365 \times \frac{\text{avg acct payable}}{\text{cost of goods sold}} = 365 \times \frac{\$585}{\$10,675} = 20.0 \text{ days}$$

The cash conversion cycle equals the operating cycle (74.0 days) less the accounts payable deferral period (20.0 days), or 54.0 days.

Solution 12

An inventory turnover period of 30 days (40 – 10) is equivalent to inventory turnover of (365/30) = 12.17 times per year. With cost of goods sold equal to $10,675 per year, the average level of inventory which would be required is the value of x in the following equation: $10,675/x = 12.17. The solution is $877.16, which is a reduction of ($1,170 – $877.16) = $292.84 in the average level of inventory. Consequently, the firm will require, on average, $292.84 less short-term financing with this reduction in the inventory turnover period.

Solution 13

An accounts receivable turnover period of 29 days (34 – 5) is equivalent to accounts receivable turnover of 12.59 times per year. The average level of accounts receivable is determined by solving for x in the following equation: $15,000/x = 12.59. Therefore, the new level of accounts receivable is $1,191.42, which represents a reduction of ($1,420 – $1,191.42) = $228.58 in the average level of accounts receivable and, consequently, in the average amount of short-term financing required by the firm.

Solution 14

An accounts payable deferral period of 25 days (20 + 5) is equivalent to accounts payable turnover of (365/25) = 14.60 times per year. The average level of accounts payable which results from this increase is indicated by the value of x in the following equation: $10,675/x = 14.60. The new level of accounts payable increases to $731.16, which is an increase of ($731.16 – $585) = $146.16 in the level of accounts payable and consequently a decrease in the amount of short-term financing required from other sources.

Solution 15

The new operating cycle is 59 days and the cash cycle is 34 days. These new values reflect the reduction in the inventory turnover period, accounts receivable turnover period, and increase in the accounts payable deferral period calculated in Problems 12 - 14. However, it is important to realize that changes such as those suggested above cannot be achieved without incurring related costs. Therefore, the benefit associated with reductions in financing requirements must be weighed against costs of making these changes, such as potential loss of sales due to reduction in credit period.

Solution 16

Fresnel's sources and uses of cash statements are shown below.

<u>Sources of cash</u>

Cash flow from operations	
Net income	$1,000
Depreciation	600
New long-term borrowing	1,300

Decrease in net working capital

Increase in accounts payable	50
Increase in notes payable	100
Decrease in accounts receivable	100
Increase in taxes payable	20
	$3,170

Uses of cash

Increase in net fixed assets	$2,600
Dividends	400
Increase in net working capital	
Increase in inventory	100
Decrease in accrued expenses	20
Increase in marketable securities	50
	$3,170
Change in cash balance	$0

As the statement shows, Fresnel's cash balance is unchanged over the year. However, cash inflows (sources of cash) and cash outflows (uses of cash) occurred during the year. For example, inventory increased by $100; a net increase in inventory requires that cash be used. Similarly, accounts payable increased by $50; this means that Fresnel effectively borrowed an additional $50 (on a net basis) from its suppliers, a source of cash. Overall, net working capital decreased by ($300 − $200) = $100. Net fixed assets increased by $12,000 − $10,000 + depreciation = $2,000 + $600 = $2,600.

Solution 17

The operating cycle is the days in inventory plus the days in receivables, while the cash cycle is the operating cycle minus the days in payables. Calculations are shown below.

$$\text{days in inventory} = 365 \text{ days/inventory turnover}$$

$$= 365(\text{average inventory/cost of goods sold})$$

$$= 365(\$650/\$2,085) = 113.8 \text{ days}$$

$$\text{days in receivables} = 365 \text{ days/receivables turnover}$$

$$= 365(\text{average receivables/credit sales})$$

$$= 365(\$350/\$5,750) = 22.2 \text{ days}$$

$$\text{days in payables} = 365 \text{ days/accounts payable deferral period}$$

$$= 365(\text{average payables/cost of goods sold})$$

$$= 365(\$225/\$2,085) = 39.4 \text{ days}$$

$$\text{operating cycle} = 113.8 \text{ days} + 22.2 \text{ days} = 136.0 \text{ days}$$

$$\text{cash cycle} = 136.0 \text{ days} - 39.4 \text{ days} = 96.6 \text{ days}$$

The difference between the operating cycle (136.0 days) and the cash cycle (96.6 days) creates the need for short-term financing.

Solution 18

In the first quarter, cash collections would be the beginning receivables of $120 plus half of sales, or $220 total. Ending receivables for a given quarter would be half of sales during the quarter. Fraunhofer's cash collections are thus:

	Q1	Q2	Q3	Q4
Beginning receivables	$120	$100	$150	$125
Sales	200	300	250	400
Cash collections	220	250	275	325
Ending receivables	100	150	125	200

Solution 19

Fraunhofer's cash disbursements consist of payments to suppliers, wages and other expenses, capital expenditures, and long-term financing payments (dividends, interest, and principal paid). In the past quarter, purchases were 60% of Q1 sales: [(.60)($200)] = $120. These purchases are paid during the first quarter (Q1). Similarly, during the first quarter purchases are 60% of Q2 sales: [(.60)($300)]= $180, which are paid in quarter Q2. The cash outflows are thus:

	Q1	Q2	Q3	Q4
Payment of accounts	$120	$180	$150	$240
Wages, taxes, other expenses	40	60	50	80
Capital expenditures	0	100	0	0
Long-term financing expenses (interest and dividends)	20	20	20	20
Total	$180	$360	$220	$340

Solution 20

The forecast net cash balance is the difference between cash collections and cash disbursements, plus the cash balance at the beginning of the period. The net cash balance is determined as follows:

	Q1	Q2	Q3	Q4
Total cash receipts	$220	$250	$275	$325
Total cash disbursements	180	360	220	340
Net cash flow	40	-110	55	-15
Cumulative excess cash balance	40	-70	-15	-30
Minimum cash balance	10	10	10	10
Cumulative finance surplus(deficit)	$30	-$80	-$25	-$40

The cumulative finance surplus is the net cash flow plus the previous quarter's cumulative excess cash balance less the minimum cash balance, e.g., for Q3, -$25 = $55 + (-$70) - $10. Beginning in the second quarter, Fraunhofer has a cash shortfall. It occurs because of the seasonal pattern of sales (which are higher toward the end of the year), the delay in collections, and the planned capital expenditure.

CHAPTER 28

CASH MANAGEMENT

CHAPTER MISSION STATEMENT

The purpose of Chapter 28 is to acquaint the student with the issues surrounding the management of non-interest earning cash balances. The chapter discusses the Baumol and Miller-Orr Models of determining the optimal trade-off between the opportunity costs of holding too much cash and the transaction costs of holding too little. The chapter describes how firms can speed up the collection of cash and use delays in the disbursement of cash to its advantage. The chapter concludes by describing money market securities in which idle cash may be invested. An appendix describes innovative ways firms may manage idle cash by investing in adjustable-rate preferred stock and floating-rate certificates of deposit.

The key concepts presented in Chapter 28 are outlined below.

- ♦Reasons for holding cash
  - ●transactions motives
  - ●compensating balances
- ♦Target cash balances
  - ●Baumol model
  - ●Miller-Orr model
- ♦Collection and disbursement of cash
  - ●float
  - ●lockboxes
  - ●concentration banking
  - ●wire transfers
  - ●zero-balance accounts
- ♦Investing idle cash

CONCEPT TEST

1. Cash that is held for reasons related to normal collection and disbursement activities satisfies the _____ motive.

2. A compensating balance is cash held in a bank account as compensation for _____.

3. The costs that tend to increase as a firm increases its cash balances are the opportunity costs of _____.

4. The costs that tend to decrease as a firm increases its cash balances are the _____ resulting from the buying and selling of securities.

5. The _____ minimizes the sum of the costs in Questions 3 and 4.

6. The simplest formal model of cash management is the _____ model.

7. The _____ model involves the establishment of minimum, maximum, and target cash balances.

8. Checks written by a firm cause a decrease in _____, but no immediate change in _____.

9. Checks received by a firm cause an increase in _____, but no immediate change in _____.

10. The difference between book and bank cash is called _____.

11. Checks written by a firm generate _____ float.

12. Checks received by a firm generate _____ float.

13. The sum of the quantities described in Questions 11 and 12 is the _____.

14. The time a check spends in the postal system is the _____.

15. The time it takes the receiver of a check to process and deposit the check is the _____.

16. The time required to clear a check through the banking system is the _____.

17. The most widely used device for speeding up cash collections is the _____.

18. _____ is a system for getting cash to a firm's main bank more quickly.

19. The fastest way to move cash to the firm's main bank from another bank is a _____.

20. A _____ involves the transfer of funds into the account whenever a check is presented for payment.

21. A _____ is similar to a check except that it is drawn on the issuer instead of a bank.

22. The market for short-term securities is called the _____.

23. The least risky, most liquid short-term security is a _____.

24. An advantage of short-term securities issued by state and local governments or agencies is their exemption from _____.

25. _____ are actively-traded bank time deposits.

ANSWERS TO CONCEPT TEST

1. transactions motive
2. bank services
3. foregone interest
4. trading costs
5. target cash balance
6. Baumol
7. Miller-Orr
8. book cash; bank cash
9. book cash; bank cash
10. float
11. disbursement
12. collection
13. net float

14. mail float
15. in-house processing float
16. availability float
17. lockbox
18. concentration banking
19. wire transfer
20. zero balance account (ZBA)
21. draft
22. money market
23. Treasury bill
24. federal taxes
25. certificates of deposit (CDs)

PROBLEMS

Problem 1

Given the following information, use the Baumol model to calculate the target cash balance:

Annual interest rate:	12%
Fixed order cost:	$100
Total cash needed:	$240,000

Problem 2

Calculate the opportunity cost, the trading costs, and the total cost for holding the target cash balance determined in Problem 1.

Problem 3

Using data provided in Problem 1, calculate the opportunity cost, the trading costs and the total cost assuming that a $15,000 target cash balance is held. Calculate the costs assuming that a $25,000 target cash balance is held.

Problem 4

Suppose that the fixed order cost (F) is $100, the interest rate is .03% daily, and the standard deviation of daily net cash flows is $50. Management has set a lower limit (L) of $200 on cash holdings. Calculate the target cash balance and upper limit using the Miller-Orr model.

Problem 5

On a typical business day, a firm writes checks totaling $1,000. On average, these checks clear in 10 days. Simultaneously, the firm receives $1,300. On average, the cash is available in 5 days. Calculate the disbursement float, the collection float, and the net float. Interpret your answer.

Problem 6

A real estate firm receives 100 rental checks a month. Of these, 70 are for $300 and 30 are for $200. The $300 checks are delayed 4 days on average; the $200 checks are delayed 5 days on average. Calculate the average daily collection float, and interpret your answer.

Problem 7

Using the data from Problem 6, calculate the weighted average delay. Use the weighted average delay to calculate the average daily float.

Problem 8

Suppose that the interest rate for Problem 7 is 12% per year. Calculate the cost of the float.

Problem 9

In Problem 8, what would the firm pay to eliminate the float? What would the firm pay to reduce float by one day?

Problem 10

Your firm has an average receipt size of $125. A bank has approached you concerning a lockbox service that will decrease your collection float by 2 1/2 days. Your firm typically receives 12,000 checks per day. The annual interest rate is 9.125%. What would the annual savings be if the service is adopted?

Problem 11

The bank's fees for the lockbox service described in Problem 10 are: a fixed annual fee of $7,200 and a variable fee of $0.075 per transaction. Should the lockbox service be adopted?

Problem 12

Suppose that, in addition to the fixed annual fee and the variable fee described in Problem 11, the bank requires that the firm maintain a compensating balance of $100,000. Should the lockbox service be adopted?

Problem 13

Given the bank fees identified in Problem 11, what compensating balance would leave the firm indifferent as to whether it adopts the lockbox service?

Problem 14

A company has all of its collections handled by a bank located in the same city as its home office. The bank requires a compensating balance of $100,000 and handles collections of $750,000 per day. The firm is considering a concentration banking system which would require total compensating balances of $450,000, but which would accelerate collections by two days. The Treasury bill rate is 6%. Should the company implement the new system?

Problem 15

Try this one on your own. Your firm mails out 15,000 checks, with a total value of $500,000, during a typical day. You have determined that if the checks were mailed from Outer Mongolia, mail time would be increased by three days, on average. It would cost an extra $.10 per check in postage and handling, however. The daily interest rate is .00015. Should you do it?

Problem 16

The Wheatridge Corporation expects cash disbursements to exceed cash inflows by $360,000 per month. The firm is trying to decide how much cash it should keep on hand. Two banks have offered to set up a cash management account for the firm. Bank A charges $500 per transaction to buy and sell securities. If Wheatridge does business with Bank A, the opportunity cost of funds is 7%. Bank B, on the other hand, is aggressively seeking new clients and offers to pay 8.5% interest on invested cash, but charges $600 for each transaction to buy or sell securities. How much cash should Wheatridge keep on hand, and with which bank should the firm do business?

Problem 17

Wheatridge established its account with Bank B in Problem 16. The opportunity cost of funds was 8.5%, and the cost per transaction was $600. Annual requirements remain the same. Interest rates, however, have declined sharply in response to the Federal Reserve Bank's actions to lower interest rates. The opportunity cost of money market funds is now 3.5%. What is Wheatridge's new optimal cash balance?

Problem 18

Competitive pressures have forced Bank B to lower transaction costs to $500 per transaction. Interest rates remain at 3.5%. What is Wheatridge's new optimal cash balance?

Problem 19

The Black Hills Mining Company pays its employees twice a month. On average, the payroll is $500,000 per period. Presently, the payroll checks are written on a local bank, and are cleared the next day. The company wants to switch its account to an East Coast bank. The switch will allow Black Hills to get an extra four days interest on its funds. If Black Hills receives 0.05% interest per day, compounded daily, how much extra interest will the firm receive over one year if it makes the switch?

Problem 20

The Bad Lands Computer Company direct-markets competitively priced desktop computers for use in homes and small offices.   The firm is considering setting up a lockbox system to speed up collections from West Coast sales. A Los Angeles bank has offered to set up the lockbox system for an fee of $1,500 per month plus $.15 per transaction. The system will speed up processing by three days. The opportunity cost of funds is 8% per year. If the average computer sale is $2,500, how may computer sales per month must be processed to make the lockbox system worthwhile?

SOLUTIONS

Solution 1

The target cash balance is:

$$C^* = (2FT/K)^{1/2} =$$

$$[2(\$100)(\$240,000)/.12]^{1/2} = \$20,000$$

Solution 2

The average cash balance will be ($20,000/2) = $10,000, so the opportunity cost is [$10,000(.12)] = $1,200. There will be ($240,000/$20,000) = 12 orders during the year, so the order cost is also $1,200. The total cost is $2,400. The fact that the opportunity cost and the order cost are equal is not coincidental; the fact that this must always be true for the target cash balance identified by the Baumol model is apparent from the mathematical derivation of the model.

Solution 3

If a $15,000 balance is held, the opportunity, trading, and total costs are $900, $1,600, and $2,500, respectively. For a $25,000 balance, the costs are $1,500, $960, and $2,460, respectively. Note that the total costs for both the $15,000 and $25,000 balances are higher than the total costs for the $20,000 balance, as derived in Problem 2. This result is, of course, to be expected since the Baumol model identifies the cash balance which minimizes these costs.

Solution 4

The variance of the daily cash flows is $(50)^2 = 2,500$. The target cash balance and upper limit are thus:

$$Z^* = [(3F\sigma^2)/(4K)]^{1/3} + L =$$

$$[(3)(\$100)(2,500))/(4)(.0003)]^{1/3} + \$200 =$$

$$\$855 + \$200 = \$1,055$$

$$H^* = 3Z^* - 2L =$$

$$3(\$1,055) - 2(\$200) = \$2765.$$

Solution 5

The disbursement float is $[10(\$1,000)] = \$10,000$. The collection float is $[-5(\$1,300)] = -\$6,500$. The net float is $[\$10,000 + (-\$6,500)] = \$3,500$. At any time, the firm typically has uncashed checks outstanding of $10,000 and uncollected receipts of $6,500. Thus the firm's book cash is typically $3,500 less than its bank cash, indicating a positive net float.

Solution 6

The total float during the month is $[70(\$300)4 + 30(\$200)5] = \$114,000$. The average daily float is $(\$114,000/30) = \$3800$. On an average day, the firm has $3800 in the mail or otherwise uncollected.

Solution 7

Total monthly collections are $[70(\$300) + 30(\$200)] = \$27,000$. The weighted average delay is $[(\$21,000/\$27,000)4 + (\$6,000/\$27,000)5] = 4.2222$ days. Average daily receipts are $(\$27,000/30) = \$900$. The average daily float is $[4.2222(\$900)] = \$3,800$, as in Problem 6.

Solution 8

We first calculate the daily interest rate: $r = (.12/365) = .0003288 = .03288\%$ per day. The interest rate for 4.2222 days is $(.0003288 \times 4.2222) = .0013883 = .13883\%$. Daily receipts are $900, and the average delay is 4.2222 days. The total cost of the float is:

$$\$900 - [\$900/(1.0013883)] = \$900 - \$898.7523 = \$1.2477 \text{ per day}$$

Solution 9

The float costs $1.2477 per day. The daily interest rate is .03288%. If the firm were to eliminate the float, it would be $1.2477 better off every day for the foreseeable future. The present value of this perpetuity is $(\$1.2477/.0003288) = \$3,794.71$. If we ignore the interest for 4.2222 days, then the firm would pay up to $[4.2222(\$900)] = \$3,800$.

If the float were 3.2222 days, then, following the procedure of Problem 8, the cost of the float would be $.9525 per day. Therefore, the firm saves about $.2952 per day forever. The present value of this perpetuity is $897.78. If we ignore the interest for one day, the firm would pay $900.

Solution 10

Average daily collections are $125 ×12,000 = $1.5 million. Accelerating collections by 2 1/2 days frees [2.5($1.5 million)] = $3.75 million (ignoring 2.5 days interest). Investing this generates [$3,750,000(.09125)] = $342,187.50 interest per year. The daily saving is thus $342,187.50/365 = $937.50.

Solution 11

The bank's total fee would be [$7,200 + (.075)(12,000)(365)] = $335,700. Net earnings for the lockbox service would be ($342,187.50 – $335,700) = $6,487.50. Therefore, the service should be adopted since it is marginally profitable.

Solution 12

The cost of the compensating balance can be deducted from the results in Problems 10 and 11 in either of two ways. First, the $100,000 can be viewed as a reduction in the $3.75 million available cash calculated in Problem 10, so that the annual saving is [($3.65 million)(.00025)(365)] = $333,062.50. Since this annual saving is $2,637.50 less than the bank's fees calculated in Problem 11, the lockbox service would not be adopted. The second approach is to calculate the opportunity cost of the $100,000 as follows: [($100,000)(.00025)(365)] = $9,125. Adding this opportunity cost to the $335,700 in bank fees gives a total cost of $344,825 for the lockbox service, which exceeds the $342,187.50 annual savings.

Solution 13

The firm will be indifferent if the cost of the lockbox service (including the opportunity cost of the compensating balance) is exactly equal to the annual savings calculated in Problem 10. Therefore, the compensating balance which would leave the firm indifferent is the solution for x in the following equation:

$$\$335,700 + (x)(.09125) = \$342,187.50$$

The solution for x is $71,095.89. Given this figure, any meaningful compensating balance would make the lockbox service unattractive. However, the bank might be willing to negotiate the size of the fee per transaction to make the service with compensating balance requirements worthwhile

Solution 14

The concentration banking system would provide an additional [($750,000)(2)] = $1,500,000 which can be invested, but an additional $350,000 would be tied up in compensating balances. The net result would be that $1,150,000 can be invested at a 6% annual rate, providing net savings of $69,000. Therefore, the concentration banking system should be implemented.

Solution 15

The firm could increase its disbursement float by $1.5 million. Investing this amount generates $225 per day. The extra cost would be $1,500 per day. The firm should not adopt the plan.

Solution 16

Wheatridge would prefer to use the bank that minimizes the cash balance that must be maintained. The Baumol model is used to calculate the optimal cash balance. Over the course of one year, the cash requirements are 12 × $360,000 = $4,320,000. For Bank A, the optimal balance is

$$C^* = (2FT/K)^{1/2} =$$

$$[2(\$500)(\$4,320,000)/.07]^{1/2} = \$248,424$$

For Bank B, the optimal cash balance is

$$C^* = (2FT/K)^{1/2} =$$

$$[2(\$600)(\$4,320,000)/.085]^{1/2} = \$246,958$$

Wheatridge should go with Bank B. The optimal cash balance will be $246,958, $1,466 lower than Bank A, and in addition the firm gets a higher interest rate on its invested cash.

Solution 17

With the lower opportunity cost of funds, the optimal cash balance is

$$C^* = (2FT/K)^{1/2} =$$

$$[2(\$600)(\$4,320,000)/.035]^{1/2} = \$384,856$$

With lower interest rates, lost interest on cash balances is small, it is more important to reduce the number of transactions by maintaining a large cash balance.

Solution 18

Lower transaction costs should lower the optimal cash balance. The new balance is

$$C^* = (2FT/K)^{1/2} =$$

$$[2(\$500)(\$4,320,000)/.035]^{1/2} = \$351,324$$

Solution 19

Over four days the firm would receive interest of

$$\$500,000[(1.0005)^4 - 1]= \$1,000$$

Black Hills would receive the $1,000 interest every two weeks, or 26 times, over the next year. Each $1,000 "payment" would be invested at .05% per day compounded daily. This is just a 26-period annuity with each period being two weeks long. The two-week effective interest rate is $[(1.0005)^{14} - 1] \times 100 = 0.70228\%$. The present value of Black Hills' yearly interest is

$$PV = \$1,000 \, [1- 1/(1.0070228)^{26}](1/.0070228) = \$23,688.68$$

If the costs associated with moving the account to the East Coast bank is less than $23,688 per year, then Black Hills should make the switch.

Solution 20

The lockbox system will be worthwhile if the savings exceed the costs. Let N equal the number of customers per month. The savings, or extra interest, is

$$N \times \$2,500 \times 3 \text{ days} \times (.08/365) = \$1.6438N \text{ per month}$$

The costs of the lockbox system are

$$\text{fixed} + \text{variable} = \$1,500 + N \times \$.15 \text{ per month}$$

The break-even point occurs when the number of customers per month equals

$$\$1.6438N = \$1,500 + .15 \, N$$

$$N = 1,004$$

Thus, more than 1,004 customers per month will make the system profitable.

CHAPTER 29

CREDIT MANAGEMENT

CHAPTER MISSION STATEMENT

The purpose of Chapter 29 is to provide a basic understanding of a firm's decision to grant credit. The chapter discusses three factors affecting a firms credit policy: terms of the sale, credit analysis, and collection policy. The chapter describes the optimal credit policy as one in which the incremental cash flows from increased sales are exactly offset by the incremental carrying costs of increased receivables.

The key concepts presented in Chapter 29 are outlined below.

- ◆Terms of the sale
  - ●credit period
  - ●cash discounts
- ◆Granting credit
  - ●credit risk
  - ●information
- ◆Optimal credit policy
- ◆Credit analysis
  - ●credit information
  - ●credit scoring
- ◆Collection policy
  - ●average collection period
  - ●aging schedule
  - ●collection effort
  - ●factoring
- ◆How to finance trade credit

CONCEPT TEST

1. The three components of credit policy are the _____, _____, and _____.

2. The conditions under which a firm proposes to grant credit are called the _____.

3. Determining the likelihood that a customer will default is part of the process of _____.

4. The potential problem of actually obtaining the payment from a credit sale is related to the firm's _____.

5. If a firm grants credit, the terms of the sale usually specify the _____, the _____, and the _____.

6. If a firm offers terms of 3/30, net 90, then the full amount of the invoice is due in _____ days from the _____ date.

7.   For the terms described in Question 6, a customer can take a _____ discount if payment is made in _____ days.

8.   The credit period generally depends on the _____, the _____, and the _____.

For Questions 9-12, indicate which firm is likely to have a longer credit period.

9.   Firm A sells milk; firm B sells machine tools.

10. Firm A retails clothing; firm B wholesales to clothing manufacturers.

11. Firm A specializes in products for homeowners; firm B specializes in products for renters.

12. Firm A sells and installs central air conditioning systems; firm B sells window air conditioners.

13. Most credit is offered on _____.

14. In Question 13, the credit instrument is the _____.

15. In some instances, such as a large order from a high-risk customer, the credit instrument may take the form of a _____.

16. If a seller sends the shipping documents to the seller's bank, along with a demand for payment, then the demand for payment is called a _____.

17. In Question 16, the credit instrument is called a _____ if the payment is due immediately.

18. The carrying costs of accounts receivable include the firm's _____ on receivables, the _____, and the costs of _____.

19. The opportunity cost of not granting credit results from _____.

20. What are the 'five C's' of credit?

21. Suppose that a firm typically receives payment in 20 days after a sale. This 20 day period is called the _____.

22. A tabulation of receivables based on the length of time they have been outstanding is called an _____.

23. The sale of a firm's receivables to a financial institution is called _____.

24. The three ways to finance accounting receivables are _____, _____, and _____.

ANSWERS TO CONCEPT TEST

1. terms of sale; credit analysis; collection policy
2. terms of sale
3. credit analysis
4. collection policy
5. credit period; cash discount; type of credit instrument
6. 90 days; invoice
7. 3%; 30
8. risk of payment; account size; perishability of goods
9. firm B
10. firm B
11. firm A
12. firm A

13. open account
14. invoice
15. promissory note
16. commercial draft
17. sight draft
18. required return; bad debt losses; credit management
19. foregone or lost sales
20. character, capacity, capital, collateral, conditions
21. average collection period (ACP)
22. aging schedule
23. factoring
24. secured debt; captive finance company; securitization

PROBLEMS

Problem 1

Sutton Company currently has a credit policy of "in God we trust, everybody else pays cash." It is considering altering this policy and has estimated the following data:

	Refuse credit	Grant credit
Price per unit	$35	$38
Cost per unit	$25	$27
Quantity sold	5,000	5,500
Probability of payment	1.00	0.90

The credit period will be 60 days, and the cost of debt is 1.50% per month. Should Sutton change its credit policy?

Problem 2

For the data in Problem 1, what does the sale price have to be in order for Sutton to break even?

Problem 3

Suppose that the Sutton Company in Problem 1 could sell its product for $42 if credit were granted; assuming that all other data are unchanged from Problem 1, what is the net present value of the decision to grant credit?

Problem 4

For the data given in Problem 3, calculate the carrying costs associated with granting credit and the opportunity costs which result from the refusal to grant credit.

Problem 5

Suppose that the Sutton Company, as described in Problems 1 and 3, considers extending additional credit, so that the relevant data become: price per unit is $44; cost per unit is $28, number of units sold is 5,600, probability of payment is .88, average collection period is 90 days. Should credit be further extended?

Problem 6

Suppose that, in Problem 1, we can obtain a credit report for $.25 per customer. Assuming that each customer buys one unit and that the credit report identifies all customers who would not pay, should credit be extended?

Problem 7

Icarus Company (a well-known 'high flyer') manufactures suntan lotion. Its credit terms are 5/20, net 40. Historically, 80% of its customers take the discount. What is the average collection period?

Problem 8

In Problem 7, Icarus sells 5,000 cases of suntan lotion each month, at a price of $15 per case. What is its average balance sheet amount in accounts receivable?

Problem 9

Daedulus Company has annual credit sales of $2 million. The average collection period is 30 days. Production costs are 80% of sales. What is Daedulus's average investment (i.e., its actual cost, as opposed to the balance sheet amount) in receivables?

Problem 10

A firm offers terms of 2/10, net 30. What effective annual interest rate does the firm earn when a customer does not take the discount?

Problem 11

For each of the following credit terms, use the formula presented in Problem 10 to determine the annualized effective rate:

3/15, net 60; 1.5/20, net 45; 1/10, net 40

Problem 12

For each of the credit terms identified in Problem 11, determine whether a firm should take the discount or pay the net amount of the invoice. Assume that the firm would have to borrow from a bank at a 15% annual interest rate in order to take advantage of the discount.

Problem 13

The Kneebopper Corporation has an average collection period of 50 days. Its average investment in receivables is $3 million. What are the firm's annual credit sales?

Problem 14

Krishna, Inc., has collected the following information:

Annual credit sales	$270,000
Collection period (days)	120
Terms	net 90
Interest rate (monthly)	1%

Krishna is contemplating offering customers terms of 2/30, net 60. Krishna anticipates that 50% of its customers will take the discount, while the remainder will pay in 90 days. Therefore, the collection period will fall to 60 days. Should the new terms be offered?

Problem 15

Brahma Company is considering extending credit to a new customer. Based on past experience, there is a 50% chance that the customer will default. The item costs $100 to manufacture and sells for $200. Payment is due in 30 days and the monthly interest rate is 1.5%.

If the customer does pay, then she will place another order, and the probability of payment in 30 days is 100%. Should Brahma grant credit? (Assume that the sale will be lost if Brahma does not grant credit.)

Problem 16

Vellum Financial Printers has decided to adopt a new credit policy. Presently, the firm prints 1200 jobs per year. On average, each job costs $150 and Vellum charges $200. Current policy is net 15; however, 20% of the customers pay immediately, 70% pay on day 15, while the remaining 10% pay on day 30. The new policy under consideration is 2/10 net 30. Under this policy, Vellum estimates the number of jobs will increase to 1400 if the price remains constant. Furthermore, Vellum believes that 5% of the customers will pay immediately, 50% will pay on day 10, 40% will pay on day 30, and the remaining 5% will pay on day 60. The interest rate is 12%. What is the average collection period under the old and proposed credit policies?

Problem 17

Should Vellum adopt the new policy or stay with its existing policy?

Problem 18

Vellum Financial Printers is considering a third credit policy. This policy calls for 3/10 net 30. Vellum believes that it will have 1,400 printing jobs per year with the same cost and price structure as before. Now, however, Vellum forecasts that 50% of the customers will take the discount and pay on day 10, and that the average collection period will increase to 25 days. Should Vellum adopt this plan instead?

Problem 19

Vellum Financial Printers has learned from experience that 5% of the customers default on paying their bills. To reduce this figure, Vellum is thinking of subscribing to a credit reporting agency. The agency charges a flat fee of $5,000 and $5.00 per report. With these reports, doubtful accounts will drop to zero. If Vellum adopts the 2/10 net 30 policy and prints 1400 jobs per year, should it also subscribe to the reporting agency?

Problem 20

Vellum believes that it is unnecessary to order credit reports on all of its customers. Forty percent of Vellum's customers have long-term agreements for printing services and are unlikely to default. Thus, Vellum thinks that credit reports are only needed on the other 60% of its customers. However, while the firm expects a 5% default rate without the credit reports, subscribing to the agency will not eliminate doubtful accounts, but will reduce them to .5% Should Vellum subscribe to the credit reporting agency?

SOLUTIONS

Solution 1

If the company does not grant credit, the cash flows at the time of sale are [($35 − $25)5,000] = $50,000. If credit is granted, the cash inflow two months (60 days) from the sale is expected to be [$38(5,500)(.90)] = $188,100. The present value (at time of sale) is: [$188,100/(1.015)^2] = $182,581.47. The certain costs incurred at time of sale are [5,500($27)] = $148,500, so the net present value is ($182,581.47 − $148,500) = $34,081.47. Since the net present value of the alternative is $50,000, credit should not be extended.

Solution 2

For Sutton to grant credit and still have the same net present value from its credit policy, the net present value of this policy must be $50,000. Therefore, S is the sale price in the following equation:

$$[S(5,500)(.90)/(1.015)^2] - \$148,500 = \$50,000$$

Solving for S, we find that the sale price would have to be $41.31 per unit in order to break even.

Solution 3

The cash flows and net present value for the decision to refuse credit are the same as in Problem 1, so that the net present value of this alternative is $50,000. The present value of the decision to grant credit is now $[(\$42)(5,500)(.90)/(1.015)^2] = \$201,800.58$ and the net present value is $(\$201,800.58 - \$148,500) = \$53,300.58$. As we would expect, given the result from Problem 2, it is now beneficial for Sutton to extend credit.

Solution 4

By granting credit, the firm incurs three kinds of carrying costs: the required return on the investment in receivables, losses from bad debts, and the costs of managing credit. The required return on the investment in receivables is the difference between the total revenue collected and the present value of that revenue, discounted for two months. Total expected revenue is $[(.90)(\$42)(5,500)] = \$207,900$, so that the required return is:

$$(\$207,900) - [(207,900)/(1.015)^2] = \$6,099.42$$

Losses from bad debts are $[(.10)(5,500)(\$42)] = \$23,100$. The firm's costs of managing credit are equal to $[(\$27 - \$25)(5,500)] = \$11,000$. (We assume here that the increase in per unit cost exactly offsets the cost of managing credit.)

The opportunity costs resulting from the refusal to grant credit are equal to the difference between the revenue for the policy of granting credit and revenue for the policy of refusing credit:

$$[(\$42 - \$25)(5,500)] - [(\$35 - \$25)(5,000)] = \$43,500$$

The net result for the policy of granting credit is an increase in profit of $43,500, less additional costs of $(\$6,099.42 + \$23,100 + \$11,000) = \$40,199.42$ for a net gain of $3,300.58. This is exactly equal to the difference in net present values in Problem 3. The solution here is simply an alternative way of viewing the previous calculations.

Solution 5

We can analyze this problem by calculating the carrying costs and opportunity costs for this extension of credit in relation to the decision to grant credit presented in Problems 3 and 4. Extending credit allows us to sell more units at a higher price, but this comes at the cost of more doubtful accounts and a longer payment period. Total revenue is $[(.88)(\$44)(5,600)] = \$216,832$, so that the required return on the investment in receivables is:

$$(\$216,832) - [(\$216,832)/(1.015)^3] = \$9,471.87$$

Losses from bad debts are $[(.12)(5,600)(\$44)] = \$29,568$. The firm's costs of managing credit are equal to $[(\$28 - \$25)(5,600)] = \$16,800$. The total of these carrying costs is $55,839.87, which is an increase of $(\$55,839.87 - \$40,199.42) = \$15,640.45$ compared to the initial extension of credit. The opportunity costs resulting from the refusal to grant credit are equal to:

$$[(\$44 - \$25)(5,600)] - [(\$35 - \$25)(5,000)] = \$56,400$$

This is an increase of (\$56,400 - \$43,500) = \$12,900 over the initial credit decision. The net result for the extension of additional credit is an increase in profit of \$12,900, and an increase of \$15,640.45 in costs, so that the additional extension of credit should not be offered.

The optimal credit policy for Sutton is a moderate extension of credit. In general, additional credit should be extended as long as the opportunity cost associated with the refusal to grant additional credit is greater than the additional carrying costs incurred when extending additional credit.

Solution 6

If we eliminate sales to those who would default, we will sell [.90(5,500)] = 4,950 units. The cash inflow will be [\$38(4,950)] = \$188,100 and the present value is \$182,581.47, as before. The costs, however, are 4,950(\$27) + 5,500(\$.25)] = \$135,025. The net present value is now \$47,556.47, still less than the \$50,000 no credit alternative, so credit should not be extended.

Solution 7

The average collection period is [.80(20 days) + .20(40 days)] = 24 days.

Solution 8

Icarus has average daily sales of [\$15(5,000)/30] = \$2,500. With an average collection period of 24 days, receivables average [(\$2,500)(24)] = \$60,000.

Solution 9

Annual costs are \$1.6 million, or \$4,444.44 per day. With an average collection period of 30 days, Daedulus has \$133,333.33 in costs tied up in receivables.

Solution 10

Suppose the product costs \$100. The firm receives \$98 if the discount is taken. If the discount is not taken, then the firm receives \$2, or (\$2/\$98) = 2.04%, more. This 2.04% is earned by extending (30 - 10) = 20 additional days credit. There are approximately (360/20)= 18 such periods per year. The annualized interest rate is a hefty $[(1.0204)^{18} - 1] = .43836 = 43.836\%$. The calculation here does not depend on the cost of the product since the 2.04% figure derived above would apply regardless of purchase price.

The annualized effective rate when foregoing a discount is often determined as follows:

$$[d/(1 - d)] \times [360/(\text{net period} - \text{discount period})]$$

where d is the discount expressed as a percent of the invoice price. However, this approach does not consider the effect of compounding in determining the annual rate. For the terms of 2/10, net 30, this alternative approach indicates that the annualized effective rate is 36.735%, rather than 43.836% as derived previously.

Note that the interest rate the firm earns is the same as the interest rate the customer pays by not taking the discount. Consequently, from the customer's point of view it is generally not reasonable to pay an interest rate in excess of that which would be paid by financing the purchase through an alternative source.

Solution 11

For terms of 3/15, net 60, d is .03, and the annualized effective rate is:

$$[.03/(1 - .03)] \times [360/(60 - 15)] = .24742 = 24.742\%$$

For terms of 1.5/20, net 45, d is .015, and the annualized effective rate is:

$$[.015/(1 - .015)] \times [360/(45 - 20)] = .21929 = 21.929\%$$

For terms of 1/10, net 40, the annualized effective rate is 12.121%.

Solution 12

For terms of 3/15, net 60, the firm would have to borrow 97% of the invoice amount in order to take advantage of the discount. Interest on the loan would then accumulate at the rate of 1.5% per month, or approximately 2.25% for 45 days, at which time we assume that the firm would repay the bank loan. Let x represent the net amount, so that the bank loan is .97x and interest plus principal of $[(.97x)(1.0225)] = .9918x$ is repaid to the bank after 45 days. Since this is less than the net amount of the invoice, the firm is better off borrowing from the bank than paying the net amount. In general, if the annualized effective rate is greater than the rate at which the firm borrows, the firm is better off borrowing from the bank in order to take advantage of the discount. Therefore, for terms of 1.5/20, net 45, the firm should borrow in order to take the discount, but for terms of 1/10, net 40, the firm should pay the net amount.

Solution 13

Average daily sales equals accounts receivable divided by average collection period: ($3 million/50) = $60,000 per day. Annual sales are thus [$60,000(360)] = $21.6 million.

Solution 14

Under the current policy, average daily sales are ($270,000/360) = $750. On average, this amount is collected in three months, so the present value is $[\$750/(1.01)^4] = \$720.74$.

Under the new policy, $375 of daily credit sales will be collected 30 days after the sale; since a 2% discount will be taken, $367.50 will actually be received by the company. The present value is thus $[(\$367.50/1.01) + (\$375/1.01)^3] = \$727.83$. The new terms should be offered.

Solution 15

If Brahma grants credit, the expected value of future payments is $[(.50)(\$200)] = \$100$, expected in 30 days. If this were a one-time sale, the net present value would be:

$$[(\$100/1.015) - \$100] = -\$1.48$$

However, if payment is made, Brahma will make another sale. Therefore, there is a 50% chance of an additional sale. The net present value of this second sale is:

$$[.50(\$200)/(1.015)^2] - [.50(\$100)/1.015] = \$47.81$$

The net present value of extending credit is $46.33. This example illustrates the importance of considering repeat business when analyzing the credit-granting decision.

Solution 16

Under the existing policy, the average collection period is

$$.20 \times 0 \text{ days} + .70 \times 15 \text{ days} + .10 \times 30 \text{ days} = 13.5 \text{ days}$$

Under the proposed credit policy, the average collection period is

$$.05 \times 0 \text{ days} + .50 \times 10 \text{ days} + .40 \times 30 \text{ days} + .05 \times 60 \text{ days}$$

$$= 20 \text{ days}$$

Solution 17

Vellum should adopt the policy which has the highest present value.

The present value of the existing policy is

$$PV(old) = .20 \times 1,200 \times \$200 + .70 \times 1200 \times \$200/[1 + .12(15/365)]$$

$$+ .10 \times 1,200 \times \$200/[1 + .12(30/365)]$$

$$= \$238,941$$

The present value of the proposed policy is

$$PV(new) = .05 \times 1,400 \times \$200 \times .98$$

$$+ .50 \times 1,400 \times \$200 \times .98/[1 + .12(10/365)]$$

$$+ .40 \times 1,400 \times \$200/[1 + .12(30/365)]$$

$$+ .05 \times 1{,}400 \times \$200/[1 + .12(60/365)]$$

$$= \$275{,}106$$

Vellum should adopt the new policy since its present value is higher, \$275,106 versus \$238,941.

Solution 18

If the average collection period is 25 days and 50% of the customers pay on day 10, then the collection period for customers not taking the discount, N, is $(25 - .50 \times 10 \text{ days}) = .5N$ or $N = 40$ days. The present value of this credit policy is

$$PV = .50 \times 1{,}400 \times \$200 \times .97/[1 + .12(10/365)]$$

$$+ .50 \times 1{,}400 \times \$200/[1 + .12(40/365)]$$

$$= \$273{,}538$$

This policy is better than the existing policy, but is inferior to the alternate new policy.

Solution 19

Vellum should subscribe if the fixed and variable costs of the credit reports are less than the bad debts. The cost of the doubtful accounts (or potential savings) is

$$\text{bad debts} = .05 \times 1{,}400 \times \$150 = \$10{,}500$$

The cost of the credit reports is

$$\text{credit reports} = \$5{,}000 + 1{,}400 \times \$5.00 = \$12{,}000$$

Vellum should not subscribe to the credit agency since it would cost more than it would save.

Solution 20

The savings associated with subscribing to the credit agency are

$$.045 \times 1{,}400 \times \$150 = \$9{,}450$$

The cost of subscribing is

$$\$5{,}000 + .60 \times 1{,}400 \times \$5.00 = \$9{,}200$$

Under these assumptions, Vellum should subscribe since the savings more than offset the costs.

CHAPTER 30

MERGERS AND ACQUISITIONS

CHAPTER MISSION STATEMENT

The purpose of Chapter 30 is to introduce the basic legal, accounting, and tax considerations of acquisitions. The chapter discusses the various ways by which one firm can acquire another, and the tax and accounting implications of these methods. The chapter describes and illustrates how to evaluate the net present value of an acquisition, and how to determine the proper exchange ratio for a stock-swap merger. The chapter discusses defensive tactics that some firms use to avoid being taken over. Whether shareholders benefit from acquisitions is an empirical question; the chapter discusses recent evidence on the shareholder wealth effects of takeovers.

The key concepts discussed in this chapter are outlined below.

- ♦ Forms of acquisition
  - merger
  - consolidation
  - tender offer
  - acquisition of assets
- ♦ Types of mergers
  - horizontal
  - vertical
  - conglomerate
- ♦ Tax considerations
  - tax free acquisition
  - taxable acquisition
- ♦ Accounting treatment
  - purchase method
  - pooling of interests
- ♦ Synergy
  - revenue enhancement
  - cost reduction
  - tax reduction
  - cost of capital reduction
- ♦ Value of an acquisition
  - tax gains
  - operating efficiencies
  - strategic fit
- ♦ Risk shifting
  - coinsurance effect
- ♦ NPV of a merger
  - cash acquisition
  - stock exchange
- ♦ Defensive tactics
- ♦ Empirical evidence on acquisitions

CONCEPT TEST

1.   The three basic procedures a firm can use to acquire another firm are: _____, acquisition of _____, and acquisition of _____.

2.   The complete absorption of one firm by another is called a _____.

3.   If an entirely new firm is created by an acquisition, then the event is called a _____.

4.   If two firms that compete in the same product market merge, the acquisition is said to be _____.

5.   If a firm were to merge with its major supplier, the acquisition would be _____.

6.   A _____ acquisition involves two firms in completely unrelated lines of business.

7.   In an acquisition, the firm attempting the takeover is called the _____. The other firm is called the _____.

8.   Takeovers can occur by _____, _____, or _____.

9.   A _____ occurs when a dissident shareholder group solicits proxies in an attempt to gain control of a firm.

10. If the shareholders in an acquired firm receive shares of stock as compensation, the acquisition would normally be _____.

11. A _____ is a general transfer of control from one group to another.

12. An advantage of a cash acquisition is the fact that the assets of the acquired firm can be _____.

13. A disadvantage of a cash acquisition is the fact that the shareholders of the acquired firm are generally obligated to pay _____.

14. The _____ method of accounting reports the assets of the acquired firm at fair market value on the balance sheet.

15. The _____ method of accounting reports the balance sheet of the acquired firm as the total of the balance sheets of the acquired and the acquiring firm.

16. For the procedure described in Question 14, the difference between the purchase price and the fair market value would be reported on the balance sheet as _____.

17. Revenue enhancing benefits from mergers may come from _____, _____, and _____.

18. If a merger reduces the average production cost for a product, then an _____ is said to exist.

19. Net operating losses, debt capacity, and surplus funds are all possible sources of _____ in a merger.

20. When two leveraged firms merge, the new firm may have a lower cost of debt and a higher debt capacity because of the _____.

21. If an acquisition has a positive NPV, then, all other things equal, the cost of the acquisition will be higher if _____ is used to pay for the acquisition.

22. An amendment to the corporate charter requiring, for example, that 80% of the stockholders must approve a merger is called a _____ provision.

23. With a _____ agreement, a target firm agrees to buy back its own stock, at a premium, from the bidder, in exchange for the bidder's terminating the takeover attempt.

24. With an _____, a target firm offers to buy its own stock, at a premium, from all stockholders except the bidding firm.

25. Going-private transactions are frequently arranged by existing management with the help of outside investors. Such transactions frequently take the form of a _____.

26. In an unfriendly takeover, the bidding firm can bypass existing management and acquire the stock by using a _____.

27. A _____ refers to compensation paid to top management in the event of a takeover.

28. A _____ refers to a defensive tactic designed to make a firm an unattractive target for acquisition.

29. The _____ are major assets that a target firm sells or threatens to sell in an effort to fend off a takeover.

30. Empirical evidence suggests that the shareholders of _____ firms benefit substantially from takeovers, whereas the shareholders of _____ do not benefit.

ANSWERS TO CONCEPT TEST

1. merger or consolidation; stock; assets
2. merger
3. consolidation
4. horizontal
5. vertical
6. conglomerate
7. bidder; target
8. acquisition; proxy contest; going private
9. proxy contest
10. a tax-free acquisition
11. takeover
12. written up
13. capital gains taxes
14. purchase
15. pooling of interests
16. goodwill
17. marketing gains; strategic benefits; market power
18. economy of scale
19. tax gains
20. coinsurance effect
21. stock
22. super majority
23. repurchase standstill
24. exclusionary self-tender
25. leveraged buyout
26. tender offer
27. golden parachute
28. poison pill
29. crown jewels
30. acquired; acquiring

PROBLEMS

Use the following information to solve Problems 1-9. Assume that Firms A and B have no debt outstanding.

	Firm A	Firm B
Total earnings	$6,000	$2,700
Shares outstanding	1,000	600
Price per share	$50	$15

Problem 1

Firm A is considering the acquisition of Firm B. Firm A has estimated that the value of the combined firm will be $64,000. Firm B has indicated that it would accept a cash purchase offer of $20 per share. Should Firm A proceed with the acquisition?

Problem 2

For the data of Problem 1, what is the synergy from the merger? What is the premium paid for the acquisition? Use the synergy and the premium to determine the net present value of the acquisition.

Problem 3

For the data of Problem 1, what is the price of Firm A's stock after the merger?

Problem 4

For the data of Problem 1, what is the net present value of the merger if Firm A pays for the acquisition with common stock, based on the current market prices?

Problem 5

For the data of Problem 4, what is the post-merger price if Firm A pays for the acquisition with stock based on a price of $22 per share for Firm B? What is the cost of the merger? What is the net present value of the merger?

Problem 6

For the data of Problem 5, what is the synergy from the merger? What is the premium paid for the acquisition? Use the synergy and the premium to determine the net present value of the acquisition. Why is the net present value lower for the acquisition through exchange of stock in Problem 5 compared to the acquisition for cash in Problem 1?

Problem 7

Problem 1 indicates that the shareholders of Firm B are willing to accept $12,000 for the acquisition. How many shares of Firm A stock should Firm B stockholders receive so that they actually receive the $12,000 price?

Problem 8

Assume that Firm A acquires Firm B in exchange for stock valued at $17.50 per share. How will this affect earnings per share for Firm A?

Problem 9

For the data of Problem 8, what is the price per share of the new firm if the market is 'fooled' by this earnings growth? What will the price/earnings ratio be if the market is not 'fooled?'

Problem 10

Blizzard Manufacturing, producer of snow-removal equipment, is analyzing the possible acquisition of Max Motors, manufacturer of engine components. Blizzard forecasts that the purchase would result in incremental after-tax cash flows of $10,000 per year for the foreseeable future. The current market values of Blizzard and Max are $500,000 and $200,000, respectively. The relevant opportunity cost of capital for the incremental cash flows is 20 percent. What is the synergy from the merger?

Problem 11

Suppose that, for the data of Problem 10, Blizzard is considering an offer of $220,000 cash for the acquisition of Max Motors. What is the premium of the merger? What is the NPV of the merger?

Problem 12

As an alternative to the $220,000 offer described in Problem 11, Blizzard is considering offering 25 percent of its stock to the stockholders of Max Motors. What is the net present value of this offer?

Use the following information to solve Problems 13 and 14.

Pinot Vineyards ($ in thousands)

Current assets	$100	Current liabilities	$60
Fixed assets	900	Long-term debt	200
		Equity	740
Total	$1,000		$1,000

Noir Vineyards ($ in thousands)

Current assets	$200	Current liabilities	$140
Fixed assets	600	Long-term debt	100
		Equity	560
Total	$800		$800

Problem 13

Assume that the balance sheets above are in terms of book values. Construct the balance sheet for Pinot assuming that Pinot purchases Noir to form Pinot Noir Vineyards, and the pooling of interests method of accounting is used.

Problem 14

Suppose that the fair market value of Noir's fixed assets is $900, in contrast to the $600 book value shown. Pinot pays $1,200 for Noir and raises the needed funds through an issue of long-term debt. Construct the balance sheet assuming that the purchase method of accounting is used.

Problem 15

Firm A manufactures umbrellas. Firm B manufactures suntan lotion. The values of the two firms depend on the weather and are shown below:

Weather	Probability	Value of A	Value of B
Rainy	.5	$100	$50
Sunny	.5	60	90
Expected value		$80	$70

Each firm has debt outstanding with a face value of $66. Calculate the value of the equity and the value of the debt for each weather condition, and the expected values of the equity and the debt.

Problem 16

Firms A and B have proposed a merger. There is no synergy. How would the stockholders view this proposal? Why?

Use the following information to answer Problems 17-20

The following table presents information about companies X and Y. Company X proposes to acquire firm Y at $55 per share in cash. Firm X believes that after the acquisition, it can increase Y's growth rate to 12%.

	X	Y
Stock price	$25	$48
Dividend (t=1)	$1.25	$1.92
Shares outstanding	1 million	400,000
Growth rate (g)	7%	10%
Cost of capital (r)	12%	14%

Problem 17

What is the NPV of the proposed acquisition?

Problem 18

What is firm X's share price after the announced takeover?

Problem 19

If firm X decides to acquire firm Y by means of a stock swap equal to $22 million, how many shares must X swap for the 400,000 shares of firm Y?

Problem 20

Firm X acquires firm Y by exchanging 531,401 of its shares for all 400,000 shares of Y. Assume that X manages to increase Y's growth rate to 11%, rather than the planned 12%, what is X's share price?

Problem 21

Hatteras Ltd. is evaluating acquiring the Pamlico Company. Pamlico's post acquisition pro forma income statement is shown below. Pamlico invests just enough to offset depreciation, and maintains a debt-to-equity ratio of 3/7. Pamlico's cost of equity is 20%. Both firms face a pre-tax borrowing rate of 10%, and a tax rate of 40%. Hatteras is all equity financed, and its cost of capital is 16%. If Hatteras acquires Pamlico today, in two years the assets will be sold for their book value of $500,000. What is the most that Hatteras should pay for Pamlico?

Income Statement
($ in thousands)

	Year 1	Year 2
Revenue	$500	$600
Costs	375	450
Depreciation	40	40
EBIT	85	110
Interest	15	15
EBT	70	95
Tax	28	38
Net income	42	57

SOLUTIONS

Solution 1

At $20 per share, Firm A is paying [($20)(600)] = $12,000 to acquire Firm B. The value of Firm A after the acquisition is equal to the value of the combined firm less the cash paid for Firm B, or ($64,000 – $12,000) = $52,000. The net present value of the acquisition is ($52,000 – $50,000) = $2,000, so that the acquisition is beneficial to the stockholders of Firm A. Firm A should proceed with the acquisition.

Solution 2

The synergy is equal to the value of the combined firm less the total value of the two separate firms:

$$\$64,000 - [(\$50)(1,000) + (\$15)(600)] = \$5,000$$

The premium is the difference between the purchase price and the market value of the acquired firm:

$$(\$20)(600) - (\$15)(600) = \$3,000$$

Therefore, the net present value is the synergy minus the premium, or ($5,000 - $3,000) = $2,000, as indicated in Problem 1.

Solution 3

The net present value of the merger is $2,000, so the stock will increase in value by ($2,000/1,000) = $2.00 per share. The stock price will be $52. Alternatively, Firm A is worth $50,000 prior to the merger. After the merger, it is worth [$50,000 + ($14,000 - $12,000)] = $52,000, where $14,000 is the increase in firm value and $12,000 is what is paid. The per share value is thus ($52,000/1,000) = $52.00, as previously calculated.

Solution 4

At current values, Firm A will exchange one of its shares for every 3 1/3 shares of Firm B [($50/$15) = 3 1/3]. In total, Firm B stockholders will receive (600/3 1/3) = 180 shares. The combined firm will thus have 1,180 shares outstanding, of which (180/1,180) = 15.25% are held by the former shareholders of Firm B. The combined firm is worth $64,000, so the cost of the merger is [(.1525)($64,000)] = $9,762.71. The net present value is ($12,000 - $9,762.71) = $2,237.29 when financed with stock.

Solution 5

Firm A will have to give ($20/$50) = .40 shares of its stock for every share of B, or [(.40)(600)] = 240 shares. [Note that this result is also equal to the cash price of the acquisition divided by the current market value of a share of Firm A stock: ($12,000/$50) =240.] The new firm will have a total of 1,240 shares outstanding. The combined firm is worth $64,000, so the per share value is ($64,000/1,240) = $51.6129. The cost of the merger is [(240/1,240)($64,000)] = $12,387.10, so the net present value is $387.10. (Note that the cost of the merger is also equal to the per share value of the merged firm times the number of shares received by the stockholders of Firm B: ($51.6129)(240) = $12,387.10.)

Solution 6

The synergy is $5,000, as indicated in Problem 2. The premium is the difference between the purchase price and the market value of the acquired firm:

$$(\$12,387.10) - [(\$15)(600)] = \$3,387.10$$

The net present value is the synergy minus the premium, or ($5,000 - $3,387.10) = $1,612.90. This NPV is $387.10 less than the $2,000 NPV of the acquisition for cash. The stockholders of Firm B receive [(240/1,240)($2,000)] = $387.10 of the net present value when the acquisition is paid for with an exchange of stock. This difference can also be viewed as the increment in the value of the shares of Firm A which is given to the stockholders of Firm B; that is, [($51.6129 - $50)(240)] = $387.10.

Solution 7

In order for the Firm B stockholders to receive $12,000, they must receive stock which has a total value equal to ($12,000/$64,000) = .1875 = 18.75% of the merged firm. Therefore, the new shares issued must represent 18.75% of the outstanding shares of the merged firm. This value is determined by solving for x in the following equation:

$$[x/(1,000 + x)] = .1875$$

The number of new shares which should be issued to the stockholders of Firm B is 230.769, so that the total number of shares outstanding will then be (1,000 + 230.769) = 1,230.769. The price per share will be ($64,000/1,230.769) = $52.00. The stockholders of Firm B receive 230.769 shares worth $52, for a total value of [(230.769)($52)] = $12,000.

Solution 8

The new firm will have total earnings of $8,700. At $17.50 per share, Firm A will have to give [($17.50/$50)(600)] = 210 shares to the shareholders of Firm B, so that the new firm will have 1,210 shares outstanding. Thus, EPS will be ($8,700/1,210) = $7.19 per share; this is an increase of $1.19 from the pre-merger level of $6 per share.

Solution 9

Before the merger, A had a P/E ratio of ($50/$6) = 8 1/3. If the market is fooled, in the sense that this P/E ratio is unchanged after the merger, the stock will rise in value to [(8 1/3)($7.19)] = $59.92.

If the market is not fooled, then the P/E ratio will fall to ($64,000/$8,700) =7.356, and the price per share will be [(7.356)($7.19)] = $52.89. This result is also equal to the value of the firm divided by the number of shares: ($64,000/1,210) = $52.89.

Solution 10

The synergy is the present value of the perpetual annuity of $10,000 per year: ($10,000/.20) = $50,000. Therefore, Max's value to Blizzard is ($200,000 + $50,000) = $250,000.

Solution 11

The premium is ($220,000 - $200,000) = $20,000. The net present value is the synergy minus the premium, or ($50,000 - $20,000) = $30,000. The net present value can also be determined as the difference between the value of the acquisition and the cost: ($250,000 - $220,000) = $30,000.

Solution 12

Twenty-five percent of the combined company is worth [(.25)($250,000 + $500,000)] = $187,500. The net present value of this acquisition would be ($250,000 − $187,500) = $62,500. Blizzard would prefer to acquire Max Motors for 25 percent of the firm's stock rather than the $220,000 cash offer described above in Problem 11.

Solution 13

With a pooling of interests, the balance sheets are added together, so the new balance sheet appears as follows:

Pinot Noir Vineyards ($ in thousands)

Current assets	$ 300	Current liabilities	$ 200
Fixed assets	1,500	Long-term debt	300
		Equity	1,300
Total	$1,800		$1,800

Solution 14

Noir's fair market value is $900 plus $200 in current assets, or $1,100 total. The $100 premium paid ($1,200 − $1,100) is goodwill. Pinot's fixed assets would be $900 (the book value of Pinot's pre-merger fixed assets) plus $900 (the market value of Noir's assets), or $1,800 total. The balance sheet appears as follows:

Pinot Noir Vineyards ($ in thousands)

Current assets	$ 300	Current liabilities	$ 200
Fixed assets	1,800	Long-term debt	1,260
Goodwill	100	Equity	740
Total	$2,200		$2,200

Solution note: Noir's assets are $1,100. Assuming that the current liabilities and long-term debt are shown at market value, the equity in Noir is worth ($1,100 − $140 − $100) = $860. Pinot pays a $100 premium, so the total amount of debt that Pinot must raise is $960. The total long-term debt after the merger is ($960 + $100 + $200) = $1,260, as shown.

Solution 15

The bonds are worth either $66 or the value of the firm, whichever is less. The stock is worth either zero or the value of the firm less $66, whichever is more. Thus:

Weather	Probability	Firm A		Firm B	
		Stock	Debt	Stock	Debt
Rainy	.5	$34	$66	$0	$50
Sunny	.5	0	60	24	66
Expected value		$17	$63	$12	$58

Notice that the value of Firm A is ($17 + $63) = $80, and the value of Firm B is ($12 + $58) = $70.

Solution 16

Before the merger, the total value of the stock in the two firms is ($17 + $12) = $29. The total value of the bonds is ($63 + $58) = $121. Since there is no synergy, the value of the merged firm will be $150. The values of the equity and debt are shown below:

Weather	Probability	Firm value	Debt value	Equity value
Rainy	.5	$150	$132	$18
Sunny	.5	150	132	18
Expected value		$150	$132	$18

This problem illustrates the coinsurance effect. The merged firm has a certain value of $150. The bonds are worth $11 more ($132 – $121) than before the merger, and, as a result, the equity is worth $11 less than before the merger.

Solution 17

The net present value of the acquisition is the value of Y to X minus what X pays for Y. The stock price of Y if the growth rate increases to 12 % is

$$\text{Price(Y)} = \$1.92/(.14 - .12)$$

$$= \$96.00 \text{ per share}$$

$$\text{or } \$96.00 \times 400,000 = \$38,400,000$$

Firm X proposes to offer $55.00 per share, or in total $55.00 × 400,000 = $22,000,000. The net present value is

$$\text{NPV} = \$38,400,000 - \$22,000,000 = \$16,400,000$$

Solution 18

Firm X's stock price will increase by the NPV per share. Thus, the increase will be $16,400,000/1,000,000 = $16.40 per share. The new stock price will be $25.00 + $16.40 = $41.40 per share.

Solution 19

Since firm X's stock price after the announced takeover is $41.40, the number of shares X must issue is $22 million/$41.40 = 531,401 shares. Another approach is to consider the fractional ownership, α, of firm Y's shareholders of the combined firm.

$$\alpha \times (\$25 \text{ million} + \$38.4 \text{ million}) = \$22 \text{ million}$$

$$\alpha = .347003$$

and

$$\alpha = \# \text{ new shares issued}/(\text{old} + \text{new shares})$$

Combining the two formulas and solving for the number of new shares:

$$\# \text{ new shares} = \alpha(\# \text{ old shares})/(1 - \alpha)$$

$$= (.347003) \times 1 \text{ million}/.652997 = 531,401 \text{ shares}$$

Solution 20

If Y's growth rate is 11%, then other things equal, the value of Y to X is

$$\text{Value (Y)} = 400,000 \times \$1.92/(.14 - .11)$$

$$= \$25,600,000$$

The value of the combined firms is $25.0 million + $25.6 million = $50.6 million. Firm X has 1,531,401 shares outstanding, thus the stock price is

$$P_x = \$50.6 \text{ million}/1.531401 = \$33.04$$

Thus, Y's shareholders received only $17.6 million, not $22 million, for their firm. Y's shareholders suffer along with X's shareholders from the incorrect forecast growth rate. Note that with $g = 11\%$, the NPV per share is ($25.6 - $22)/1.0 = $3.60. Firm X's stock price should be $28.60, and X should have exchanged $22,000,000/$28.60 = 769,231 shares.

Solution 21

The most that Hatteras should pay for Pamlico is the present value of future cash flows. There are three risk classes, requiring three different discount rates, of cash flows that Hatteras must discount: interfirm dividends, terminal asset value, and repayment of debt. Dividends should be discounted at Pamlico's cost of equity, asset value (reflecting value of an ongoing business with same capital structure) should be discounted at the weighted average cost of capital, and debt should be discounted at the cost of debt. Since investment equals depreciation, Pamlico's net income represents the dividends that Hatteras will receive, the present value is

$$PV\ (Div) = \$42/(1.20) + \$57/(1.20)^2 = \$74.58$$

Pamlico's WACC is $.3(.10)(1-.4) + .7(.20) = .1580$. The present value of the terminal asset value is

$$PV\ (assets) = \$500/(1.158)^2 = \$372.87$$

Since Pamlico maintains a debt-to-equity ratio of 3/7, or a debt ratio of 3/10, the debt outstanding when the assets are sold at time 2 is $.30(\$500) = \$150$. The present value of the debt repayment is

$$PV\ (debt) = \$150/(1.10)^2 = \$123.97$$

Thus, the most that Hatteras should pay is $\$74.58 + \$372.87 - \$123.97 = \$323.48$, or $\$323,480$.

CHAPTER 31

FINANCIAL DISTRESS

CHAPTER MISSION STATEMENT

The purpose of Chapter 31 is to describe the institutional details of financial distress, bankruptcy, private workouts, and prepackaged bankruptcy. The chapter discusses the definition of financial distress and what happens to a firm in distress. Bankruptcy liquidation is described, along with the rules for determining the priority of claims. Bankruptcy reorganization is discussed along with the violation of the absolute priority rule. The chapter compares private workouts with bankruptcy, and discusses the combination of the two - prepackaged bankruptcy. The chapter concludes by discussing the Revco decision to file for bankruptcy. An appendix discusses using the Z-score model to predict bankruptcy.

The key concepts presented in Chapter 31 are outlined below.

- ♦Financial distress defined
  - ●stock-based
  - ●flow-based
- ♦Bankruptcy
  - ●liquidation (Chapter 7)
  - ●reorganization (Chapter 11)
  - ●priority of claims
- ♦Private workout
- ♦Prepackaged bankruptcy

CONCEPT TEST

1. A firm is in _____ when its cash flows are not sufficient to satisfy current obligations.

2. The inability to pay one's debts is known as _____.

3. Negative net worth is an example of _____ insolvency.

4. Cash flow insufficient to meet one's obligations is an example of _____ insolvency.

5. Financial distress may involve _____ restructuring and _____ restructuring.

6. Bankrupt firms may either _____ or _____.

7. Chapter 7 of the Bankruptcy Reform Act of 1978 deals with _____.

8. Chapter 11 of the Bankruptcy Reform Act of 1978 deals with _____.

9. Bankruptcy petitions may be filed _____ by the firm or _____ by creditors.

10. Creditors with claims totaling _____ may file a petition for involuntary bankruptcy.

11. Disposition of assets in bankruptcy is determined by the _____.

12. An exception to the absolute priority rule involves _____.

13. The firm ceases to exist in a _____, while the firm may continue as an ongoing concern in a _____.

14. Financial restructuring without bankruptcy is known as a _____.

15. On average, a _____ is less costly than a _____.

16. Generally, the more complex the capital structure, the more likely _____, rather than _____, will be used in financial distress.

17. A combination of private workout and legal bankruptcy is known as _____.

18. A reorganization plan forced by the court on one or more unwilling creditor classes is known as a _____.

ANSWERS TO CONCEPT TEST

1. financial distress
2. insolvency
3. stock-based
4. flow-based
5. asset; financial
6. liquidate; reorganize
7. liquidation
8. reorganization
9. voluntarily; involuntarily

10. $5,000
11. absolute priority rule (APR)
12. liens on property
13. liquidation; reorganization
14. private workout
15. private workout; formal bankruptcy
16. bankruptcy; private workout
17. prepackaged bankruptcy
18. cramdown

PROBLEMS

Problem 1

The balance sheets for companies A and B are shown below. Both book and market values are shown. Company A has earnings before interest and taxes of $10.0, while Company B's EBIT is $2.0. All debt carries a coupon rate of 10% and matures several years in the future. Both firms are insolvent. Describe whether the firms are insolvent on a flow basis or a stock basis.

Firm A

Assets			Liabilities and Equity		
	Book	Market		Book	Market
Cash	$40	$40	Debt	$100	$60
Fixed assets	160	40	Equity	100	20
Total	$200	$80	Total	$200	$80

Firm B

Assets			Liabilities and Equity		
	Book	Market		Book	Market
Cash	$4	$4	Debt	$80	$60
Fixed assets	196	96	Equity	120	40
Total	$200	$100	Total	$200	$100

Problem 2

The Nadir Company filed for bankruptcy under Chapter 7 of the U.S. Bankruptcy Code. The firm's balance sheet is shown below. As trustee what distribution of liquidating value would you propose?

Liquidating value		Claims	
Cash	$100	Payables	$50
Assets	200	Mortgage bonds	200
		Senior debentures	100
		Junior debentures	50
		Equity	(100)
Total	$300	Total	$300

Problem 3

The Phoenix Corporation has just filed for reorganization under Chapter 11 of the Bankruptcy Code. The firm's balance sheet is shown below. As trustee what reorganization plan would you accept from management?

Assets		Claims	
Going concern value	$500	Payables	$100
		Mortgage bonds	250
		Senior debentures	200
		Junior debentures	50
		Equity	(100)
Total	$500	Total	$500

Problem 4

The balance sheets for General Manufacturing and General Emporium are shown below. Both firms have experienced low earnings over the past few years and are in financial distress. Each firm plans to undergo financial restructuring in order to continue in business. Should they restructure under Chapter 11 of the Bankruptcy Code, or should they try a private workout? What advice would you give each firm?

General Manufacturing

Assets		Liabilities	
Assets	$100,000	Mortgages	$40,000
		Debentures	30,000
		Equity	30,000
Total	$100,000	Total	$100,000

General Emporium

Assets		Liabilities	
Assets	$100,000	Payables	$10,000
		Trade credit	10,000
		Mortgages	30,000
		Senior debentures	10,000
		Junior debentures	10,000
		Equity	30,000
Total	$100,000	Total	$100,000

Problem 5

The Hiccup Company is privately held and is seeking a loan at your bank. As the bank's loan officer, determine if Hiccup Company is credit worthy, or on the verge of bankruptcy. Hiccup reported EBIT of $96 million last year; its balance sheet is shown below.

Assets		Liabilities and equity	
Net working capital	$240	Debt	$1,440
Fixed assets	1,680	Common stock	288
		Retained earnings	192
Total	$1,920	Total	$1,920

SOLUTIONS

Solution 1

Firm A is insolvent on a stock basis. Firm A has $100 debt outstanding, however, the value of the firm is only $80. But, since the debt doesn't mature for several years, and the firm has sufficient resources to pay interest on the debt (cash plus earnings exceed the $10 interest), the firm cannot be forced into bankruptcy. Firm B, on the other hand, is insolvent on a flow basis. The market value of the firm, $100, exceeds the $80 debt outstanding. However, the firm does not have sufficient resources to pay the $80 x .10 = $8 interest (cash plus earnings only equal $4). Thus, the firm could be forced into bankruptcy by bondholders if Firm B does not raise additional cash, through the sale of assets or new equity, to pay interest on the bonds.

Solution 2

The following proposal abides by the absolute priority rule:

Claims		Payoff
Payables	$50	$0
Mortgage bonds	200	200
Senior debentures	100	100
Junior debentures	50	0
Equity	(100)	0
Total	$300	$300

Payables are unsecured debts and fall just above equity in the absolute priority rule. Debentures are unsecured debt and fall below the secured mortgage bonds. However, evidence suggests that the absolute priority rule is frequently violated. Thus, an alternative proposal is:

Claims		Payoff
Payables	$50	$0
Mortgage bonds	200	200
Senior debentures	100	80
Junior debentures	50	20
Equity	(100)	0
Total	$300	$300

In this proposal, since Senior Debenture holders are not fully paid while Junior Debenture holders get some payoff, the APR is violated. Although there are sufficient resources to give Senior holders 100 cents on the dollar, they get only 80 cents per dollar of claims while Junior claimants get 40 cents on the dollar. Needless to say, if the absolute priority rule is going to be violated, then the final distribution of assets depends on the relative bargaining power of the claimants.

Solution 3

A possible reorganization plan that would not violate the absolute priority rule is indicated below:

Claims		New claim	New security
Payables	$100	$0	Senior debentures
Mortgage bonds	250	250	Subordinated debentures
Senior debentures	200	200	Common stock
Junior debentures	50	50	
Equity	(100)	0	
Total	$500	$500	

Studies show, however, that about 80% of the time the absolute priority rule is violated. Equity holders and unsecured creditors may insist on some compensation before agreeing to the reorganization plan. An alternative plan which violates the absolute priority rule is shown below:

Claims		New claim	New security
Payables	$100	$50	Cash and subordinated
Mortgage bonds	250	250	debentures
Senior debentures	200	150	Senior debentures
Junior debentures	50	40	Subordinated debentures
Equity	(100)	10	Preferred and common stock
			Common stock
Total	$500	$500	

In this plan all claimants and equity holders get something. Since the firm intends to stay in business, compensating suppliers 10 cents on the dollar may be necessary to get an agreement. Likewise, letting existing shareholders maintain an equity interest in the reorganized firm may facilitate reaching a mutually satisfactory agreement. As in almost all cases, secured creditors are fully paid before unsecured creditors get paid.

Solution 4

Evidence suggests that the direct costs of private workouts are about 10% of the direct costs of formal bankruptcies. Thus, other things equal, private workouts seem like the preferred method to reorganize. However, a private workout requires that all creditors and equity investors agree to the plan. Agreement is more likely with fewer creditors. Thus, since General Manufacturing has a relatively simple balance sheet, agreement among creditors is likely, a private workout is the best course of action. General Emporium, on the other hand, has many creditors, particularly unsecured payables and trade credit accounts, and agreement is much more in doubt. Thus, a successful reorganization in General Emporium's case is more likely with formal bankruptcy proceedings.

Solution 5

We use Altman's revised Z-score model to determine Hiccup's credit worthiness since it is not a publicly traded firm. From balance sheet and EBIT figures we find the financial statement variables for the Z-score model.

$$\frac{\text{Net working capital}}{\text{Total assets}} = \frac{240}{1,920} = .125$$

$$\frac{\text{Accumulated retained earnings}}{\text{Total assets}} = \frac{192}{1,920} = .100$$

$$\frac{\text{EBIT}}{\text{Total assets}} = \frac{96}{1,920} = .050$$

$$\frac{\text{Book value of equity}}{\text{Total liabilities}} = \frac{480}{1,440} = .333$$

The revised Z-score is

$$Z = 6.56 \times .125 + 3.26 \times .100 + 1.05 \times .050 + 6.72 \times .333$$

$$Z = 3.439$$

A revised Z-score above 2.90 suggests that Hiccup is in no immediate danger of bankruptcy. Any deterioration of the firm's financial condition, however, would put the firm in financial distress.

CHAPTER 32

INTERNATIONAL CORPORATE FINANCE

CHAPTER MISSION STATEMENT

The purpose of Chapter 32 is to provide an introduction to the basic relationships governing international finance. The chapter discusses the law of one price, also known as the purchasing-power parity theorem, the expectation theory of exchange rates, and the interest-rate parity theorem. The chapter applies these theorems to financing decisions in foreign currencies. The chapter also discusses how to apply the net present value rule in international capital budgeting problems. The chapter concludes by describing the accounting treatment of currency translation gains and losses on financial statements.

The key concepts presented in this chapter are outlined below.

- ◆Exchange markets
- ◆Exchange rates
  - ●direct or American terms
  - ●indirect or European terms
  - ●triangular arbitrage
  - ●spot trades
  - ●forward trades
- ◆Law of one price
  - ●purchasing-power parity
  - ●relative purchasing-power parity
- ◆Interest-rate parity
- ◆International capital budgeting
- ◆International financial decisions
- ◆Reporting foreign operations

CONCEPT TEST

1. A security issued in the United States which represents a share of stock in a foreign firm is called an _____.

2. A _____ is the exchange rate for two non-U.S. currencies.

3. Bonds denominated in a particular currency and simultaneously issued in several countries are called _____.

4. A _____ is money deposited in financial institutions outside of the country whose currency is involved.

5. Dollars on deposit in a London bank are called _____.

6. A _____ is a basket of 10 European currencies intended to serve as a monetary unit for the EMS.

7. A U.S. firm issues pound-denominated bonds in England. Such bonds are generically called _____.

8. A bond issued in the United States by a foreign country or company are known as _____.

9 A British government security is called a _____.

10. The overnight interest rate banks charge each other on Eurodollar loans is the _____.

11. A currency _____ refers to an exchange of one currency for another.

12. The _____ is the world's largest financial market.

13. The price of one country's currency expressed in terms of another's is called the _____.

14. _____ is a means of profiting from inconsistencies in exchange rates by converting currencies.

15. Foreign exchange trades that are settled in two business days are called _____ trades and take place at the _____ rate.

16. Foreign exchange trades that settled in sixty days are called _____ trades and take place at the _____ rate.

17. The _____ states that a particular commodity has the same price regardless of the country in which it is selling.

18. An implication of the concept identified in Question 17 is that the price of a 'market basket' of goods is the same in all countries and currencies. This is called _____.

19. _____ states that the relative inflation rates in two countries determine the rate of change in the exchange rate.

20. The _____ theorem states that the difference between the spot and forward exchange rates depends on relative interest rates.

21. If it takes more dollars to buy a foreign currency in the forward market than in the spot market, the foreign currency is said to be selling at a _____ in the forward market.

22. The uncertainty associated with changes in the value of future cash flows resulting from changes in exchange rates is called _____.

23. The cost of capital for international investments may be increased because of _____.

24. The cost of capital for international investments may be decreased because of gains from
_____.

25. Current accounting rules require that all balance sheet items must be translated into dollars at the
_____ exchange rate.

ANSWERS TO CONCEPT TEST

1. American Depository Receipt (ADR)
2. cross rate
3. Eurobonds
4. Eurocurrency
5. Eurodollars
6. European Currency Unit (ECU)
7. foreign bonds
8. Yankee bonds
9. gilt
10. London Interbank Offer Rate (LIBOR)
11. swap
12. foreign exchange market
13. exchange rate

14. triangular arbitrage
15. spot; spot
16. forward; forward
17. law of one price (LOP)
18. purchasing power parity (PPP)
19. relative purchasing power parity (RPPP)
20. interest rate parity
21. premium
22. exchange-rate risk
23. political risk
24. diversification
25. current

PROBLEMS

Problem 1

You can exchange 40 Baht for 1 dollar. What is the direct exchange rate? What is the indirect exchange rate?

Problem 2

The direct exchange rate for the South African Rand is .20. How many South African Rands do you receive in exchange for 1 U.S. dollar?

Problem 3

The direct exchange rate for German marks is .50. The direct exchange rate for British pounds is 1.5. If you have 1 mark, how many pounds can you buy? (That is, what is the cross rate?)

Problem 4

Suppose that, for the data in Problem 3, the cross rate is 3.3 marks = 1 pound, rather than the calculated result of 3 marks = 1 pound. Describe the triangular arbitrage opportunity which would exist under these circumstances.

Problem 5

Suppose that, for the data in Problem 3, the cross rate is 2.7 marks = 1 pound. Describe the triangular arbitrage opportunity which would exist under these circumstances.

Problem 6

An ounce of silver costs 5 dollars in the U.S. or 800 yen in Japan. The exchange rate is 150 yen = 1 dollar. Is this an equilibrium situation? Suppose that a trader has $500 available. Can the trader make an arbitrage profit?

Problem 7

Suppose that, for the data in Problem 6, the price of silver in Japan is 700 yen per ounce. Describe the arbitrage profit opportunity for a trader with $500 available.

Problem 8

Suppose that, for the data in Problem 6, the price of silver in the U.S. and Japan remains constant, but the exchange rate adjusts in accordance with the law of one price. What is the equilibrium exchange rate?

Problem 9

The direct spot exchange rate for marks is .50 and the 90-day forward rate is .51. Is the mark selling at a premium or discount?

Problem 10

Suppose that, in Problem 9, the U.S. 90-day risk-free rate is 3%. What is the German risk-free rate, i_G?

Problem 11

Suppose the Swiss inflation rate is forecast to be 2% during the coming year and the United States rate over the same period will be 5%. The current exchange rate is SF 1 = $ 1.50. What is the expected spot exchange rate in one year?

Problem 12

The current yen/dollar exchange rate is 150. The risk-free interest rate in Japan is 6% and in the United States is 8%. What is the expected spot exchange rate in one year?

Problem 13

Suppose that, for the data in Problem 12, the U.S. inflation rate is expected to be 4%. What is the expected spot exchange rate in five years, $E[S(5)]$?

Use the following information to solve Problems 14 and 15.

You have been asked to evaluate a proposed investment in the country of Westfield. Westfield's home currency is the Sar, abbreviated SA. The current exchange rate is 1 Sar = $2. The inflation rate in Westfield is expected to be 10% higher than in the United States; that is, $\Pi_W/\Pi_{US} = 1.10$.

The project will cost SA 1,000 and is expected to generate SA 300 per year for three years. The project will then be sold for an estimated SA 400. The appropriate discount rate for dollar flows of this risk level is 12%.

Problem 14

What is the expected exchange rate at the end of the project's life?

Problem 15

Try this one on your own. What is the net present value of the proposed investment, in dollars? In Sars?

Use the following table to answer Problems 16-20.

	US $ equiv	Currency per US $
Swiss Franc (SFr)	.6652	1.5033
30-Day Forward	.6676	1.4979
90-Day Forward	.6722	1.4877
180-Day Forward	.6789	1.4730
Denmark Krone (DKr)	.1454	6.8776

Problem 16

Is the price of a Swiss Franc (SFr) at a premium or discount to the US dollar ($) in the forward market?

Problem 17

What is the spot exchange cross rate between Swiss Francs and Danish Krone?

Problem 18

Suppose that you are an importer of Swiss watches. In six months you must pay SFr 100,000 for a shipment of watches. How much would the shipment cost in dollars if you locked in the price today with a forward contract? Would you buy or sell Swiss Francs forward?

Problem 19

Suppose that you are offered an investment in Switzerland that costs SFr 1,000,000 and produces cash flows over the next three years of SFr 500,000, SFr 600,000, and SFr 700,000. Similar investments in the US have a 14% opportunity cost of capital. Interest rates in the US are 6%, while in Switzerland they are 10%. What is the NPV of this investment in dollar terms?

Problem 20

Calculate the net present value of the investment in Swiss Francs. Assume that the risk premium in the opportunity cost of capital does not change across currencies.

SOLUTIONS

Solution 1

The direct (or American) rate is quoted as dollars per unit of foreign currency, so the direct rate is .025 dollar per 1 Baht. The indirect (or European) rate is units of foreign currency per dollar, or 40 Baht per 1 dollar.

Solution 2

Each South African Rand costs .20 U.S. dollar, so you receive 5 in exchange for one U.S. dollar.

Solution 3

Your one mark will buy .50 dollar. With .50 dollar, you can buy 1/3 of a pound. The cross rate is 3 marks = 1 pound.

Solution 4

Use the one mark to purchase .50 dollar and then exchange the .50 dollar for 1/3 pound. At the cross rate of 3.3 marks = 1 pound, 1/3 pound can be exchanged for 1.1 mark, or an arbitrage profit of 10%.

Solution 5

Exchange one mark for (1/2.7) = .37037 pounds and then purchase [(.37037)(1.5)] = .55556 dollar. At the exchange rate of .50 dollar = one mark, .55556 dollar can be exchanged for [(.55556)(2)] = 1.1111 marks. This result represents an arbitrage profit of 11.11%.

Solution 6

The trader can purchase ($500/$5) = 100 ounces of silver in the U.S. This can then be sold for [(100)(800 yen)] = 80,000 yen in Japan. At the exchange rate of 150 yen = 1 dollar, the trader can exchange 80,000 yen for (80,000/150) = $533.33, so that the arbitrage profit is $33.33. This is not an equilibrium situation because the demand for silver in the U.S. will cause the dollar price of silver to increase and the supply of silver will decrease the price in Japan. Also, the exchange rate will increase due to the increased demand for dollars and the decreased demand for yen.

Solution 7

In this situation, the trader can exchange $500 for [(500)(150)] = 75,000 yen. With 75,000 yen, the trader can then purchase (75,000/700) = 107.1429 ounces of silver in Japan. He can sell the silver for [($5)(107.1429)] = $535.71, for an arbitrage profit of $35.71.

Solution 8

According to the law of one price, the stated prices and/or exchange rate adjust in such a way as to eliminate the arbitrage profit. This profit is eliminated if:

$$P^{US}(t) = S_Y(t)\, P^Y(t)$$

where $P^{US}(t)$ and $P^Y(t)$ are the price of silver, in dollars and yen, respectively, and $S_Y(t)$ is the exchange rate for dollars in terms of yen. The equilibrium exchange rate equals $S_Y(t)$ in the following equation:

$$5 = [S_Y(t)] \times 800$$

Therefore, the equilibrium exchange rate is 160 yen = 1 dollar.

Solution 9

It takes more dollars ($.51 compared to $.50) to buy a mark forward than it does to buy a mark today. Therefore the mark is selling at a premium.

Solution 10

From the interest rate parity theorem:
$$1.03/(1 + i_G) = .51/.50$$

Therefore, the German risk-free rate is .9804%, or approximately 1%.

Solution 11

From relative purchasing power parity:

$$(1.05/1.02) = E[S(1)]/1.5$$

Therefore, $E[S(1)] = 1.544$.

Solution note: You must be careful here to use the exchange rate expressed as dollars per unit of foreign currency. It costs $1.50 to buy a Swiss franc today. The difference between the U.S. and the Swiss inflation rates is 3%, so the price of a Swiss franc will rise by approximately 3%: $[(\$1.50)(1.03)] = \$1.545$.

Solution 12

The current exchange rate, expressed as dollars per yen, is $(\$1/150) = \$.006667$. Based on IRP:

$$(1.08/1.06) = F(0,1)/(.006667)$$

Therefore, the forward rate is $.0067925, or 147.22 yen per dollar. This result is based on the assumption that the forward rate is equal to the expected spot rate.

Solution 13

Using the IRP and RPPP, the Japanese inflation rate, Π_J, can be determined as follows:

$$(1.08/1.06) = (1.04/[1 + \Pi_J])$$

$$\Pi_J = 2.074\%$$

Using RPPP, the expected spot exchange rate in five years is:

$$E[S(5)] = (.006667)(1.04/1.02074)^5 = .00732$$

This is equivalent to approximately 137 yen per dollar.

Solution 14

The current exchange rate is $.50. This is expected to decline by $(1/1.10) = .9091$ per year. In three years, the exchange rate is expected to be:

$$.50(.9091)^3 = \$.376.$$

Solution 15

The cash flows and exchange rates are:

Year	Cash flow (SA)	Exchange rate	Cash flow ($)
0	SA −1,000	.50000	$ −500.00
1	300	.45454	136.36
2	300	.41322	123.97
3	700	.37566	262.96

At a 12% discount rate, the NPV in dollars is −$92.25. The NPV in Sars is −184.50 Sars.

Solution 16

The forward price of a SFr in dollars per Swiss Franc is higher than the spot price, thus the SFr is selling forward at a premium to the dollar. For example, 180-day forward price is $.6789 per SFr while the spot price is $.6652 per SFr.

Solution 17

The cross rate between SFr and DKr should be

$$S(SFr/\$) \times S(\$/DKr) = 1.5033 \times .1454 = .2186 \text{ SFr/DKr}$$

$$\text{or } 4.5750 \text{ DKr/SFr}$$

Solution 18

The 180-Day Forward price is .6789 $/SFr, thus your price in dollars is SFr 100,000 x .6789 $/SFr = $67,890. Since you need Swiss Francs in six-months to pay for the watches, you are short Swiss Francs. To hedge against a the SFr strengthening, you would buy Swiss Francs forward.

Solution 19

To find the net present value of this investment in dollar terms, the SFr cash flows must be converted to dollars. First, however, we must use the interest rate and purchasing power parity relationships to find expected spot rates, E[S(t)], for years 1, 2, and 3. The following relationship (International Fisher Effect) is useful

$$E[S_{\$/sfr}(t)] = [(1 + i_{us})/(1 + i_{sfr})]^t \, S_{\$/sfr}(0)$$

	0	1	2	3
Cash flow (SFr)	−1,000	500.0	600.0	700.0
Spot rate ($/SFr)	.6652	.6410	.6177	.5952
Cash flow ($)	−665.2	320.5	370.6	416.6
PV (@14%)	−665.2	281.1	285.2	281.2

NPV = $182.3 thousand

Where, for example, the spot rate at time 2 is given by

$$E[S_{\$/sfr}(t)] = [\frac{(1 + i_\$)}{(1 + i_{sfr})}]^t S_{\$/sfr}(0)$$

$$= [\frac{(1.06)}{(1.10)}]^2 \times 0.6652 = 0.6177$$

Solution 20

We need the SFr equivalent of 14% to calculate NPV in SFr. The interest rate and relative purchasing power parity relationships are useful here. In US currency, the risk premium is [(1.14)/(1.06) − 1] = .0755. Thus, in Swiss currency the opportunity cost of capital is

$$1 + r_{sfr} = (1.14) [(1.10)/(1.06)] = (1.10)(1.0755) = 1.1830$$

Then,

$$NPV (SFr) = -SFr1000 + SFr500/(1.1830)$$

$$+ SFr600/(1.1830)^2 + SFr700/(1.1830)^3$$

$$= SFr\ 274.19$$

Converting to dollars, the dollar NPV is

$$NPV (\$) = .6652 \times SFr\ 274.19 = \$182.39$$

This is the same answer, within rounding error, as in Problem 19. The answers must be the same, for example consider the dollar cash flow for year two (from Problem 19):

$$SFr600 \times E[S_{\$/sfr}(2)] /(1.14)^2$$

$$= SFr600 \: [(1 + i_{us})/(1 + i_{sfr})]^t \: S_{\$/sfr}(0)/(1.14)^2$$

$$= SFr600 \: [(1.06)/(1.10)]^2 (.6652)/(1.14)^2$$

$$= (.6652) \: SFr600/[(1.14)(1.10)/(1.06)]^2$$

$$= (.6652) \: Sfr600/[1.1830]^2$$

$$= \$285.19$$

Each year would have a similar form - the spot rate times the cash flow in SFr all discounted at 18.30%. Thus, without the spot rate we get NPV in SFr, with the spot rate we get NPV in $ terms.

NOTES

NOTES

NOTES

NOTES